Primordial Truth
and
Postmodern Theology

SUNY SERIES IN
CONSTRUCTIVE POSTMODERN THOUGHT
DAVID RAY GRIFFIN, EDITOR

David Ray Griffin, editor, *The Reenchantment of Science:
Postmodern Proposals*

David Ray Griffin, editor, *Spirituality and Society:
Postmodern Visions*

David Ray Griffin, *God and Religion in the Postmodern World:
Essays in Postmodern Theology*

David Ray Griffin, William A. Beardslee, and Joe Holland,
Varieties of Postmodern Theology

David Ray Griffin and Huston Smith, *Primordial Truth and
Postmodern Theology*

PRIMORDIAL TRUTH

AND

POSTMODERN THEOLOGY

DAVID RAY GRIFFIN
HUSTON SMITH

STATE UNIVERSITY OF NEW YORK PRESS

Published by
State University of New York Press, Albany

© 1989 State University of New York

For information, address State University of New York
Press, State University Plaza, Albany, N.Y., 12246

Library of Congress Cataloging-in-Publication Data

Griffin, David Ray, 1939-
    Primordial truth and postmodern theology / David Ray Griffin and
Huston Smith.
        p.   cm. — (SUNY series in constructive postmodern thought)
    Bibliography: p.
    Includes index.
    ISBN 0-7914-0198-7. — ISBN 0-7914-0199-5 (pbk.)
    1. Religion—Philosophy. 2. Science—Philosophy.
3. Postmodernism. 4. Griffin, David Ray, 1939-   . 5. Smith,
Huston.   I. Smith, Huston. II. Title. III. Series.
BL51.G735   1989
200'.1—dc19   89-4388
                                                        CIP

10   9   8   7   6   5   4   3   2

*To Ann and Kendra,
the loves of our lives.*

CONTENTS

vii

ACKNOWLEDGMENTS

Earlier versions of the first round of our dialogue were presented at a forum sponsored by the Center for a Postmodern World in Santa Barbara in January, 1988. We wish to thank the members of the center and other friends who attended for their stimulating questions and comments. Their sense that we were debating important issues gave us added incentive to continue.

David Griffin wishes to thank Dean Allen J. Moore, President Richard C. Cain, and the trustees of the School of Theology at Claremont for released time; President John D. Maguire and Claremont University Center and Graduate School, as well as the School of Theology, for continued support of the Center for Process Studies; and Nancy Howell and John Cobb for making absence from the center possible.

We both acknowledge our greatest indebtedness to our delightful companions, to whom we dedicate this book.

D. R. G. AND H. S.

INTRODUCTION TO SUNY SERIES IN CONSTRUCTIVE POSTMODERN THOUGHT

The rapid spread of the term *postmodern* in recent years witnesses to a growing dissatisfaction with modernity and to an increasing sense that the modern age not only had a beginning but can have an end as well. Whereas the word *modern* was almost always used until quite recently as a word of praise and as a synonym for *contemporary,* a growing sense is now evidenced that we can and should leave modernity behind—in fact, that we *must* if we are to avoid destroying ourselves and most of the life on our planet.

Modernity, rather than being regarded as the norm for human society toward which all history has been aiming and into which all societies should be ushered—forcibly if necessary—is instead increasingly seen as an aberration. A new respect for the wisdom of traditional societies is growing as we realize that they have endured for thousands of years and that, by contrast, the existence of modern society for even another century seems doubtful. Likewise, *modernism* as a worldview is less and less seen as The Final Truth, in comparison with which all divergent worldviews are automatically regarded as "superstitious." The modern worldview is increasingly relativized to the status of one among many, useful for some purposes, inadequate for others.

Although there have been antimodern movements before, beginning perhaps near the outset of the nineteenth century with the Romanticists and the Luddites, the rapidity with which the term *postmodern* has become widespread in our time suggests that the antimodern sentiment is more extensive and intense than before, and also that it includes the sense that modernity can be successfully overcome only by going

xi

beyond it, not by attempting to return to a premodern form of existence. Insofar as a common element is found in the various ways in which the term is used, *postmodernism* refers to a diffuse sentiment rather than to any common set of doctrines—the sentiment that humanity can and must go beyond the modern.

Beyond connoting this sentiment, the term *postmodern* is used in a confusing variety of ways, some of them contradictory to others. In artistic and literary circles, for example, postmodernism shares in this general sentiment but also involves a specific reaction against "modernism" in the narrow sense of a movement in artistic-literary circles in the late nineteenth and early twentieth centuries. Postmodern architecture is very different from postmodern literary criticism. In some circles, the term *postmodern* is used in reference to that potpourri of ideas and systems sometimes called *new age metaphysics,* although many of these ideas and systems are more premodern that postmodern. Even in philosophical and theological circles, the term *postmodern* refers to two quite different positions, one of which is reflected in this series. Each position seeks to transcend both *modernism* in the sense of the worldview that has developed out of the seventeenth century Galilean-Cartesian-Baconian-Newtonian science, and *modernity* in the sense of the world order that both conditioned and was conditioned by this worldview. But the two positions seek to transcend the modern in different ways.

Closely related to literary-artistic postmodernism is a philosophical postmodernism inspired variously by pragmatism, physicalism, Ludwig Wittgenstein, Martin Heidegger, and Jacques Derrida and other recent French thinkers. By the use of terms that arise out of particular segments of this movement, it can be called *deconstructive* or *eliminative postmodernism.* It overcomes the modern worldview through an anti-worldview: it deconstructs or eliminates the ingredients necessary for a worldview, such as God, self, purpose, meaning, a real world, and truth as correspondence. While motivated in some cases by the ethical concern to forestall totalitarian systems, this type of postmodern thought issues in relativism, even nihilism. It could also be called *ultramodernism,* in that its eliminations result from carrying modern premises to their logical conclusions.

The postmodernism of this series can, by contrast, be called *constructive* or *revisionary.* It seeks to overcome the modern worldview not by eliminating the possibility of worldviews as such, but by constructing a postmodern worldview through a revision of modern premises and traditional concepts. This constructive or revisionary postmodernism involves a new unity of scientific, ethical, aesthetic, and religious intuitions. It rejects not science as such but only that scientism in which the data of the modern natural sciences are alone allowed to contribute to the construction of our worldview.

The constructive activity of this type of postmodern thought is not limited to a revised worldview; it is equally concerned with a postmodern world that will support and be supported by the new worldview. A postmodern world will involve postmodern persons, with a postmodern spirituality, on the one hand, and a postmodern society, ultimately a postmodern global order, on the other. Going beyond the modern world will involve transcending its individualism, anthropocentrism, patriarchy, mechanization, economism, consumerism, nationalism, and militarism. Constructive postmodern thought provides support for the ecology, peace, feminist, and other emancipatory movements of our time, while stressing that the inclusive emancipation must be from modernity itself. The term *postmodern,* however, by contrast with *premodern,* emphasizes that the modern world has produced unparalleled advances that must not be lost in a general revulsion against its negative features.

From the point of view of deconstructive postmodernists, this constructive postmodernism is still hopelessly wedded to outdated concepts, because it wishes to salvage a postive meaning not only for the notions of the human self, historical meaning, and truth as correspondence, which were central to modernity, but also for premodern notions of a divine reality, cosmic meaning, and an enchanted nature. From this point of view of its advocates, however, this revisionary postmodernism is not only more adequate to our experience but also more genuinely postmodern. It does not simply carry the premises of modernity through to their logical conclusions, but criticizes and revises those premises. Through its return to organicism and its acceptance of nonsensory perception, it opens itself to the recovery of truths and values from various forms of premodern thought and practice that had been dogmatically rejected by modernity. This constructive, revisionary postmodernism involves a creative synthesis of modern and premodern truths and values.

This series does not seek to create a movement so much as to help shape and support an already existing movement convinced that modernity can and must be transcended. But those antimodern movements which arose in the past failed to deflect or even retard the onslaught of modernity. What reasons can we have to expect the current movement to be more successful? First, the previous antimodern movements were primarily calls to return to a premodern form of life and thought rather than calls to advance, and the human spirit does not rally to calls to turn back. Second, the previous antimodern movements either rejected modern science, reduced it to a description of mere appearances, or assumed its adequacy in principle; therefore, they could base their calls only on the negative social and spiritual effects of modernity. The current move-ment draws on natural science itself as a witness against the adequacy of the modern worldview. In the third place, the present movement has even more evidence than did previous movements of the ways in which modernity and its worldview *are* socially and spiritually destructive. The fourth and probably most decisive difference is that the present move-ment is based on the awareness that *the continuation of modernity threat-ens the very survival of life on our planet.* This awareness, combined with the growing knowledge of the interdependence of the modern worldview and the militarism, nuclearism, and ecological devastation of the modern world, is providing an unprecedented impetus for people to see the evidence for a postmodern worldview and to envisage postmodern ways of relating to each other, the rest of nature, and the cosmos as a whole. For these reasons, the failure of the previous antimodern move-ments says little about the possible success of the current movement.

Advocates of this movement do not hold the naively utopian belief that the success of this movement would bring about a global society of universal and lasting peace, harmony, and happiness, in which all spirit-ual problems, social conflicts, ecological destruction, and hard choices would vanish. There is, after all, surely a deep truth in the testimony of the world's religions to the presence of a transcultural proclivity to evil deep within the human heart, which no new paradigm, combined with a new economic order, new child-rearing practices, or any other social arrangements, will suddenly eliminate. Furthermore, it has correctly been said that "life is robbery": a strong element of competition is inherent within finite existence, which no social-political-economic-ecological order can overcome. These two truths, especially when contemplated together, should caution us against unrealistic hopes.

However, no such appeal to "universal constants" should reconcile us to the present order, as if this order were thereby uniquely legitimated. The human proclivity to evil in general, and to conflictual competition and ecological destruction in particular, can be greatly exacerbated or greatly mitigated by a world order and its worldview. Modernity exacer-bates it about as much as imaginable. We can therefore envision, with-out being naively utopian, a far better world order, with a far less dangerous trajectory, than the one we now have.

This series, making no pretense of neutrality, is dedicated to the success of this movement toward a postmodern world.

David Ray Griffin
Series Editor

1

INTRODUCTION: HOW THIS DISCUSSION TRANSPIRED

David Ray Griffin and Huston Smith

This book is a dialogue between two people, both of whom are highly critical of the modern worldview. Both are keenly interested in the relation between science and religion, and between Christianity and other religions. And both, at some point in their odysseys, abandoned the position the other now holds for the one he presently espouses. This puts us in a favorable position, we felt, to work on the deep-lying differences between our two positions—one perennial, the other postmodern. Our discussion also held the prospect, it seemed to us, of bringing the outlines of our two positions into sharper relief by virtue of the contrasts we would be mainly focusing on.

We agree on far more than divides us, but in this book we only allude to our commonalities so we can get on with the differences. In this introduction, we enter the portions of our respective stories that bear on the discussion that ensues.

1

DAVID GRIFFIN'S STORY

I grew up actively participating in a conservative church in a small town. After high school, I entered the University of Oregon in 1957 as a music major. I soon decided to become a minister, however, and transferred the next year across the street to Northwest Christian College, a Bible college of my denomination, where a conservative-to-fundamentalist theology was taught. During my final years I became restless with this outlook, particularly with its exclusivism conjoined with an Anselmian doctrine of atonement.

In the 1962-63 academic year, while I was back at the university getting a master's degree in counselling, I came into contact with a wider world of thought. I went to Berkeley to hear Paul Tillich give the Earl Lectures at Pacific School of Religion, and decided to focus on philosophical theology when I went to seminary instead of pastoral counseling. I took a class from Douglas Straton who introduced me to Reinhold Niebuhr, among others. In the class I met George Nordgulen, who praised the virtues of Alfred North Whitehead, Charles Hartshorne, and various process theologians. His attempts to interest me were mainly in vain, but I do recall trying to read *God's Grace and Man's Hope* by Daniel Day Williams.

Later that year, however, George and I visited the School of Theology at Claremont. There I met John Cobb, and, on the basis of his paper "A Personal Christology," decided to attend Claremont.

I also encountered a quite different world of thought while still in Eugene that same year. A professor in a philosophy course mentioned "Flying Father Joseph of Copertino," who was a contemporary of Leibniz and allegedly levitated on a regular basis. Looking up the account of him in the *Journal of the American Society for Psychical Research* was my first brush with that world of thought—and my only brush with the *academic* study of such phenomena for many years to come. A friend introduced me to peyote (which in those days he had to get from Texas), and to Aldous Huxley's *Doors of Perception*. Although I took peyote only twice, and belladonna once (this was several years before hallucinogenic drugs were made illegal), I did learn the meaning, before I knew the words, of "altered states of consciousness." I also learned of the existence of a Theosophy library in the neighborhood, and read quite extensively, especially books based on Edgar Cayce's "life readings" and other books about reincarnation. More generally, a Theosophical blend of Hinduism and Christianity became my world of thought. It seemed to be based on good evidence, and the doctrine of universal salvation through reincarnational evolution was ethically and rationally much more satisfying than the exclusivistic Anselmian idea of atonement I had been taught since childhood. It seemed much more exciting and illuminating than not only the conservative theology I was fast leaving behind but also the new blend of Tillich, Niebuhr, and process theology that had been its initial replacement. I recall, while on the way to Claremont, trying to reread Dan Williams's book and finding it tepid fare, indeed, too dull to read. That experience provided a basis for understanding many years later Huston Smith's statement that, after he first came upon Vedanta, he found that his "interest in process theology dropped markedly." I felt the same thrill with the Vedantic world of thought, as I understood it, that he says he felt when he first encountered Whitehead.

Through these influences, I had decided to make Eastern religions my major field of study, and immediately enrolled in a history of religions course. This course happened to be at the same time as John Cobb's seminar on "Whitehead's Philosophy and its Religious Relevance," however, and I soon found myself skipping class about every other time to attend Cobb's seminar. I had not yet read Whitehead himself, but I found that his thought, as expounded by Cobb, spoke to my concerns. I remember, for example, Cobb's saying that this philosophy provided a way between the old supernaturalism, according to which God miraculously interrupted the normal causal processes now and then, and a view according to which God is something like a cosmic hydraulic jack, exerting the same pressure always and everywhere (which described rather aptly the position to which I had come). Through this influence, I returned to my plan to study philosophical theology, and started becoming a process theologian, eventually writing my dissertation on "Jesus, Revelation, and Truth," which, after some years and considerable revision, was published as my first book, *A Process Christology,* in 1973.

As that book reveals, my interests had shifted greatly. I saw process theology as providing a good basis for a social (and ecological) gospel, and treated the resurrection of Jesus as an optional feature of Christology and of Christian faith in general. Salvation was regarded, in good modern liberal fashion, as a this-worldly state. A future existence was not necessarily denied, it was simply ignored, as being too uncertain to be the focus of faith and too irrelevant to the main issue, which was to bring about the Kingdom of God, or at least a more just and survivable way of life, on this planet.

This change of interests and outlook was based partly on evidence. Edgar Cayce had been my primary authority for my semi-Vedantic convictions, and for not wholly bad reasons. When in trance, he apparently had remarkable clairvoyant powers, being somewhere near 90 percent accurate with his medical diagnoses and prescriptions. But when, with more historical sophistication, I learned that it was very unlikely that Jesus, *contra* Cayce, had spent several years in India, I came to distinguish between the accuracy of his medical readings and that of his historical and theological assertions. While this distinction left the validity of clairvoyance intact, I quickly lost interest in that whole complex of ideas, having found a better, more sophisticated world of thought that seemed quite satisfactory, if not fully so (Easters were not glorious).

Sociological factors were important in this change. Liberal theological circles were dominated by Bultmannian and other antimystical schools of thought. More importantly, the general state of the culture during those years, between 1963 and 1968, can best be recaptured by recalling the assassinations of John and Bobby Kennedy at the beginning and the end, and the assassination of Martin Luther King, Jr., and the driving of Lyndon Johnson from office over the Vietnam war, in between. My focus, like that of the culture in general, was outward.

Several developments during the five years I taught in the theology department of the University of Dayton are relevant to this series on postmodern thought in general and to this dialogue with Huston Smith in particular. First, after the rise of ecological awareness about 1969, I devoted considerable attention to a process theology of nature, becoming convinced that anthropocentrism and dualism are errors that must be rooted out if we are to survive. Second, this was the heyday of the death-of-God theologies, and I focused on the ontological and epistemological sources of atheism in modern philosophy. Third, I began coediting a book on John Cobb's theology with Thomas Altizer (Mr. God-is-Dead himself), and entitled my introduction "Post-Modern Theology for a New Christian Existence," thereby picking up the key term in Cobb's 1964 response to the death-of-God theologies, "From Crisis Theology to the Post-Modern World." In my mind, both ecological and spiritual survival became associated with the possibility of a widespread adoption of a new worldview in which nonsensory experience is primary in us and in which experience is attributed to all individuals, even those without sensory organs. Fourth, a colleague who had organized a local conference on immortality asked me to write a paper. I wrote positively of "The Possibility of Subjective Immortality in Whitehead's Philosophy"; while I believed that life probably did not continue after bodily death, I thought it important for people not to think that philosophical reflection ruled out the possibility. The fact that I did not really believe was made abundantly clear by my reaction to the death of my then-wife's younger brother in Vietnam. The normal grief was greatly intensified by the fact that this delightful boy, after having been unhappy for a long period, had just begun to find himself—having been found by love—and then before he had a chance to live was killed in a war he considered wrong. Fifth (moving right along), the opportunity arose to spend an entire year teaching nothing but Asian religions, and I jumped at it. This decision allowed for an immersion in the literature of Hinduism and Buddhism, and for some reflection about the relation of Whiteheadian philosophy to some of the philosophies produced by these traditions. Sixth, the invitation came to return to Claremont to establish, with John Cobb, the Center for Process Studies.

My major task for the center has been to plan conferences to relate Whiteheadian philosophy to various areas of thought. Most of the conferences have involved either Eastern religious philosophies or the natural sciences, especially physics and biology, which enabled me to become acquainted with some of the most creative thinkers in these areas. Through these interchanges in the latter part of the 1970s, I became more convinced than ever of both the possibility and the necessity of a postmodern worldview (although I was not yet using the word) based primarily upon a synthesis of Whiteheadian philosophy and the best of more recent thinking in these and other areas.

A research leave in 1980-81 provided the final stimulus to make the contrast between modernity and postmodernity central to my work. A semester at Cambridge University in England was crucial in several respects. I devoted much of my time to studying the emergence of modern ways of thought in the seventeenth and eighteenth centuries. In studying the furor in England surrounding *The Myth of God Incarnate,* written by John Hick and others, I saw that the reaction was due not solely to supernaturalistic reactionaries maintaining a virtual identification of Jesus with God but also to the modern presuppositions of the authors, which led to a denial of divine presence in Jesus altogether. I delivered a paper at Cambridge speaking of the need for a postmodern christology. In discussions resulting from this and other presentations, I became even more convinced of the need to relate talk of nature, human nature, and divine action to contemporary sciences and philosophical reflection thereon, rather than simply presupposing the general adequacy of the Whiteheadian framework. In particular, the attempt to use the mind-brain relation as an analogue for the God-world relation failed to communicate because so many hearers assumed an identity between brain and mind. I began reading extensively about the mind-brain relation to see if identism really had the solid empirical support its advocates claimed for it. Besides seeing that it did not, this study brought me into contact, by chance (evidently), with parapsychology. This contact began my first study of serious parapsychological research (as distinct from my earlier exposure to occult literature and psychical research of the softest kind).

I spent the second half of my leave in Berkeley (where Huston now lives, but did not at that time). I had decided to spend most of my time on physics (I went to Berkeley partly because Henry Stapp is there) and evolutionary biology, and to read parapsychology in the evenings. But I soon decided that the parapsychological evidence was not only more interesting but also more important for philosophical theology, partly because it was a largely untapped source. I was amazed to learn of the quantity of good work, the quality of the best work, and the number of first rate thinkers who had explored the evidence seriously and found it credible. Some of the evidence related to the question of life after death (this generally being considered, with extrasensory perception and psychokinesis, one of the three main areas of psychical research). I began reading this literature with the confidence that all the data could be explained, especially from a Whiteheadian perspective, in terms of extrasensory perception and psychokinesis ("the super-ESP-PK hypothesis"). But the quantity and quality of the evidence, and the complexity of the theories needed to explain it away, finally overcame me, and I, against my original intention (at least consciously), became a "believer." I did not become absolutely convinced of the truth of life after death, just as I had never been absolutely convinced of its falsity; but I came, intellectually and emotionally, to believe it about as strongly as I had previously disbelieved it. This inversion of probability involved no major change with regard to philosophical possibility; I had always recognized that Whitehead's philosophy allowed for the possibility of survival. But even here there was some change; I saw that the possibility was supported by more features of this philosophy than I had previously realized. I came to see these features, which are those features that support parapsychological influences in general, as among the distinctively postmodern features of this philosophy. My lecture at the Center for Process Studies' annual banquet after my return to Claremont was entitled "Parapsychology and the Need for a Postmodern Philosophy."

My next discovery involved more historical work in the seventeenth century. I learned that the mechanistic worldview associated with the rise of "modern science" was based less on empirical facts than upon theological-sociological motivations, and that the mechanistic worldview did not replace a decrepit Aristotelianism, as the textbooks had taught us, as much as a vibrant "magical" worldview, in which action at a distance, internal relations, and divine immanence were central, and which was the real cradle of most of those breakthroughs associated with the "rise of modern science," including Newton's theory of gravity as well as

Gilbert's of magnetism. I came to see that the modern worldview, as expressed in scientific, philosophical, and theological thought (which were then not separated), was most centrally a rejection of precisely those types of powers and influences that are now called parapsychological. And I came to see Whitehead's philosophy, especially when its support for these influences is emphasized, to be a twentieth-century recrudescence of that Renaissance worldview which spawned modern science only to be rejected in the name of reactionary theological and sociological interests. My sense of the Whiteheadian philosophy as a postmodern worldview thereby increased, along with my interest in stressing its distinctively postmodern features. In 1983, I started the Center for a Postmodern World in Santa Barbara.

It was in the context of all these developments that I received, after a brief conversation with Huston at a conference, a copy of his article, "Science and Theology: The Unstable Detente," which had been published in the *Anglican Theological Review*. It was inscribed: "David, admitting I might be wrong, this marked copy, p. 377, with regards, Huston." Turning to said page, I saw that his inscription was an allusion to a statement once made by Kennett Roshi that she was working on a new *ko'an*, "I could be wrong." Getting ready to criticize various forms of the "theological innovations of modernity" because of the loss that has been suffered through them, Huston said that he wanted that *ko'an* to apply to his remarks. After mentioning personalism, Bultmann's demythologizing, the theology of hope, and Teilhard de Chardin, he devoted most of his attention to process theology. His major criticisms were these: (1) process theology deprives God of ultimacy (giving it instead to creativity, eternal objects, and the structure of actual occasions); (2) it rules out a concrete, timeless perfection and divine simplicity; (3) it rejects life after death (in favor of objective immortality in God) on the basis of a naturalism it wrongly assumes to be forced on us by natural science. For these reasons, he said, process theology involves a great loss in comparison with the classical expressions of Christianity (which he found to include everything of importance he had discovered in the Upanishads). He asks, in fact: "Why, then is this loss—Process Theology—being inflicted on Christians? (That is a strong charge. I keep repeating to myself, like the Jesus Prayer, 'I could be wrong. I could be wrong!')"

I was convinced that he *was* wrong—to some extent about process theology in general, but especially about its more postmodern possibilities: It should not be classified as an example of *modern* theology. It does not deprive God of ultimacy. And it does not—which seemed to be the main criticism—accept a naturalistic worldview on the basis of modern science, at least not the type of naturalism that rules out life after death, but criticizes that form of naturalism. I believed that my new theological position was sufficiently different from the image of process theology being rejected by Huston that, once he saw it, he would consider any remaining differences trivial. Knowing that he was keenly interested in parapsychological phenomena, I assumed that my Whiteheadian defense of such phenomena would especially win him over. I resolved to write a response, but then, being preoccupied with a host of other matters, did not.

When I became aware, somewhat belatedly, of his book *Beyond the Post-Modern Mind,* and learned that the article he had sent me was reprinted therein, I renewed my intention to write a response, but now in the context of a response to his position as a whole. One important point to make was that the postmodern mind he wanted to get beyond is not the postmodernity I was advocating. More time passed, but finally an invitation was issued for Huston to come to Santa Barbara in January 1988 to lecture for the Center for a Postmodern World and to engage in a dialogue with me. I wrote the critique that appears here as Chapter 1 and sent it to Huston, who prepared a brief response. After our face-to-face exchange, we finished the dialogue through the mail. As is obvious, the unanimity I had at one time expected did not result. That it would not had become clear to me after I began a serious study of Huston's position, seeing that the differences were deeper than I had originally thought. I still hoped, nevertheless, that we might end up with more agreement than we thought we had when we began.

I now turn the floor over to Huston, but will return for a joint statement with him at the close of this introduction.

HUSTON SMITH'S STORY

I was born of missionary parents, in China, and spent my formative years there. I don't suppose one ever gets over that.

Because we were the only Americans in our small town, my parents were my only role models, so I grew up assuming that missionaries were what Westerners grew up to be. When I left for college in America, therefore, it was with the settled expectation that I would be back as soon as I had my theological credentials in hand. I had not reckoned with the West's dynamism. Never mind that *my* West was initially Central Methodist College (enrollment 600), set in Fayette, Missouri (population 3,000). Compared with Changshu, China, it was bright lights and the big time. Within weeks, China had faded into a happy memory; it would not be my future. The consequence for my career, however, was slight. Instead of being a missionary, I would be a minister.

My junior year in college brought another surprise: ideas jumped to life and began to take over. To a certain extent they must have slipped up on me gradually, but there was a night when, with the force of a conversion experience, I watched them preempt my life. Returning from a meeting of a small honor society, which met monthly for dessert and discussion in the home of its faculty sponsor, several of us lingered in a corridor to continue arguments the evening had provoked—as unlikely a knot of peripatetics as ever assembled. My excitement had been mounting all evening, and around midnight it exploded, shattering mental stockades. It was as if a fourth dimension of space had opened, and ideas—now palpable—were unrolling like carpets before me. And I had an entire life to explore those endless, awesome, portentous corridors! Unhappiness might return, but I knew that I would never again be bored. I wonder if I slept at all that night.

In retrospect it seems predestined, but at the time I could only see it as good fortune that the faculty sponsor of our discussion group was a protégé of Henry Nelson Wieman. Wieman was at The University of Chicago, so I naturally chose it for my graduate study. Having earlier shifted my vocational intent from missionary to minister, I now moved next door again by opting for the teaching rather than the pastoral ministry—administrative and promotional demands of the latter would leave too little time for ideas. Because these vocational adjustments were not only logical but small, they occasioned no soul-searching; but as I think back on the matter I am surprised that the collapse of my youthful supernaturalism seems to have caused no trauma either. I entered The Divinity School of The University of Chicago a convinced Wiemanite, which is to say, a naturalistic theist. Robert Maynard Hutchins, the university's president, had chosen as his motto for the university Walt Whitman's "Solitary, alone in the West, I strike up for a new world," and I responded to his idealism—with some smug elitism admixed. Hutchins insisted that the "The" in The University of Chicago be capitalized to underscore its distinctiveness, and we were fond of quoting William James's alleged observation that whereas Harvard University had thought but no school, and Yale University, a school but no thought, Chicago had both. Chicago was an exciting place, and despite World War II—I had ministerial deferment and was headed for the chaplaincy—the early 1940s were a heady time for me. Through naturalistic theism, the two most powerful forces in history—science and religion— were about to be aligned, and it would be my life's mission to help effect the splice. I was a very young man and fresh to the world's confusions.

I can remember as if it were yesterday the night in which that entire prospect, including its underlying naturalistic worldview, collapsed like a house of cards. It was five years later, in Berkeley—but before I relate what happened, I need to explain how I got there. Chicago proceeded as planned, with one major surprise. Although in my first year I would not have believed that such a thing was possible, in the second year I discovered something better than Wieman's theology, namely his daughter. Two years later we were married, and for forty-five years she has been a delightful and stimulating companion.

Having married into Wieman's family, I needed to find a new advisor, so Bernard Loomer, a newly appointed instructor, saw me through my dissertation. It was Wieman, however, who suggested its topic. Stephen Pepper at the University of California had followed his book on metaphysics, *World Hypotheses*, by focusing on pragmatism (or *contextualism*, as he called it), and, as that worldview underlay Wieman's theology, he was interested in having someone explore the fit. So with recent bride and more recent first child in tow, I set off for a year in Berkeley to write (under Pepper's guidance) "The Metaphysical Foundations of Contextualistic Philosophy of Religion."

That year, I bumped into the question of how a philosophy that placed the premium on quality that contextualism did would handle the quality called *pain*, and, having given pain little direct thought up to then, I set off to the library for instruction. Rummaging under *pain* in the card catalogue, I found four titles that looked as if they might be relevant. One of them—Gerald Heard's *Pain, Sex and Time*—carried the most interesting title of the four, so I began with it. It proved to be one of the two most important reading experiences of my life. By page two, I discovered the book had nothing to do with my dissertation, but I kept reading. When I finished, I made two resolves. First, I would not read another line by this author until I had completed my doctoral studies—I obviously feared that if I did, I might quit the university. Second, when my diploma was in hand, I would read everything Gerald Heard had written.

What "grasped" me that night, as Tillich would say, was the mystic's worldview. Never before—not during my four years as an undergraduate religion major, nor during the four subsequent years as a graduate student of philosophy and theology—had mysticism been sympathetically presented to me, and when it was, I instantly cathected. The naturalistic world I had loved and lived in since my mind's arousal was, with a single stroke, relativized. It was but part of the whole. An island—lush to be sure, but rimmed round about by an endless, shining sea.

The dissertation was completed, and I began to teach the philosophy of religion (at the University of Denver and then the University of

Colorado) in the framework of Pepper's *World Hypotheses*. Pepper argued that the things in the world look differently according to the worldview through which they are seen. In *The Basis of Criticism in the Arts* he applied this thesis to aesthetic criticism, showing how evaluations of poems and paintings differ according to whether the critic is a Platonist, a mechanist, a contextualist, or an idealist. My courses simply extended that approach to religion. Initially, Wieman provided my specimen of the way religion looks to a contextualist, but as Wieman turned from metaphysics to the social sciences, and Hartshorne and Loomer convinced me that Whitehead's "philosophy of organism" was the strongest worldview for a naturalistic theist, this philosophy replaced pragmatism (contextualism) in my metaphysical spectrum. Already I was suspecting that Pepper's dismissal of mysticism as an imprecise worldview was uninformed, but I was still too unschooled in that outlook to enter it as a fifth option in my metaphysical spectrum.

That changed when I moved to Washington University in St. Louis in 1948 at the beck of its chancellor, Arthur Compton, who somehow heard of me through Wieman, whom he had come to respect while the two of them were at The University of Chicago. Before the move placed more distance between us, I decided to visit Gerald Heard who I had learned was living in southern California. During the course of the visit, he introduced me to his friend and neighbor, Aldous Huxley, whose *The Perennial Philosophy* had been under my arm on the journey. On seeing me off for my return journey, Heard remarked: "So you're moving to St. Louis. There's a very good swami there."

Swami? I'm not sure I recognized the word. At that point, however, Heard and Huxley were my guiding lights, so I asked for the swami's name and looked up *Satprakashananda* in the St. Louis telephone directory the week that I arrived. He turned out to be with the Ramakrishna Order of Vedanta, which Swami Vivekananda had established in America after taking the 1893 Chicago Parliament of Religions by storm. Learning that he was conducting a Tuesday evening discussion group on the Katha Upanishad, I dropped in on a session and returned home with a copy of the text. It occasioned the second of the two distinctive reading experiences I alluded to above. I have met teachers of world religions who confess that after fifteen years they still do not understand the Upanishads. For me it was otherwise. Their teachings were self-evident, including their insistence that there was more to be comprehended than could be rationally conceived.

For ten years, my Western philosophy marked time as I apprenticed myself to my new-found mentor. In weekly tutorials he taught me the Vedanta and at the same time set me to work meditating. There was a time—about five or six years into this regimen—when in return for a monthly sermon I was listed as associate minister of my local Methodist Church and while (less publicized) I served as president of the St. Louis Vedanta Society. While this might have seemed odd, I experienced no conflict. In addition to keeping my ancestral ties intact, my church connection kept me "in love and charity" with my ostensible community and offered outlets for good works. To add, though, that the theological concerns of my congregation did not run deep enough to satisfy me would be to put the matter mildly, and its spiritual exercises stopped with pietism—in Vedic idiom, *bhakti.* There was one day each year when the two poles of my religious life were sharply joined. The church pageant on Christmas Eve was pitched early to accommodate young children, and its magic regularly worked to rebind me to my family and heritage, for what can rival a "Silent Night" that is imprinted in memory's deepest recesses? I could *sense* the mystery of the Incarnation in that service, but nothing in its ambiance underwrote for me the ontological foundations of that mystery to the extent that Swami Satprakashananda's annual meditation on "Jesus Christ, the Light of the World," delivered late at night after the children were put to bed, did. That Christ was one of multiple avatars for him was incidental compared with his certitude that in Christ's birth something ontologically dramatic had *happened.*

In my tenth year at Washington University, a bid came from the Massachusetts Institute of Technology (M.I.T.). Its president, Carl Compton—brother of my own chancellor—wanted to strengthen M.I.T.'s humanities program, and felt that the time had come to add philosophy to its existing tracks in English and history. My St. Louis colleagues argued that the dream of humanizing scientists was romantic, but the task seemed worth attempting. Moreover, Cambridge was an intellectual magnet.

M.I.T. proved to be my longest tenure. Its fifteen years were intense, tumultuous, and above all instructive. The edge with science that it offered me was pure gain, but the edge with philosophy in the northeastern United States was ambiguous. Analytic philosophy was in its heyday then, and M.I.T. was in its Harvard/Princeton/Cornell "Bermuda Triangle"—likening it to that Caribbean trap, which is rumored to consume planes that unsuspectingly enter its mysterious vortex, seems quite appropriate. It was not the brand of philosophy that I—or for that matter the administrators who had brought me to M.I.T.—felt our students most needed, however. In time, I grew weary of the polemics and the need to justify my philosophical interests to my colleagues, so when Syracuse University came into an endowed chair that was more open to those interests and would give me greater access to graduate students, I accepted the invitation to be its first occupant.

As for my Asian education, my move to the eastern seaboard added Buddhism to the Vedantic foundation St. Louis had laid down. Before leaving Washington University I had brought to its campus D. T. Suzuki and then a Zen priest, who was a Fulbright exchange scholar, with whom I taught a semester's course on Zen. The experience "hooked" me and, because the priest insisted that Zen could not be grasped by the rational mind alone, I decided to go to Kyoto for a summer of meditation, *ko'an* training, and residence in Myoshinji monastery—Gary Snyder was my *dharma* brother there. Thus it was that Zen became my contemplative practice for my M.I.T. years. In switching, I did not feel as if I was deserting Vedanta. Śunyata seemed very similar to nirguna Brahman and the Buddha-nature similar to Atman—so much so that I felt I was encountering the same truth in different idiom. Another sea-change of the same order—same sea—occurred a decade or so later when Seyyed Hossein Nasr introduced me to the mystical dimension of Islam in pre-Khomeini Iran. Again, it felt as though I was learning yet another language in which the same truths could be couched.

Only one more episode needs telling. In my Introduction to Frithjof Schuon's *The Transcendent Unity of Religions*, I relate how, while conducting students on an academic year around the world, I chanced in Japan, India, and Iran successively upon books of his that dramatically deepened my understanding of the religions at hand. Pursuing Schuon's writings after I returned home, I discovered that he situated the world's religious traditions in a framework that enabled me to honor their significant differences unreservedly while at the same time seeing them as expressions of a truth that, because it was single, I could absolutely affirm. In a single stroke, I was handed a way of honoring the world's diversity without falling prey to relativism, a resolution I had been seeking for more than thirty years.

Turning from this account of "where I'm coming from" to the discussion with David Griffin that follows: although it is not one that I would myself have initiated, I am grateful to him for having brought it to pass. Because I am writing this concluding paragraph after our substantive discussion has been completed, I can say with knowledge of hindsight that I have learned vastly more from it than I expected I would—not only about David's position, but about my own. And pleasures have accrued. Neither I nor my wife could have wished for more gracious hosts than David and his wife, Ann, during the Santa Barbara weekend to which he alludes, or for a more worthy and civil antagonist in this written dialogue that has ensued.

JOINT STATEMENT

Although, in fact because, most of our attention in the book is devoted to our differences, we want here to emphasize our agreement, which we consider more fundamental. The central agreement is that we must, for individual, social, and planetary health and even survival, move beyond the modern worldview, including the relativistic, nihilistic postmodern mind-set that is indicated in Smith's book title, *Beyond the Post-Modern Mind.* The first section of Chapter 1, in which Griffin summarizes Smith's "Critique of the Modern Worldview," can for the most part be considered a joint critique (especially if the adjective *modern* is always inserted before *science*).

We also agree that, in spite of all our criticisms of each other's position, that other position is far superior to any version of the modern worldview and to any of the fully relativistic, nihilistic stances, sometimes called *postmodern,* that have resulted from taking certain modern presuppositions to their logical conclusion.

The major value of this book, we expect, is that it provides readers who are dissatisfied with modernity and relativistic postmodernity an inside look at two alternatives, or, we should say, two versions of two of the major alternatives available today. Each position is presented and defended by an advocate and criticized by a sympathetic critic—one who affirms its basic intention and wishes it well—in fact, wishes to help make it better! Through the process of response and counterresponse, the reader is enabled to observe a process that usually occurs in letters or private conversations. Occasionally, this type of extended interchange can be heard at academic meetings or read in scholarly journals, but even there the time or space is usually far too limited to allow more than a brief interchange on isolated issues. We have each tried to see the other's position whole and to show how our various criticisms come from our own position as a whole. Through this back-and-forth process of presentation, critique, clarification, defense, and countercritique, the reader should have a sufficient basis to evaluate the respective viability of these two alternatives to the dominant worldview of modernity.

Neither of us expects all readers to come down on one side rather than the other—and we know that some readers will say "a plague on both your houses!" We recognize that worldview is a matter not simply of logic and evidence but also of social conditioning. We recognize with William James that worldview is also partly a matter of temperament, and that, even beyond social conditioning, people have fundamentally different temperaments. We recognize with Whitehead that "others may require a proportion of formulation different from that suitable for ourselves," so that our pet dogmas may not strike a chord with others. We offer our ideas for those who find them helpful.

2

PREMODERN AND POSTMODERN PHILOSOPHICAL THEOLOGY: A RESPONSE TO HUSTON SMITH'S PROGRAM

David Ray Griffin

Huston Smith has become an important and influential critic of the modern worldview and of the relativistic postmodern outlook to which it has led. He is influential because he writes in an engaging manner and because he is an important critic. He is important partly because he is influential but also because he has a number of other virtues. As a philosopher of science who taught many years at M.I.T., he has an intimate knowledge of modern science, which has been at the root of the modern world. As a philosopher in general, he is conversant with the relativistic postmodernism that has resulted from taking the premises of modern thought to their logical conclusions. As a philosopher and historian of religion,

he understands well the extent of the contrast between the modern outlook and the worldviews in terms of which all previous peoples have
lived. As a man with intense religious sensitivity, he realizes the devas-
tating impact that this change has had on the self-image and, therefore,
the behavior of human beings. Finally, as a theologian,[1] he is an articu-
late and effective spokesman for that philosophical-theological position
he calls the primordial tradition. He convincingly points out the pragmatic and intellectual weaknesses of the modern and relativistic postmodern outlooks and portrays the primordial worldview as very attractive
by comparison.

In this evaluation of Smith's program, I first present a summary of
his criticism of the modern worldview and the relativistic postmodernism[2]
to which it has led. I then present his reclamation program to recover
the "forgotten truth" of a premodern vision of reality.[3] In the third and
fourth sections, I argue that some of the premises upon which Smith's
program is based lead to several problems. In the final section, I suggest
a (nonrelativistic) postmodern approach to recovering the central truths
and values that modernity lost.

I. THE CRITIQUE OF THE MODERN WORLDVIEW

Smith can sum up the modern worldview either as the loss of faith in
transcendence[4] or as the acceptance of a lifeless universe.[5] These two
descriptions come to the same thing, which is reductionism, the belief
that every higher thing is explainable in terms of lower things. All causation is upward, from the lower to the higher. This outlook implies that
we derived not from a transcendent, divine reality but from lifeless bits
of matter. This worldview comes to fullest expression in the neo-Darwinian theory of evolution, according to which we are the products of a
blind, material process, from which all divine influence is in principle
excluded.[6] This modern worldview involves a complete reversal of the
traditional viewpoint.

Smith believes that this modern worldview involves an incalculable loss, and he is concerned primarily with its effects upon our self-
image.[7] Growing up with this worldview, modern men and women are
deprived of the beliefs and values in terms of which virtually all previous
peoples lived their lives.[8] Earlier people saw their world as an enchanted
garden, whereas moderns see it as a meaningless machine. Earlier people believed their origin and therefore their very essence to be spiritual;
modern people are taught that their origin and therefore their very
essense is material. Modern people are the first to believe they origi-

nated not from gods but from savages.[9] Earlier people tried to live up to their self-image; modern men and women have been busy living down to theirs.

The loss involved in this modern worldview is doubly tragic in that it was based on a mistake. This mistake (which will be explained below) was closely related to the overriding myth of modernity, the myth of progress. In our century, the illusory nature of this faith in progress has been realized.[10] The modern mind, with its faith in order and progress, is evolving into a postmodern mind that is relativistic and nihilistic. This postmodern mind rejects the modern belief that human reason can discover the true order of the world; it even rejects the belief that there is a true order.[11] The ideal of a comprehensive vision of reality is, hence, completely rejected.[12] Neither philosophy, theology, nor science can provide any support for values or any sort of orientation for life.[13] Theologians have acquiesced to this situation, toning their theologies down to fit the secular mind-set.[14] The most we can be told by philosophers or theologians is that we must decide for ourselves.[15] But we are then told that everything is meaningless, which implies that our decision will itself be meaningless.

This relativistic postmodernism is, Smith believes, a transitional phase, because the will to order is fundamental to the human spirit. A comprehensive vision, providing a sense of meaning and orientation, is a basic human need.[16] Relativism is unlivable and finally self-subverting.[17] Some people think that the solution is to tell stories. But a story or narrative only works as long as it is assumed to be true, which means as long as it has no effective competitor. When two or more stories clash, Smith argues, we must move to the more abstract level, where the truth of the matter can be sorted out. We must, in other words, turn to metaphysics.[18]

The first step in recovering an orienting metaphysic, Smith holds, is to provide a critique of the modern worldview. It can be criticized both formally and substantively. The point of the formal critique is that this worldview was based on a mistake. A limited method was turned into a metaphysic.[19] This limited method is the scientific method. It is limited because it is useful for studying only the lowest realm of existence, Smith maintains, the material realm we know through our physical senses.[20] This realm can be fruitfully studied and described, he says, in purely mechanistic, quantifiable, reductionistic terms. The modern worldview results from turning this science into scientism, the doctrine that nothing exists except what can be studied in terms of this method. This conclusion is wholly unjustified. The fact that a flashlight, which can reveal the existence of dirt beneath your feet, does not reveal the existence of stars above your head does not prove that only dirt exists.[21] Modernity's conceit that it has a "scientific world-view" therefore reflects a contradiction in terms. Science by its very nature deals with only part of reality, not the whole.[22] The assumption that modernity has discovered that transcendence does not exist, and that we do not live in an enchanted garden, is therefore based on a colossal mistake.[23]

This scientistic metaphysic meant that science became the only way to know. This conclusion did not emerge overnight. Science and religion engaged in a long warfare, but science won.[24] Scientific reason thereby replaced revelation as the basis for culture, and art as well as religion were marginalized.[25] In terms of the politics of culture, this victory meant that professionalized scientists wrested cultural power from the church.[26] As for philosophy, it became ontologically naturalistic, assuming all existence to be rooted in space, time, and matter, and epistemologically sensationist, rejecting any supersensual way of knowing.[27]

This modern metaphysic reflected a Promethean epistemology. Modern science is based upon the will to power, the desire to control. Whereas previous spiritualities were oriented toward self-control, the control of inner nature, modern spirituality reflects the desire to control outer things.[28] This desire is closely related to the modern faith in this-worldly progress, both reflecting and supporting it.[29]

When examined in terms of its substantive assertions, the reductionistic worldview of modernity is easily found wanting. Neo-Darwinism as an explanation for evolution is a failure. (Smith even believes that evolution as a *description* of how our world came about is problematic.[30]) Furthermore, the basic premise of the reductionistic worldview, that the more emerges from the less, is incredible, because it means that something comes out of nothing.[31] Psychosomatic medicine and parapsychology both reflect downward causation from mind to matter,[32] and the evidence for the Gaia hypothesis suggests downward causation from the planet as a whole to its parts.[33] Not only parapsychology but also recent physics suggests influence at a distance, which is impossible within the materialistic worldview.[34] Finally, as Lewis Thomas and other scientists have suggested, consciousness may be pervasive throughout nature, meaning that the Cartesian view of matter as "vacuous actuality" would be false.[35]

The negative task of criticizing the scientistic worldview is only the first step in recovering an orienting philosophy of life. Because the positive task, which involves thinking about reality as a whole, is too vast for an individual mind, Smith says, we need help.[36] Where should we turn? At this point the crucial feature of Smith's program appears.

II. The Recovery of Forgotten Truth

Smith says that the best way to overcome modernity is to return to premodernity. "The wave of the future," he suggests, "will be a return to the past."[37] More specifically, he has in mind a return to what has been called the "perennial philosophy," which he prefers to call the "primordial tradition." The word *primordial* indicates that this philosophy has been present in every time and every place in human history.[38] It is, he maintains, the "natural," the virtually universal way, of seeing,[39] so common to premodern peoples that it can be called "the human unanimity."[40] To speak of this unanimity does not mean that all premodern religious philosophies were identical; that assertion would be obviously false. It means that beneath the great differences in the explicit doctrines lies a common core. This common core constitutes the primordial tradition and provides a basis for overcoming the complete pluralism, that is, relativism, which pervades contemporary philosophy.[42] Unlike some Vedantist apologists, Smith does not believe that all of our modern knowledge was possessed by the ancients. But they erred only in details, he maintains, "not in their basic surmises."[42] Smith's convictions are summed up in his statement that "our hope lies in returning to an outlook which in its broad outlines is carried in the bloodstream of the human race."[43]

What are the "basic surmises" or "broad outlines" of this view? The main conviction is that divine reality is at the root of everything and that everything in our universe is a consequence of something superior.[44] Reality is ordered hierarchically; things with less reality and value are dominated by things with greater reality and worth. Causation runs downward. The universe is teleologically ordered, being persuaded from above, not determined mechanically from below.[45] Rather than assuming that consciousness and values have emerged only late in the day, through the workings of chance and determinism, the primordial vision places them at the beginning and sees everything in our world as derivative therefrom. The universe is, therefore, seen as a meaningful, spiritual place, in which values, purposes, and qualities are central, rather than being illusions or mere by-products of matter, efficient causes, and quantities, and in which human beings are seen to have a spiritual, divine core.[46] This worldview reflects a will to participate, or to embrace, not a will to control. Insofar as it does provide knowledge for control, it is ethical knowledge in terms of which to control ourselves.[47]

While this primordial vision provides human beings with a comprehensive vision in terms of which they can lead a happier, healthier life, Smith says that its practical consequences cannot be the main reason for accepting it. The main reason for changing to a different outlook must be that we have become convinced of its truth. And truth is not to be defined pragmatically but in terms of correspondence: to believe that a statement is true is to believe that it correctly represents the way things are. Our primary concern must be to adjust ourselves to the way things are.[48]

The belief that we can reach truth involves rejection of the assumption of the postmodern relativists that we are necessarily prisoners of a culturally conditioned perspective. That view assumes that all our perceptions are conditioned from the outset by our language, with its inherent worldview, so that we have no means for getting at reality in itself. Reason, from that point of view, is limited to reasoning about culturally conditioned perceptions. Truth, therefore, can be nothing more than coherence with the majority viewpoint; it cannot be correspondence with reality in itself. The social sciences, therefore, become the final arbiters of "truth."[49] But that view is false. We do have direct, unmediated experience of reality. We are not limited to sensory perception and reasoning thereon. Rather, through what Plato called the "eye of the soul," we have nonsensuous, preconceptual, prelinguistic, metaphysical intuitions into the nature of reality.[50] Because we have these intuitions, our context is not our social collectivity but the generically human. Through these intuitions, which are grounded in human nature as related to its source, universal and therefore nonrelative truths are discovered.[51] These truths constitute the human unanimity, the primordial tradition. Through a return to this primordial tradition we find a worldview that not only can be accepted as true but that also provides us with an inspiring picture of the universe and thereby of ourselves.

My summary of Smith's criticism of the modern worldview and his statement of the essence of the primordial worldview, to which he suggests we return, has been sympathetic. I believe his criticism of the modern worldview is in most respects justified. I also believe that there are primordial truths that are in principle available to human beings in all times and places, and that among them are the ideas summarized above. However, I also believe that, when Smith's position is examined more closely and the content of his primordial vision specified in more detail, problems arise.

III. SMITH'S PREMODERN VISION:
INTERNAL PROBLEMS

Most of my criticisms of Smith's position follow from one or both of two features of his program to reclaim past truths and values. First, he proposes an undialectical return to a premodern vision, rather than a dialectical "return forward" to a postmodern vision in which modern and premodern truths and values would be creatively synthesized. Second, Advaita Vedanta seems to be normative for the premodern vision he advocates. Although Smith and those upon whom he builds speak of an esoteric core that is common to all great religious traditions, the teachings of Advaita Vedanta seem to provide the criterion for discerning this common core. Any doctrines inconsistent with Advaita Vedanta are relegated to the category of illusion or at best provisional truth.

Some of my criticisms point to internal problems in Smith's position. That is, some of his statements seem to be inconsistent with other statements, or at least with implications of other statements. Other of my criticisms are externally based. That is, Smith's position seems to be inadequate to certain facts or values of which I, seeing reality from a somewhat different perspective, am convinced. I treat internal problems in this section, saving external criticisms for the next.

1. Personal God and absolute reality. One internal problem involves a tension between Smith's Advaita Vedantist vision and his conviction that deity must be "superior to ourselves by every measure of worth we know."[52] In Smith's hierarchy, reality is first divided into two basic levels, which can be called the transcendent and the immanent, the absolute and the relative, the infinite and the finite, or reality and appearance. Each of these two realms is then divided into two planes, so that four planes result. The finite level is divided into matter and spirit, or visible and invisible, with spirit or the invisible higher. The infinite level is divided into the personal God and the transpersonal absolute, with the absolute higher.[53] The personal dimension of the Godhead does not include the transpersonal; rather, it is included within it. We can speak of a personal God, but we must be aware that the personal aspect of the divine is one of "those qualified and provisional realities," which are exceeded by the absolute.[54] The personal deity is the God of Western theism, who "creates the world by deliberate intent, presides over history providentially, and knows and loves his creatures."[55] Theism in this sense is said to be true, "but not the final truth; God's personal mode is not his final mode," which means that humans must realize that "in the last analysis God is not the kind of God who loves them."[56] In the last analysis, God is nirguna Brahman, an infinite, undifferentiated reality devoid of all attributes. "The Infinite . . . is undifferentiated."[57] "It is not enough to say that God's attributes exceed ours inexhaustibly; the attributes themselves must be transcended."[58]

If deity, however, is ultimately devoid of attributes or qualities such as love and knowledge, how can we say that deity is "superior to ourselves by every measure of worth we know?" Does Smith not think that, at the finite level, mind is higher than matter insofar as mind knows and feels? Does he not think that humans are higher than other animals insofar as we have more capacity to know and to love? The idea that deity is ultimately *beyond* all knowing and loving seems to contradict the entire hierarchical view, according to which lesser things originate from higher things. The Advaita Vedantist view seems strangely similar to the modern materialistic view. In both, the personal arises from, and is less real than, the impersonal. One can *say*, of course, that the infinite reality is not subpersonal, but transpersonal or suprapersonal; but unless some significant difference can be specified, the terminological distinction is merely verbal.[59]

2. Orientation and ineffability. A second internal problem is that Smith's statement of the primordial vision is in tension with his recognition that we need an orienting vision. He says that "orientation always includes a sense of what is important and what is not: what we should emphasize and move towards and what we should avoid." We need "knowledge of the right direction."[60] Against relativistic postmodernists, he asks rhetorically: "How can we know what kinds of sacrifices and surrenders are appropriate if we don't know what kind of universe is requiring them of us?"[61]

When we come to Smith's own statement about the nature of reality, however, we are told that it is ineffable, that is, indescribable: "the final reality, the infinite, is radically ineffable."[62] It must be, of course, if it is devoid of all attributes. Nothing can be appropriately attributed to that which transcends all attributes.

Given Smith's hierarchical view, his calling the infinite ineffable does not mean that merely one feature of reality is indescribable. Rather, the infinite, or the absolute, *is* reality, in comparison with which everything else is mere appearance. Everything else is finally included within the infinite. To call the infinite ineffable is thereby to say that reality as a whole is indescribable. How then does this worldview provide us with orientation? I do not see how we can decide what is truly important, and what the right direction for our lives is, apart from some idea as to qualities, purposes, and values that are central from the divine perspective, or that are otherwise of central importance in the nature of reality. Smith tells us, however, that the divine reality is devoid of all purposes and qualities, and that reality cannot be described. I fail to see how this viewpoint provides any more orientation than does the explicit relativism of the postmodernists that Smith opposes.

3. Immortality and undifferentiated reality. Closely related to the previous two points is a tension in Smith's statements about the ultimate meaning of our lives. He is critical of a form of theology that "replaces subjective human immortality with an objective version in which we are remembered by God." That view is said to be a "loss" compared with "the traditional teaching that we must all one day awaken from life's dream into other dimensions in which the lie shrivels, the fiction is destroyed, and all deceptions are swept away."[63] In Smith's own statement about immortality, however, he says that selves take "the final step of relinquishing their individuality entirely" as they "simply dissolve into the Godhead."[64] Just as the personal God is not ultimately real, neither is the personal self. We are immortal only insofar as we are Spirit, which is what lies below our "specifically human overlay—body, mind, and soul."[65] What is Spirit? "Spirit is the Atman that is Brahman, . . . that something in the soul that is uncreated and uncreatable."[66] As we have seen, Brahman is undifferentiated; it is devoid of all attributes. That in us which is immortal is accordingly the undifferentiated reality, which is devoid of any attributes. This view makes it very difficult to see that I am immortal in any sense that gives my life ultimate meaning. "From undifferentiated reality to undifferentiated reality" seems little improvement over "from dust to dust." It certainly provides no basis from which to describe as a "loss" the view that we are preserved everlastingly in the divine experience.

4. Truth and incoherence. A fourth internal problem involves the issue of truth. As we saw, Smith accepts the correspondence account of truth, and says that we should accept the primordial philosophy primarily because it is true, not because it is more appealing pragmatically. But what grounds are we given for thinking that this premodern worldview is more true than the modern? Some theologians appeal to revelation, saying that we should believe their doctrines because they are based on revelation. For example, conservative Christian theologians point to miracles and fulfillments of prophecy as extrinsic proof that the Bible is or contains God's revealed word, whose contents can therefore be believed without further ado. Christian doctrines need not, according to this approach, prove themselves true in terms of their intrinsic capacity to provide a consistent and adequate view of reality. Smith does believe that the primordial vision is revealed, but I am not sure how this claim functions in relation to the question of our acceptance of the primordial vision as true. Smith may mean that, insofar as the primordial vision is universal, being present in every major human tradition, its truth is proved. But if this were his claim, then very detailed historical work would be needed to prove that this vision is indeed at the esoteric heart of every major tradition, and this certainly has not been part of Smith's project. I assume, then, that the claim that the primordial vision is universal does not function, analogously to miracles and fulfilled prophecies, as extrinsic proof of the truth of the vision's content. I assume, rather, that the relation between truth and revelation goes the other way. That is, we can believe that the primordial vision is revealed because we have good reason to think it true. The apparent universality of the vision is a desideratum in favor of its truth but not by itself proof. The case for the truth of this vision must be, therefore, based upon the intrinsic merits of this vision itself. How can this case be made?

The usual philosophical criteria for a philosophical position are self-consistency and adequacy to the facts of experience. Smith accepts these criteria, at least implicitly, in that he uses them to argue against the truth of the modern worldview. We have already seen his use of the criterion of adequacy to the facts, as he uses evidence from physics, parapsychology, and psychosomatic medicine to show that the modern worldview is inadequate to the mind's influence on matter and action at a distance. His rejection of reductionism as incredible is based upon the fact that the reductionist's explanation of emergence "so ill accords with our direct experience."[67] He also uses the criterion of self-consistency or coherence. For example, he criticizes the modern worldview insofar as its deterministic behaviorism results in a paradox:

> Out of the practical side of our mouths we continue to urge people to exercise their freedom and take responsibility. . . . Meanwhile, out of the theoretical side of our mouths we serve notice on these attributes and place them in jeopardy . . . [saying that] human beings are not free at all.[68]

Smith also uses the test of coherence against relativism:

> Relativism sets out to reduce every kind of absoluteness to a relativity while making an illogical exception for its own case. In effect, it declares it to be true that there is no such thing as truth; that it is absolutely true that only the relatively true exists. This is like saying that language does not exist, or writing that there is no such thing as script. Total relativism is an incoherent position.[69]

As Smith approaches his own position, however, he becomes more tolerant of paradox and incoherence, and even criticizes others for their intolerance. For example, he criticizes process theologians for rejecting classical theism on the grounds of incoherence. "Had their notion of coherence ruled at Nicea and Chalcedon," he says chidingly, "the creeds could not have come down to us as they have."[70] Contradictions are involved in the proposition that "God and man are infinitely different" but that Christ is nevertheless fully both, he agrees, and in the proposition that the persons of the Trinity are completely distinct and yet completely fused; but these propositions are not to be rejected on that account. Against those who claim that "whatever can be neither imaged nor coherently conceived . . . does not extist," Smith replies: "truth does not need us and is in no way dependent upon our powers of conceptualization."[71] Smith defends the paradoxes of classical theism by analogy with the paradoxes of modern physics. He asks rhetorically, "is there any 'incoherence' in classical theism . . . that does not have its analogy in the paradoxes of quantum mechanics, and cannot, with deep discernment, be brought under Niels Bohr's claim that, whereas the opposite of a small truth is false, the opposite of a great truth is another great truth?"[72]

The incoherences of classical theism, however, are not those with which Smith is finally concerned. Theistic assertions apply only to the penultimate plane of reality, not the ultimate. Smith's defense of incoherence is finally applicable to the relation between the absolute plane and the planes below it. Having said that the personal dimensions of the divine are not unreal, he says that they "are caught up and assume their place in the abysmal infinity of the Godhead which our rational minds can no more fathom than a two-dimensional mind could fathom the nature of a sphere." Smith says that kataphatic theology, which deals with the theistic level of reality, "inevitably produces paradoxes analogous to the ones that turn up on two-dimensional maps of our three-dimensional earth."[73] More generally, he says:

> There is an Absolute, which is likewise Infinite. This Infinite both includes and transcends everything else. . . . The way the Absolute transcends the relative is to integrate the relative into itself so completely that even the Absolute/relative distinction gets annulled. . . . How the opposition is resolved we cannot, of course, imagine or even consistently conceive, which is one reason the Absolute is ineffable.[74]

Why should we believe this? In fact, the more basic question is, What does it mean to "believe" something that is neither imaginable nor coherently conceivable? To ask these rhetorical questions is not necessarily to say, as Smith seems to think, that whatever we cannot coherently conceive does not exist. It is only to say that, if an assertion does not express or evoke a consistently conceivable proposition in our minds, we at the least have no reason to believe the assertion. The more radical claim is that no "assertion" has in fact been entertained, so that it is meaningless to talk about believing or not believing it. But even without this more radical claim, we can wonder why we should believe an assertion the meaning of which cannot be consistently conceived. After all, no end of such assertions can be made. Smith himself rejects some assertions because of their incoherence, such as the assertion that "relativism is absolutely true" and the simultaneous assertion of both determinism and freedom. And Smith criticizes relativism for making an exception for its own case. But is not Smith implying that other positions should be rejected if they are found incoherent, whereas incoherences in his own position are no grounds for its dismissal? Does he not indeed seek to make a virtue out of a necessity, suggesting that only an incoherent position can express the ultimate truth? But again, why except *Smith's* incoherent position rather than some other one?

To recall the nature of the present argument: I am asking on what grounds we should accept the primordial vision of reality as portrayed by Huston Smith. I have pointed out that Smith himself says that it is to be accepted not primarily because of its pragmatic benefits but because it is true. And I have assumed that Smith is not saying that we should accept it as true because of its alleged universality or divine origin. These excluded bases seemed to leave only the normal philosophical criteria for accepting a position: coherence and adequacy. But the primordial vision, by Smith's own admission, does not provide a coherent vision of reality. Smith thereby seems to be asking us to accept it as true even though it fails one of the tests he himself applies to other positions.

The test of adequacy to the facts also counts against the acceptance of Smith's vision as true. I have in mind here the problem of evil. Smith is critical of those who believe that the world's evil means that we must deny either the goodness or the omnipotence of the divine reality. He believes that we should hold to both.[75] Traditionally—for example in St. Augustine—this move has meant the denial of the reality of evil. That is, evil in one sense is admitted: sin, suffering, and ugliness do abound.[76] But it is claimed that somehow all these evils contribute to a higher good than would have been possible without them. The evil is hence only apparently evil; it is not genuinely evil, if by "genuine evil" we mean something without which reality as a whole would have been better. Smith adopts this position, affirming the East's attitude that "it is as it should be."[77] He endorses Augustine's view that evil is simply the absence of good, and an assertion by Augustine in which the reality of genuine evil is denied: "I no longer desired a better world, because I was thinking of creation as a whole: and in the light of this more balanced discernment, I had come to see that higher things are better than the lower, but that the sum of all creation is better than the higher things alone."[78] Not to affirm Augustine's position, Smith says, "is to complain about the admittedly-inferior-while-essentially-noble condition that is ours."[79] Smith's position involves the hierarchical, great chain-of-being idea that lower beings have less being and goodness than higher beings. God is the most real being and accordingly has the most being and goodness, having in fact *infinite* being and goodness. But it is nevertheless good that finite beings exist as well. Even though they are not as good as God, reality as a whole is richer through the fact that every possible level of being is actualized.[80]

This position, however, does not really solve the problem of evil. The only form of evil that this position justifies is what Leibniz called "metaphysical evil," which is the evil allegedly inherent in a finite being by virtue of the fact that it is not infinite and divine.[81] The idea that being finite is *ipso facto* to be in some sense evil is a peculiar idea, peculiar to those who think in terms of degrees of being and think that these degrees are correlated with degrees of goodness. In any case, even if this so-called metaphysical evil should be considered a form of evil, it is entirely distinct from physical evil (suffering) and moral evil, which are what we usually have in mind when we are troubled by the problem of evil. That is, we ask not why human beings are not God or why cells are not human beings. Rather, we ask why some human beings are so sinful, or why some humans or other sentient beings suffer so much, or why some cells become cancerous. The problem is not why some things have less being than others, but why things do not more perfectly fulfill their own level of being. In explaining why so-called metaphysical evil exists, Smith has therefore in no way responded to the real problem of evil. If he intends moral and physical evil to be included under metaphysical evil, meaning that no genuine evil of any kind exists, his position is simply not adequate to reality. The idea that no genuine evil exists is as counterintuitive as the idea that something arises out of nothing. Smith's position, accordingly, fails the test of adequacy to the facts as well as that of coherence.

In saying this, I have shifted from internal to external criticism of his position. But not entirely: Smith himself clearly implies that genuine evil occurs. One cannot read his criticism of the modern worldview, and of the effects it has had upon human beings, without seeing that Smith believes the existence of the modern worldview to be a great evil that should be overcome. To paraphrase Smith's own criticism of those who speak incoherently about freedom quoted above (26): Out of the practical side of his mouth Smith urges people to overcome the evil of the modern worldview, while out of the theoretical side of his mouth he denies that any genuine evils exist. Smith's response to the problem of evil, therefore, seems to involve incoherence as well as inadequacy to obvious facts of experience.

On the question of truth, then, Smith seems to leave us with a purely pragmatic basis for choosing the primordial philosophy. Interestingly, in one place Smith seems to say as much. In spite of his criticism elsewhere of postmodern relativists who claim that there is no objective basis for preferring one worldview to another, Smith says: "It is not possible to adjudicate between contending outlooks objectively, but it is possible to say which is the more interesting. And on this count [the primordial vision] wins over the MWM [Modern Western Mind-set] hands down, for it allows for everything in the latter and vastly more besides.[82] On the very next page, Smith does say that "we are tracking truth not for its practical consequences but for its intrinsic worth. . . ."[83] But unless Smith has an argument that the "more interesting" view is more likely to correspond with reality, the previous statement seems to say that no objective basis exists for deciding whether one worldview corresponds to reality more than any other, which is precisely what the relativistic postmodernists contend.

5. Dualism or nondualism. Turning from the formal question of truth to the substantive question of ontology, I find that Smith seems to be of two minds on the question of dualism. On the one hand, he is critical of the dualism between humanity and nature that lies at the root of the modern worldview. I referred earlier to his approving quotation of Lewis Thomas's remark that we may share consciousness with all other things of the biosphere. He also says that "the man/world divide that Descartes and Newton first moved into place" does not describe "the actual nature of things" but is one of "science's working principles, no more, no less." He points out that the uncritical acceptance of this divide "drove the existentialists into an alienated, embattled, egocentric depiction of the human condition."[84] He says, further, that "no culture save our own has disjoined man from his world, life from what is presumed to be nonlife, in the alienating way we have," and he quotes approvingly a statement that "dualism is the great 'schizomorphic' structure of Western intelligence."[85] Given all this, plus his rejection of the materialistic alternative to dualism, we would expect to be told that the primordial tradition involves a panpsychic, animistic vision. And indeed Smith says that, if humans and all other things issue from a single, unqualifiedly good source, "it is impossible that its offspring not be kin.

In a single stroke the self-world divide, laid wide by Descartes' mind/ matter disjunction and the slash between primary and secondary qualities, is mended."[86] He also endorses the view that "heaven and earth are pervaded with sentience, infused with feeling."[87]

Elsewhere, however, dualism is asserted. His hierarchical view of reality, one will recall, involves a division within the finite world between matter and spirit. This division seems to be not merely epistemic (according to which all things are sentient from within while appearing to be material from without), but ontological. He endorses the view that our being consists of "two fundamental elements," and describes them, as Descartes did, as spatial and nonspatial. He speaks of an infinite gulf between insentient matter and sentience and indicates that these two realms must be linked by the infinite.[88] This statement recalls the appeal by Descartes and his followers to God to explain the apparent interaction of mind and matter. With regard to panpsychism, at one place Smith suggests that its possible truth is not important to his program;[89] at another place he apparently rejects it, saying that matter can no more be reduced to mind than mind to matter.[90] In any case, rather than appealing to panpsychism to combat reductionistic materialism, he makes the dualistic comment that "our thoughts and feelings are . . . too different from what we experience matter to be, to be reduced to it."[91] He adds that the elemental parts of nature can be "pushed around" because they possess "neither mind nor freedom in the genuine sense."[92]

Smith even seems to go beyond dualism, suggesting that there are *four* ontologically different types of substances, corresponding to Aristotle's divisions into mineral, vegetable, animal, and human. "The differences between inanimate and animate, plant and animal, and animal and human, are so momentous," he says, "that it makes more sense intuitively to recognize that different qualities, powers, and even substances are involved." He rejects the attempt "to account for differences in kind as if they were only differences in degree." Smith evidently believes that these differences in kind require the postulation of a life-force, of consciousness, and of self-awareness in higher types of substances.[93] In any case, whether there be two, three, or four ontologically different kinds of substances, I cannot see how this view is consistent with Smith's assertion that all things are kin, and that the nature-human divide is overcome in the primordial vision. I also wonder if he is now comfortable with the appeal to deity to explain the apparently natural interactions between mind and body.

   6. Science and theology. Smith's two minds about the ontological issue of dualism is paralleled by two attitudes about the formal issue of the relation between science and theology. This relation is central to his project. He cites approvingly Whitehead's prediction that the future will be shaped most decisively by the way in which science and religion settle into relation with each other.[94] Smith clearly rejects an accommodation of religious thought to the materialistic worldview with which modern science has been associated.[95] What is not clear is whether, beyond this negative relation, he sees the possibility for a positive relation, a relation of mutual support, between theology and certain developments in recent scientific thought.

On the one hand, Smith seems to deny this possibility. He rejects the idea that scientists and theologians should make joint statements on the nature of reality, and cites approvingly the statement that "to hitch a religious philosophy to contemporary science is a sure route to its obsolescence."[96] This rejection is buttressed by Smith's contention that the word *science* refers only to the natural sciences, and that science has been normatively defined by *modern* natural science.[97] Jacques Monod is accordingly said to be "exactly right" in declaring the systematic exclusion of the notion of final causation or purpose to be the basis of the scientific method.[98] Science is also said by its very nature to exclude all reference to downward causation, qualities, values, meanings, and transcendence.[99] It explains all phenomena solely in terms of efficient causation, upward causation, and quantities,[100] and limits itself to data knowable through sensory experience.[101] It seeks objectivity, mathematical precision, and the ability to predict and control.[102] As such, science cannot deal with life, consciousness, and self-consciousness, but is limited to the lowest level of the world, the material level.[103] This is so because the very crux of science, according to Smith, is the controlled experiment, and the necessary control is possible only with material things.[104]

From this standpoint, Smith rejects the call for a more holistic kind of science, which would deal with normative values, final causes, and intrinsic qualities. This development would, he says, decrease the effectiveness of science.[105] Smith also rejects the idea of a theistic account of evolution, according to which we could say that we are the products of both God and evolution, having issued from both above and below.[106] As he sees it, only the Darwinian account of evolution, which excludes all purposes and divine influence, is scientific.[107] The scientific and the religious viewpoints are thereby diametrically opposed. We should not look forward to a new era in which the differences between them would be overcome and in which they would speak with one voice about the nature of reality. Any collaboration would force religion to conform to science's method and its exclusions.[108]

On the other hand, many of Smith's statements point to a more positive relation between science and theology. He believes that science stands "in *supporting* relation to the traditional outlook."[109] I have found eight examples from contemporary science that he takes to support the primordial philosophy. First, as mentioned, he uses the paradoxes of contemporary quantum physics as support for the paradoxes of traditional religious thought.[110] How does this use of contemporary physics differ from that tendency "to hitch a religious philosophy to contemporary science" which he finds objectionable? He objected to this hitching on the grounds that scientific theories continually change. Is it not probable that physics in the future will overcome the paradoxes of the current dominant theories? That is at least the opinion and hope of David Bohm, to whom Smith often appeals approvingly.[111]

Second, as evidence for the integrated, holistic vision of the universe, Smith points to the fact that "science has found nature to be unified to a degree that ... we would not have surmised without its proofs." He refers here to the ideas that matter and energy are one, that time and space are one, with "time being space's fourth dimension," and that space and gravity are one with the latter's being "simply space's curvature."[112] Besides the fact that he has appealed to very specific theories, those of Einstein's, as support for his theological vision, his statement of each of the three unities is controversial.[113]

Third, against process theology, which makes time real for God, Smith appeals to physics to support his own view that God as absolute is eternal, beyond time. He says that process theology is "out of step with the growing suspicion in science that time is derivative and dependent," and quotes Einstein's well-known comment: "People like us, who believe in physics, know that the distinction between past, present and future is only a stubbornly persistent illusion."[114] Smith's negative comments about hitching theology to science were occasioned by the alleged fact that Whitehead and therefore process theologians modelled their cosmology on Einstein's relativity theory.[115] But insofar as Einstein's views support Smith, the appeal to them seems to be all right.

Fourth, Smith appeals to science, namely quantum mechanics, chemistry, and astronomy, to support his hierarchical model of reality. He says that "it is not likely that it would figure so prominently there [in the empirical world] if it were not embedded in the structure of reality itself."[116]

Fifth, as more specific support for the hierarchical model, he appeals to the Gaia hypothesis as evidence for downward causation from the animate to the inanimate.[117]

Sixth, Smith argues that power stands in inverse ratio to size from the law that, the shorter the wavelength of a light corpuscle, the greater its energy. From this principle he suggests that "the energy of something that has no size at all—God—might be infinite."[118] Smith adds that he included these two items from science to support the view that the more rather than the less has greater influence because "help from every quarter is useful."[119]

Seventh, in spite of his statements elsewhere that neo-Darwinism states *the* scientific theory of our origins, he points to developments that suggest that changes in the scientific theory will soon occur that will bring evolutionary theory into more accord with his own viewpoint.[120]

As an eighth example, I refer again to his positive citation of Lewis Thomas's suggestion that consciousness of a sort may pervade the biosphere. More generally, Smith buttresses his argument against materialism with evidence that contemporary physics seems to be abandoning materialism.[121]

Smith seems to reconcile this positive use of science to support a religious philosophy with his negative statements by thinking of the positive significance of science as merely symbolic. He says, for example: "If, instead of rummaging through science for direct, literal clues to the nature of reality, we could outgrow this fundamentalism and read science allegorically, we would find sermons in cloud chambers," and he refers to chapter five of his *Forgotten Truth* as an example,[122] which indeed it is. Most if not all of the examples cited above, however, seem to appeal to science for quite "literal clues to the nature of reality." It is hard not to believe that Smith, as do most of us, finds the appeal to science meaningful when it supports his intuitions and only frowns upon it when it is used to support contrary ideas. (To illustrate: The first, second, third, and sixth examples of Smith's positive use of science could tempt even me to make warning noises about hitching one's religious philosophy to contemporary scientific ideas.)

I suspect that Smith's two attitudes toward the relation between science and religious thought are related to his two views about dualism. On the one hand, his dualistic tendency to regard matter as wholly insentient supports and is supported by his tendency to regard science as restricted to mechanistic, reductionistic theories. On the other hand, his desire to overcome dualism and to portray a kinship between humans and the rest of nature supports, and is supported by, his desire to find positive evidence for his religious vision from the findings of recent science.

Smith's ambivalences about science and ontological dualism are related to the distinction between sensory and nonsensory perception. On the one hand, Smith generally writes as if science were necessarily restricted to the data of sensory perception, which would mean that life, consciousness, and self-awareness are beyond its purview.[123] Science, therefore, would be restricted to matter, and Smith evidently thinks of this "matter" as a distinct level of being, rather than simply an abstraction produced by sensory perception. On the other hand, he believes that nonsensory perception, which he alternatively calls "intuition," "intellect," and the "eye of the soul," is fundamental to our relation to reality and can be compared with the tropism of plants toward light.[124] Thus understood, this nonsensory perception would not be higher than sensory perception and the empirical reason based upon it, as Smith usually says, but more fundamental than it. This dimension of his thought supports a nondualistic ontology and perhaps opens him to a postmodern science, in which experience can be attributed to the inner nature of the things studied by biology, chemistry, and physics.

IV. SMITH'S PREMODERN VISION: PROBLEMS FROM A POSTMODERN PERSPECTIVE

I turn now to some features of Smith's position that do not seem to involve inconsistency but that are nevertheless problematic from my viewpoint. The fact that the issues in the previous section were subjected to internal rather than external critique does not mean that I do not find objectionable many of his positions summarized there. Indeed, I dislike his subordination of the personal God to an impersonal, ineffable absolute, his defense of incoherence, his denial of genuine evil, his tendency toward dualism, and his tendency to limit science to modern science. But because those stances all brought him into tension with other features of his thought, the criticisms of them could be made as internal criticisms, which is the type most authors take more seriously. In this section, the criticisms are made from the outside. I say that from my perspective, Smith's position on seven issues does not seem credible, helpful, or both.

1. Premodern versus postmodern. The first and overarching feature of Smith's program that I find problematic is his advocacy of a simple return to a premodern worldview. While I advocate a postmodern worldview, in which truths and values from modern and premodern outlooks are combined, Smith seems to think that the modern world has nothing to contribute at the level of basic truths. Premodern thought needs to be corrected and supplemented with regard to details, says Smith, but not with regard to basic surmises.[125] He quotes with approval Frithjof Schuon's statement that "everything has been said already. . . . There can therefore be no question of presenting 'new truths'."[126] Smith's position here reflects a strong distinction between cumulative and noncumulative truth. In history and science, he holds, truth is cumulative; progress is made through the discovery of new truths. But in metaphysics, religion, and art, he says, truth cannot be cumulative; nothing more exists to be discovered. "What, twenty-five hundred years later," Smith asks rhetorically, "do we know about evil that Job did not know?"[127]

What Smith's option for premodernity means concretely has to some extent been illustrated in the previous section, and more examples are examined below, but first two general questions must be asked. First, is the distinction between cumulative and noncumulative disciplines as absolute as Smith suggests? On the one hand, if, as postpositivistic philosophy of science suggests, science cannot be completely separated from an encompassing metaphysic, how can we say that science can make progress while metaphysics cannot? It would seem that either both can, as I hold, or neither can, as the relativistic postmodernists hold. On the other hand, has there been no progress in metaphysics and theology even in areas that are less directly related to the natural sciences? Some of us, for example, believe that an advance beyond Job in understanding the relation between God and evil *has* been made. (I return to this point below.) A second question: in rejecting modernity *in toto*, implying that it has discovered nothing essential, has Smith not simply repeated modernity's error, insofar as it rejected premodern thought and practice *in toto* as unenlightened superstition? Smith endorses the principle that philosophical positions are usually right in what they affirm, wrong only in what they deny.[128] Should that principle not be extended to modernity? And has not modernity, besides denying much, also affirmed much? Smith believes that every major tradition—every one that has evoked loyalty from a large number of people and endured for a considerable period—must contain important truths. Modernity is a major tradition. It has endured for several hundred years and has spread further and more rapidly than any previous tradition. Are we to say that this tradition's affirmations are all at the level of superficial detail, that none of them embody fundamental truths and values that need to be retained in the new worldview that supersedes the modern one? In other words, do we not need to go forward to a postmodern worldview, rather than trying to return to a premodern vision?

Having raised these general questions about a simple acceptance of a premodern vision, I turn now to some specific issues.

2. Causation: downward and upward. At the heart of Smith's contrast between the modern and the premodern visions is the contrast between upward and downward causation. In rejecting modern reductionism, according to which all causation goes upward from elementary particles, and the evolution of complex organisms is due entirely to material interactions, Smith presents a picture in which all causation is seemingly downward, from mind to body, from God to the world. He thereby advocates inverse reductionism. Reductionism's error, he says, "does not lie in its attempt to understand one type of reality in terms of another." The error is only "its attempt to explain the greater in terms of the less." Against this modern outlook, Smith affirms tradition, "where the drift is always the reverse: to explain the lesser by means of the more."[129]

At the level of the mind-body relation, Smith hence replaces modern epiphenomenalism, which regards mind as a passive by-product of the body, with the opposite view, according to which the body is a by-product of the mind, with no causal power of its own *vis-à-vis* the mind. At the level of cosmology, his position moves toward absolute idealism, according to which all finite things are wholly derivative from, or even aspects of, the infinite or absolute, with no causal power in relation to it. "Thus," says Smith, "everything derives, ultimately, from the Infinite. And since 'derives' cannot in this last case involve separation— the Infinite is like a celestial void: nothing escapes from it—everything abides in the Infinite's luster."[130] In a few passages, Smith seems to affirm a more complex view, in which there is both upward and downward causation. He speaks of "body-mind interaction," and refers to objects that "cooperated in bringing us into being,"[131] which seems to imply the both-and position on God and evolution that he usually resists. But most of his rhetoric suggests downward causation alone. He says, for example, that "everything in the bubble of our universe is the consequence of things superior to it . . . . Causation throughout is downward—from superior to inferior, from what is more to what is less."[132] The idea that everything derives from the infinite or, in theological language, that God is omnipotent, is what leads Smith to "solve" the problem of evil with the counterintuitive assertion that no genuine evil exists.

With regard to the mind-body relation, Smith's position would support the position of Christian Science, according to which all apparent physical illness is induced by the mind. This view is, of course, as Smith is aware, diametrically opposed to the presuppositions of modern medicine.[133] These modern presuppositions surely need revision. Should we revise them, however, by turning them completely upside down, as if modern medicine had been a complete failure? Smith surely agrees that modern medicine, working with its assumption that causation runs upward, from elemental to complex, from body to mind, has made great advances. Should this agreement not be reflected in a worldview that consistently portrays causation as running in every direction—upward and sideways as well as downward?

3. Gnostic dualism. Closely related to the issue of downward causation and to the problem of ontological dualism discussed earlier is a position that can be called *gnostic dualism.* Besides saying that mind is ontologically different from the body, and that causation goes only (or at least primarily) downward from mind to body, Smith also says that life and minds "do not depend on the physical bodies that sometimes 'house' them."[134] Given Smith's stress on downward causation and his doubts about evolution even as a description of how we got here, I take it he means that human-like minds or souls can be created (or emanated) directly. Devolution, he says, is more true than evolution.[135] That is, not only do the human minds or souls now have the ability to survive apart from their physical bodies; they did not really need those bodies in the first place. That Smith leans toward this view is supported by his surmise—which he admits not being sure how literally to intend—that early humans, being "close to provenient spirit," were more "ethereal" and thus left few ossified remains.[136] If this is Smith's position, it would be the strongest possible example of the rejection of modern thought. The physical world and the historical process would, on this view, be completely unnecessary for the creation of the highest forms of finite being and value-realization. I do not believe that the modern sensibility is so completely wrong. Furthermore, the gnostic position implies that the whole temporal process, with its at least apparent reality, is all wasted motion, unnecessary for the emergence of finite greatness. This waste would constitute an enormous problem of evil.

4. The unimportance of time. Closely related to the previous point is Smith's acceptance of the premodern view that time is of no ultimate importance in the scheme of things and is, in fact, ultimately unreal. He endorses the notion of deity as "concrete, timeless perfection,"[137] which implies that the temporal process is not needed for the divine realization of value. He says this explicitly: "nothing turns on time, for the limitless landscape is there from the start."[138] He endorses the view that time is a human invention,[139] and repeatedly quotes the statement by Einstein, cited earlier, that time, in the sense of a distinction between past, present, and future, is an illusion. Because the absolute is above time, the idea that the personal God is derivative from the absolute implies that "time derives from nontime."[140] The idea that the personal God is finally unreal in comparison with the absolute implies that time is finally unreal. When we awaken to our true self, which is identical with the absolute (Atman is Brahman), we will "pass beyond all space and time."[141]

Smith's position on this issue illustrates especially well the point I made at the outset, that he takes some premodern traditions, such as

Advaita Vedanta, to be superior to others, such as the biblical tradition, in which time was real and the historical process was regarded as essential to the realization of important values. Smith rejects this interpretation, to be sure. He claims that the primordial tradition he enunciates constitutes the esoteric core of all the great traditions, including the Hebrew tradition. I will not here try to solve this issue, which has been debated countless times. I only register my opinion that the Judeo-Christian view—which became fundamental to modernity—that time is ultimately real, and that real progress in the realization of values can be achieved in the temporal process, contains truth. This truth needs to be reconciled with Smith's truth, which is that all values that can possibly be realized in the temporal process are *in some sense* existent at the outset.

A serious question can be raised also about Smith's appeal to physics to support the unreality of time. It is indeed true that the dominant view among modern physicists has been that time is ultimately unreal, that "time's arrow" is not inherent in reality and does not exist for the most elementary physical entities. Einstein's statement, reflecting his Spinozistic vision of reality, is only a particularly strong statement of this widespread consensus. It is arguable, however, that this consensus reflects just the failure that Smith rightly says most philosophical extrapolations from physics exemplify, the failure to see that physics deals with abstractions from the real world, not the real world itself.[142] The fact that time does not matter to the physicist's abstractions does not prove that time does not exist for the real electrons, protons, and atoms in nature. In recent years, furthermore, some postmodern physicists and philosophers of science have been challenging the modern consensus, suggesting that time's arrow *does* exist for nature's most fundamental processes.[143]

5. No social progress. Because in Smith's view the notion of social progress is the cornerstone of the modern outlook, his assertion that progress is an illusion is perhaps his most pointed rejection of modernity.[144] His hope for salvation puts him at the opposite end of the spectrum from liberation theologians. While they focus on society and the future, Smith focuses on hope for the individual and says that everything necessary is already present.[145] He in particular rejects collective progress "envisioned as sociopolitical, the gradual amelioration of man's corporate lot through his collective efforts and ingenuity."[146] Smith denies both that progress in essentials will occur in the future and that it has occurred in the past. "Utopia is a dream, evolution a myth."[147] This denial is closely correlated with his view of the unimportance of time. If all important values are present from the outset, no essential progress can occur. Smith's rejection of progress is also closely related to his denial of evil. At the heading of a chapter entitled "Hope, Yes; Progress, No,"[148] Smith places the statement by Augustine, cited earlier, which begins, "I no longer desired a better world," and which Smith uses to support his belief that no genuine evil exists. Obviously, if everything is already perfect, if the world "is as it should be,"[149] sociopolitical efforts to make the world better are pointless. In a description of how he teaches religion, Smith says that he contrasts Western prophetic faith, which stresses the holiness of the *ought*, with Eastern ontological faith, which stresses the holiness of the *is*. He clearly believes that the latter form of faith is the one to stress. "With the near collapse of modernity's hopes for historical progress," he comments, "students are ready to think seriously about alternatives or complements.[150]

It again seems to me that Smith reacts to the onesidedness of modernity by advocating an equally onesided premodern outlook. Should we not emphasize the holiness of both the is and the ought? Smith, to be sure, leaves the door open for this both-and approach in the statement just quoted, saying that ontological faith could be taken as a complement, not simply as a stark alternative, to prophetic faith. And, in addressing the charge of social indifference, he says that he is calling for balance, not indifference.[151] But the force of his whole position points toward *replacing* prophetic faith with ontological faith, the holiness of the ought with that of the is, especially any ought related to the social-political-economic order. Although Smith endorses the principle that traditions are usually right in what they affirm, only wrong in what they deny, he seems to be rejecting what the Judeo-Christian tradition and the modern tradition have affirmed.

Smith's onesided emphasis seems unfortunate for a second reason. Is it not unseemly for Americans, living in the materially richest country in the world, to be belittling the importance of social progress? In arguing against the view that the development of civilization has meant progress, Smith endorses the view that it has increased rather than decreased starvation.[152] That is probably true. But this fact provides no reason for denying that we ought to take steps to try to overcome global hunger. Nor does it provide any reason to believe that we could not overcome global starvation, if we collectively set our minds to it. The fact that industrial capitalism has impoverished some people as much as it has enriched others does not prove that no system would work better. Smith is certainly correct to challenge current ideas of what constitutes progress. We who have so much material abundance will not be happier or better by having still more. But for us to cut back on our control and use of the globe's material resources so that others can have at least the basic necessities—for us to "live simply so that others can simply live"—

would be real progress. As to the call of conscience that tells us we ought to do so—that call I consider holy.

6. *The essential identity of all religions.* Another of Smith's positions with which I disagree is his claim that all the great religions are "equal revelations from, and of, the one true God," and that each is accordingly equally adequate for salvation.[153] Smith recognizes and even emphasizes that the various traditions are very different; they are manifestly not identical. This diversity, however, is a feature of their external, exoteric side; at the esoteric level, he maintains, they teach the same primordial truths. They have, to use the term of Smith's favorite author, Frithjof Schuon, a "transcendent unity."[154] Smith's claim here seems to be based less on historical, empirical facts than on deduction from the omnipotence and goodness of God. In fact, Smith states his case deductively:

> there is one God. It is inconceivable that s/he not disclose her saving nature to her children, for s/he is benevolent: hence revelation. From her benevolence it follows, too, that her revelations must be impartial, which is to say equal: the deity cannot play favorites.[155]

Just as horizontal causation among the creatures cannot bring about any genuine evil in the world for Smith, neither can it prevent saving truth from coming equally to all peoples. In fact, if such parity failed to exist, this failure would be an example of genuine evil. As Smith says of the great religions, which have endured for millennia, "God would not have permitted them to endure for such stretches had they been founded on error."[156]

If one looks at the religions without this theological presupposition, however, one is likely to see the situation differently. It does not seem plausible to me, in any case, to think of the various great religions as equally embodying revelations of the same divine reality. Judaism, Christianity, Islam and Zoroastrianism are oriented primarily to a personal deity, while much Buddhism and much of Hinduism, especially Advaita Vedanta, are oriented toward an impersonal, infinite, absolute reality. To say that the devotees of both types of religion are really worshipping the "same God" does not seem illuminating. Not sharing Smith's belief that the personal God is really derivative from, and hence less ultimate than, the impersonal absolute, I cannot agree that the God who inspired the ten commandments, liberation of people from sociopolitical captivity, and the Sermon on the Mount is really the same as the divine reality to which Shankara and Nagarjuna were oriented. To say that all religions are equally adequate for salvation seems equally unilluminating. That statement implies that the salvation sought by, say, Moslems and Mahayana Buddhists is the same. But meditation on Emptiness and submission to Allah seem to produce strikingly different types of people. While the inclusive doctrine that "we are all on the same path" seems appealing in comparison with the exclusivist claim that "there is no salvation outside of our church," it is not illuminating of the empirical realities. It is also not necessarily the only alternative.

A reason for taking issue with Smith's position here, besides the fact that it seems untrue, is that its widespread acceptance would discourage the type of religious interaction that seems to me desirable. Rather than thinking of the great religions as essentially identical, I see them as complementary, with each one focusing upon a limited set of transforming truths and values of universal import. Members of each historic tradition therefore have much to learn and appropriate from the others. The attitudes needed for this mutual appropriation and transformation would not be encouraged by Smith's view that all the traditions are, at bottom, saying the same thing.

7. Premodern worldview in a modern world. Having fleshed out the meaning of Smith's proposed return to a premodern worldview, we are now in position to expand on the first external criticism, which was that an advance to a postmodern worldview would be better than a simple return to a premodern outlook. There the point was that modernity has its distinctive truths which should be preserved, so that a simple return to a premodern worldview would not be desirable. Here the point is that a simple return is not even possible, at least not without far more extensive changes than Smith envisages.

Smith is aware that a return to a premodern *world* is not possible. He says that "our opportunity is not in any literal sense to go back, a move that in a thousand ways is impossible even if it were desirable. Bygone days really are gone." In clarifying the kind of reversion for which he is calling, he says: "The needed return . . . is in outlook only; it is in world view and sense of reality."[157] The separation between worldview and world implied here seems false. A worldview supports a particular kind of world. A particular kind of world cannot not long survive the disappearance of a worldview that supports it. Yet Smith seems to think that the social, political, economic, and technological structures of the modern world could remain essentially the same if people adopted the premodern worldview he advocates. Smith thereby underestimates the power of ideas to shape (or unshape) a world. Or perhaps, due to the fact that he believes his "perennial philosophy" to have been the esoteric core of classical Christian thought, he underestimates the great difference between the perennial philosophy and the outlook on which the modern world has been built. In any case, if the majority of the people in modernized countries became profoundly convinced of the truth of Smith's philosophy, I cannot believe that the structures and institutions of society would be basically unaffected. A people who no longer considered persons and the temporal process to be of ultimate importance in the scheme of things, who no longer thought science revealed truths about the ultimate nature of reality, and who no longer thought social progress either desirable or possible—such a people would develop a very different society. Smith does occasionally show his awareness that beliefs about the nature of reality have consequences for social structure. He points out, for example, that the erosion of religion has eroded the social order, and that the emergence of the materialistic worldview enabled professionalized scientists to wrest cultural power from the church. How can he think that the enormous change in worldview he is proposing would not have even more sweeping social effects? Distinctive features of the modern world will be preserved in the coming centuries only if the worldview that supersedes the modern one is a postmodern worldview, in which distinctive features of the modern worldview are retained.

V. A POSTMODERN RECOVERY OF PREMODERN TRUTHS

In this final section, I present a postmodern theology as an alternative way to recover those premodern truths and values that are at the center of Smith's concerns. These truths and values are: the rootage of all finite existence in divinity; an enchanted universe in which values, qualities, and purposes are primary; downward causation (especially as persuasion from above); nonsensory experience; the direct experience of values; the intuition of primordial universal truths; a noble self-image; present meaning; and hope for immortality. I suggest that these truths and values can better be recovered not by a return to a premodern vision but by an advance to a postmodern vision, in which truths and values of the modern tradition are included. This approach provides a better way, I maintain, not only because it includes modern as well as premodern truths, but also because it is devoid of the problems of inadequacy and incoherence inherent in Smith's premodern vision.

The position from which I speak, that of Whiteheadian process theology, is not unknown to Smith. He not only speaks critically of it in several places, but also indicates that it was at one time his own position.[159] These facts do not convince me, however, that the prospect for conversation is doomed from the outset, for two reasons. First, some of Smith's criticisms of Whitehead reflect misinterpretations.[160] Second, his other criticisms apply to only one type of Whiteheadian theology, a modernizing type, in which the distinctively postmodern possibilities inherent in the Whiteheadian vision and conceptuality have been ignored or denied. Whitehead's own theological writing was more modern, less postmodern, than it need have been, given his metaphysical position, while that of some of his followers is even more modern. A position that develops the postmodern possibilities in his metaphysics, in conjuction with more recent empirical evidence, might bring this form of theology much closer to Smith's primordial theology than he dreamed to be possible. I seek in this capsule statement, in any case, to suggest that this postmodern vision includes everything of central importance that Smith affirms, while excluding the negations and inconsistencies to which the premodern position had led him.

To facilitate comparison, I have discussed the various issues in roughly the same order as they were raised in the critique of Smith's position.

The key issues that differentiate this postmodern vision from Smith's, and from which the remaining differences follow, involve the metaphysical ultimate or absolute—its nature, its relation to God, and its relation to the finite world. This metaphysically ultimate reality is *creative experience*. This ultimate does not exist in itself, but only as embodied in concrete experiences. It does not as such create or experience, but all embodiments of it creatively experience. It is the absolute, or metaphysical ultimate, because it is that which is embodied in every actual or concrete thing.

Creative experience is embodied primordially in God. It could not exist without God, and God could not exist without it. They are hence equally primordial, equally ultimate. Creative experience is the metaphysical ultimate, while God can be called the axiological ultimate, in that God primordially envisages the moral, aesthetic, logical, and mathematical values that shape the ways in which creative experience is differently embodied in finite beings.[161]

Creative experience, the metaphysical ultimate, is also embodied primordially in a world of finite beings. A world could not exist without creative experience, and creative experience could not exist without a plurality of finite embodiments of it. In this sense, the world is equiprimordial with creative experience and God. God is essentially soul of the universe; God could not be the one and only embodiment of creative experience. In another sense, however, only God is equiprimordial with creative experience. God is the one and only enduring individual that exists necessarily and hence eternally. All finite beings exist contingently. *Some* world of finite beings must exist, but no particular world is necessary. No particular finite being, or set of such, exists necessarily and hence primordially.

The equal primordiality of the personal God, who creates and experiences the world, and the metaphysical ultimate, which is impersonal, means that personal qualities are not finally secondary and derivative in the nature of things. Just as God does not create creative experience, because that would imply a self-contradiction, creative experience does not create God, because it is not an agent which can create. It is agency itself, not *an* agent. The personal God is not derivative from the impersonal ultimate any more than the impersonal ultimate is derivative from God. They are distinct but equally ultimate.

This position means that the divine reality is not wholly ineffable. The metaphysical ultimate is, as Advaita Vedanta says of nirguna Brahman, the ultimate without qualities. We can have intuitive knowledge of what it is, because we embody it, but it is ineffable, in that it has no characteristics by which it could be described. This ineffability of the metaphysical ultimate does not, however, mean that *God* is wholly ineffable, because God is the *primordial characterization* of creative experience. We can understand God to some extent by analogy with ourselves and other personal beings. Analogously to us, God has (by hypothesis) an abstract essence, which means those abstract features that are instantiated in every moment of divine creative experience. These abstract features include perfect sympathy, perfect knowledge, perfect power, necessary existence, immutability (with respect to abstract essence), and changeability (with respect to concrete experiences). Ineffability virtually returns when we think of God as the concrete, all-inclusive experience of the universe at any time: we can scarcely begin to conceive what such an experience would be like. This type of ineffability does not lead, however, to a disorienting relativism. We can still describe the divine reality as creative experience, in some remote analogy with our own creative experience, and we can say that this creative experience involves perfect sympathetic knowledge.

Because the personal God is as ultimate as creative experience as such, personal qualities and therefore personal experiences are primary in the nature of things. The alpha and omega of the universe, and hence *our* beginning and end, is a personal reality. We derive from the primordial nature of God, and we are preserved everlastingly in God's all-inclusive, sympathetic, compassionate experience. (Whether we might also be immortal in the more ordinary sense is discussed later.)

Another virtue of this position is that nothing about God, the world, or their relation to the metaphysical ultimate necessarily forces us into incoherence in seeking to describe the ultimate nature of reality. Our concepts can, in principle, correspond with the reality. In practice we will surely fall far short. But, in principle, reality can (by hypothesis) be consistently understood, that is, in terms of its abstract features. This religious philosophy can rest its claim to truth on its ability to provide a more coherent, adequate, and illuminating account of reality than any of its rivals.

Neither the coherence nor the adequacy of this position is threatened by the problem of evil. God's perfect goodness and power are not contradicted by the world's evil. The idea that the world necessarily is comprised of beings with inherent creative power means that God cannot unilaterally prevent evil. Perfect power cannot mean omnipotence, if that means the power to override the creative power of the creatures or the effects thereof. God influences every event in the world but determines none—not because of a divine self-limitation, but because creative power belongs to a plurality of finite beings as primordially as it belongs to God.

The creative power of each event has three phases. The event first exercises the receptive power to receive influences (feelings) from other creative experiences. It then exercises the power of self-determination, through which it shapes its own experience. Finally, it exerts creative influence upon subsequent events by sharing some of its experiences with them. Each event is hence a product of divine influence, the creative influence of all previous events, and the event's own creative self-determination. Downward causation from God to the world occurs continually, but so does upward causation from lower to higher beings, horizontal causation between beings of the same level (for example, from person to person), and self-causation. The downward causation is therefore *necessarily* persuasion from above; it *cannot* be coercion from above. Because Perfect Goodness cannot coerce, the possibility of evil is necessary. The reality of evil therefore does not contradict the reality of Divine Perfection. We thereby perhaps know something about evil that Job did not know. This position is made possible by the distinction between creative experience as such—the metaphysical ultimate—and God—the axiological ultimate who evokes theistic worship.

The idea that all beings in the world are embodiments of creative experience rules out a dualism between humanity and nature, and between mind and body. All genuine individuals are instances of creative experience. We are thereby kin with all of nature. Existentialist alienation is precluded. The interaction between our conscious experiences and our body is thereby natural. Bodily cells share their feelings with the mind, which shares its feelings in return. No appeal to supernatural aid is therefore necessary to account for this interaction.

The fact that many things do not *appear* to be embodiments of creative experience can be accounted for in two ways. First, sensory perception involves a tremendous abstraction from the concrete individuals of the world. The rock is inert, but if we could see the atoms and subatomic entities of which it is comprised, we would not think of them as inert. Second, the complex organizations of individuals in the world can be divided, with some oversimplification, into two types—individuated and nonindividuated. In the former, a dominant individual exists which gives the whole organism a unity of experience and action—the dog has a soul. In the nonindividuated organization, no dominant individual is present. The rock has billions of molecules, but no dominant member to coordinate their motions to make a unified response to the environment possible. This distinction goes back to Leibniz (who, as Smith points out, coined the term *perennial philosophy*). Leibniz distinguished between groups of monads that have a "dominant monad" and those that do not. An updated version of that distinction allows us to explain why some things are apparently inert and are subject to complete determination by efficient causes, even though every individual of which the world is comprised embodies creative experience, is influenced by final causes, and exercises some degree of self-determination. In nonindividuated aggregates, the spontaneities of the various members, not being coordinated by a dominant individual, cancel each other out. The "law of large numbers" applies. The result is the appearance (to the naked eye) of inertness. With this account, inertness need not tempt us to adopt dualism or materialism.

The idea that creative experience is the absolute reality, embodied in all concrete existents, provides the basis for nonsensory perception as a universal and therefore natural feature of the world. Sensory perception is a very high, derivative form of perception. It presupposes nonsensory perception. The mind or soul has sensory information about outer objects only because it nonsensuously perceives the brain cells which have received this information from the sensory organs. Likewise, for the brain cells to feel the soul's feelings is for them to perceive the soul in a nonsensory way. Nonsensory perception is, in fact, the basis for all causation. Because it is universal, there is nothing extraordinary about the "extrasensory perception" studied by parapsychology, except that it is extraordinary for certain types of information perceived in a nonsensory way to become conscious. In any case, we are perceiving things nonsensuously all the time. This type of perception is at the root not only of our knowledge of our bodies, and of our occasional conscious extrasensory knowledge of other minds and places, but also of that knowledge of the past we call *memory*.

Because we have a nonsensory perception of all things in our environment, we also perceive God, who, being omnipresent, is always in our environment. We therefore have a direct, intuitive knowledge of God. When this form of nonsensory perception rises to consciousness, we speak not of extrasensory perception but of the "experience of the holy." Because God is the locus of all eternal values, we perceive such values through our intuitive perception of God. It is because we experience God, as the axiological ultimate and thereby the source of all importance, that we feel the importance of Truth, Beauty, and Goodness. The atheist believes it important, in the name of truth, to deny God, only because he or she, through an unconscious perception of God's valuation of truth, feels that truth is important.

This nonsensory, prelinguistic perception provides the basis, more generally, for a wide range of primordial truths—truths that are directly known by all humans at all places and times. These truths include the reality of causation, the "external world," partial freedom, objective values—including truth as correspondence—and a holy reality, among others. The truth of these convictions can be verified through the fact that no one can consistently deny them. They thereby provide a core set of beliefs through which complete relativism can be resisted and other ideas can be tested.

This postmodern worldview provides the basis for a new alliance between science and theology. While modern science was necessarily at odds with theology, postmodern science will be supportive of postmodern theology. Postmodern science will not be materialistic or dualistic; it will not exclude qualities, final causes, freedom, influence at a distance, or downward causation, even divine causation. It will not insist upon one method to study all things. In particular, the method for studying the interactions between nonindividuated aggregates (such as billiard balls) will not be used for the study of individuated organisms, such as humans or even amoebas. Likewise, high-level individuals, such as humans or dolphins, will not be treated as if they had no more creative power for self-determination than low-level individuals, such as atoms. Scientific study will, furthermore, not be limited to a behavioristic description of the outer features of its subjects, whether they be humans, rats, or even electrons. Although not much can be said about the inner experiences of low-grade individuals, they will not be studied as if they had no inner reality. In principle, scientific study will seek to describe both the inner and outer features of things, and to show how they are related. Science will not, finally, limit its data to sensory experience but will be open to including nonsensory data as well, whether it be extrasensory perception or the intuitive knowledge of values and the holy.

Science, in other words, will try to live up to its name, which simply means knowledge, and will not therefore arbitrarily exclude some kinds of knowledge as inherently "unscientific." It will seek the capacity to predict and control insofar as that is appropriate to the objects in question. It will not, however, say that scientific knowledge is impossible where a high degree of predictability or control is impossible. With such a science, not only the modern warfare but even the modern boundary between science and theology will, in principle at least, be overcome. It goes without saying that the absolute distinction between cumulative and noncumulative researches will be erased. The distinction will be one of degree, not kind.

The notion that every actual thing is an embodiment of creative experience means that causation runs upward, downward, and horizontally. A cell in a human body, for example, is subject to upward influences from its components, horizontal influences from neighboring cells, and downward influences from the human soul (not to mention God). Cellular pathology could therefore be a product of horizontal, upward, or downward (psychogenic) causation, or some combination, and healing likewise could come from any direction. A combination of meditation and surgical and/or chemical treatment might provide the most effective therapy. This same principle, that causation runs in every possible direction—which was already applied to the question of God and evil—applies as well to the question of God and evolution. Neither a creationist picture of downward causation alone nor a neo-Darwinian picture of upward and horizontal causation alone could be true. A role should be played not only by Darwin's chance and environmental selection, but also by Lamarck's spontaneity and purposes, and by Jung's archetypes *via* Aristotle's divine persuasion and perhaps *via* Sheldrake's morphic resonance. If everything actual exerts creative influence on everything else, causation must be multidirectional, coming from every level of reality.

If creative experience is the ultimate, and the actual world is thereby comprised exhaustively of creative experiences (and their ingredients), time must be inherent in the nature of things. If each creative experience embodies feelings from all previous experiences and *only* from all previous ones, then the distinction between the past and the future is absolute. A present experience could not embody feelings from future experiences because future experiences do not yet exist. They cannot exist "already" or "tenselessly" if all events are *creative* experiences. To be a creative experience is to exercise some self-creation in the moment, choosing between alternative possibilities. If time were ultimately unreal, so that all events—which we distinguish as past, present, and future— really existed simultaneously, then creative experience would not be the absolute. Conversely, if creative experience is the absolute, which all actual things embody, then future events do not exist. From this perspective, time is not simply a function of entropy and is, therefore, real even for an individual atom. An atom is a series of low-level creative experiences. Each such experience appropriates its predecessors and is in turn appropriated by its successors. Reality is, therefore, cumulative and time is, hence, irreversible even for the entities studied by fundamental physics.

Besides being ultimately real for physics, time is also ultimately important for the realization of value. All values must in some sense exist primordially, as the perennial philosophy holds; values could not somehow "emerge" out of a value-free universe. But as primordially existent (or subsistent), values are unrealized: they are not realized values but possible values for realization. More precisely, they exist in the primordial nature of God, where they are envisaged with appetition. God in this guise is the Divine Eros of the universe. God's appetite for these possible values to be realized in the world makes them into lures for creaturely feeling. When the creatures respond to these divine lures, the possible values become actual values, first for the creatures and then for God. As an analogy, we can imagine a particular value for our bodies— perhaps sexual, gustatory, or athletic enjoyment. Prior to the chosen activity, the value exists in our souls, but only as a possible value. As such, it serves as a lure for us to undertake the activity. Only through the bodily activity itself is the possible value realized, first for the bodily cells and then for the soul, which enjoys its body's enjoyment. If we think of God as the soul of the world, and the world as the body of God, we can see the way in which the temporal process is essential to the realization of value. We can suppose, with Whitehead, that the finite realization of truth, beauty, and goodness "provides the final contentment for the Eros of the Universe."[162]

Two other factors, besides the distinction between possible and actual value, make the temporal process essential. One factor is that some realized values are incompatible with the simultaneous realization of other values. Time is, as it were, the universe's way of getting around the fact that not everything can happen at once. Another factor is that the finite realization of more complex values presupposes the prior realization of simpler ones. Shakespeare presupposed a highly developed English language, Jesus presupposed a long development of the Hebrew tradition, Beethoven a long development of musical tradition. Likewise, living organisms presuppose rather complex forms of nonliving entities, consciousness presupposes life, and self-consciousness presupposes consciousness. The human race presupposed some four billion years of the evolution of life.

This last point raises the issue of possible life after death. In contrast with Smith's gnostic dualism, postmodern theology says that individuals with high-level experience cannot be created directly, but must be evolved through a long, slow process. A human-like soul could not have emerged apart from a human-like body. This principle does not exclude the possibility, however, that the human soul, once it has fully emerged, might be able to survive and continue to develop apart from the biological body.

Two principles of postmodern theology lie behind this possibility for continued existence beyond the body. Both of these principles are examples of the postmodern reformulation of premodern ideas. First, the fact that the soul's basic way of interacting with the world, even while in the body, is nonsensory perception means that the soul, if it could exist apart from the body, would still be able to perceive. The reverse side of this point is that, because other beings are able to perceive the soul in a nonsensory way, the soul's power to influence other beings is not limited to its bodily action. *Psychokinesis* is the term used for particularly obvious exercises of this power. If a soul found itself experiencing without its body, it might still have the capacity to interact with its environment.

The second principle of postmodern theology that makes continued experience apart from the body conceivable is the correlation between value and power in the hierarchy of creative experiences. The greater an enduring individual's capacity for experience is, the more power it has. The human soul, among all earthly creatures, is evidently the most evolved. It has the capacity not only for conscious experience but also for symbolic language and a high degree of self-conscious experience. This capacity for symbolism and self-consciousness emerged through the evolutionary process, being evoked by divinely-presented possibilities. It is possible that the emergence of this capacity brought with it, as another consequence of the same increase in power, the capacity to survive apart from the body. The belief in continued life beyond bodily death is fully compatible, then, with the view that a human soul could have been orginally created only through an evolutionary process.

The issue of progress has already been partly answered: the evolutionary process, through which the souls of humans and other higher animals have been created, has involved real progress. Social progress, once human beings emerged, can likewise be affirmed, even if every increase in the possibilities for good has entailed an increase in the possibilities for evil. Social progress is not only possible and actual but also desirable.

On this point the social or ecological viewpoint of postmodern theology contrasts strongly with Smith's premodern individualism, for three reasons. In the first place, growth toward individual perfection is not possible apart from compassion for all sentient beings and a desire for their welfare. This principle depends upon two other points, discussed earlier: genuine evil occurs, and God wills its overcoming. In the second place, because we are all interconnected at a deep level, the welfare of one soul is not fully independent of that of others. Even if moral considerations did not preclude it, I could not work for my own good apart from working for the general good. In the third place, the real dependence of souls upon their bodies and hence upon their physical context generally means that concern for their welfare entails concern for their physical environment. People without sufficient protein for proper brain development cannot progress spiritually. A world situation in which some people have not enough while others have more than enough is therefore genuinely evil. Beyond a certain level of physical well-being, to be sure, an increase provides no additional aid for the soul's growth and may even be a hindrance. But until that level is reached, intelligent compassion expresses itself by providing physical aid. In the large, this means working for social-political-economic progress. The difference between my postmodern and Smith's premodern theology on this point is related to different views about upward causation, evolution versus gnostic dualism, the importance of time, social salvation versus individualism, the reality of evil, and the ultimacy of a personal God who cares about evil and provides holy oughts to persuade us to overcome it.

The idea that the personal God as well as creative experience is ultimate brings us to the relations among the world's great religions. The idea that there are two ultimates raises the likelihood that there are at least two basic types of religion, those oriented to the metaphysical ultimate and those oriented to the axiological ultimate, the personal God. The salvation realizable through one type of religion would therefore not be the same as that realizable through the other. Because downward causation from deity cannot override human freedom, including the freedom to err, we have no deductive reason to assume that all religions essentially reflect the same truths. Various religions may focus on different, complementary truths. Devotees from different religions, therefore, may be able to enrich their religious lives, and to realize a more complete form of wholeness, by learning from each other. Theists might learn from Advaita Vedantists and Buddhists, and the latter might learn from theists. Modernists might learn from premodernists of various sorts, and the latter might learn from modernists.

Through these mutual appropriations we might come into a more adequate relation to the primordial realities, and in such a way that we can sustain and extend the positive features of the modern world.

NOTES

1. Smith does not, to my knowledge, call himself a *theologian*. But if a theologian is a person who articulates and defends a particular theological perspective, then he is one. Smith would probably resist the adjective *particular*; he considers the position he defends to be the universal core of all the particular traditions. But that view of the relations among the religions is itself one view among others. In any case, as a theologian myself I use the term as a description, not an accusation.

2. Most of the essays included in Smith's book *Beyond the Post-Modern Mind* (New York: Crossroad Publishing Co., 1982) (henceforth BPMM) criticize the modern worldview, or what Smith calls the Modern Western Mind-set. The discussion of the Post-Modern Mind is largely (although not entirely) limited to the newly written portions of the book (the preface, ch. 9, and various insertions). By the *Post-Modern Mind* he means the relativistic, nihilistic outlook called eliminative or deconstructive postmodernism in the introduction to this series. He rightly sees that this outlook results from carrying the modern mind-set through to its logical conclusions. He does not have in view the revisionary postmodernism of this series; he never uses the term *postmodern* to refer to the postmodern theology that is based primarily on the philosophy of Alfred North Whitehead and kindred thinkers. He does, to be sure, take occasional swipes at this form of thought, under the name of *process theology,* which he considers a form of modern theology. I deal with this issue at the beginning of section 5, and in note 115.

3. The allusion is to Smith's book *Forgotten Truth: The Primordial Tradition* (New York: Harper & Row, 1977) (henceforth FT). Smith describes his project as the "reclamation-of-the-lost" in "Another World to Live In, or How I Teach the Introductory Course," *Religious Studies and Theology* 7/1 (January 1987), 54-63 (henceforth "Another World"), 55.

4. BPMM, xii, 76; "Another World," 55.

5. BPMM, 95, 101.

6. BPMM, 119n, 169-71, 173.

7. BPMM, xi, xii, 13, 95, 101; "Another World," 57; "Two Evolutions," Leroy S. Rouner, ed., *On Nature* (Vol. 6 of Boston University Studies in Philosophy and Religion, Notre Dame, Ind.: University of Notre Dame Press, 1984), 42-89, esp. 46.

8. "Another World," 57.

9. "Two Evolutions," 46.

10. FT, 120-22, 131; "Another World," 62.

11. BPMM, 3, 9; "The View from Everywhere: Ontotheology and the Post-Nietzschean Deconstruction of Metaphysics," Henry Ruf, ed., *Religion, Ontotheology and Deconstruction* (New York: Paragon Press, forthcoming), ms. 4n. (Because this essay will not be published in time to indicate page numbers, I give the page references to the unpublished manuscript so that the reader can tell about where in the essay the cited passage occurs.)

12. BPMM, xii, 3.

13. BPMM, 163-67.

14. BPMM, 110, 108, 121.

15. BPMM, 11-12.

16. BPMM, 15, 16, 95; "The View from Everywhere," ms. 1-2.

17. "The View from Everywhere," ms. 21.

18. "The View from Everywhere," ms. 2-3.

19. "Another World," 57.

20. BPMM, 126, 144.

21. "Another World," 57.

22. BPMM, 109, 111.

23. BPMM, xii; "Another World," 55.

24. BPMM, 108.

25. BPMM, 108; "Another World," 56.

26. BPMM, 170n-171n.

27. BPMM, 76, 78, 132-34, 144, 168-69.

28. BPMM, 77-78, 144.

29. BPMM, 110; FT, 120, 122, 131.

30. "Two Evolutions," 50-52; FT, 130-41.

31. BPMM, 154, 165; "Two Evolutions," 56-57.

32. BPMM, 43, 138-39.

33. BPMM, 43.

34. BPMM, 174-75.

35. BPMM, 157-74.

36. "Is There a Perennial Philosophy?," *Journal of the American Academy of Religion* LV/3 (Fall 1987), 553-60, esp. 561.

37. FT, 145.

38. "Philosophy, Theology, and the Primordial Claim," *Cross Currents* XXXVIII/3 (Fall 1988), 276-88 (henceforth "Primordial Claim"), 276; "Is There a Perennial Philosophy?," 553 n2.

39. BPMM, x, 5, 18, 103.

40. FT, 5; BPMM, 150.

41. "Primordial Claim," 278.

42. BPMM, 150.

43. BPMM, 131.

44. BPMM, 36, 152.

45. BPMM, 153.

46. "Primordial Claim," 283-84.

47. BPMM, 143-46.

48. BPMM, 141-43; "Primordial Claim," 281-82; "The View From Everywhere," ms. 10-11

49. "Is There a Perennial Philosophy?," 560 n12; "Primordial Claim," 280.

50. "Is There a Perennial Philosophy?," 554; "The View from Everywhere," ms. 12; BPMM, 168.

51. BPMM, 34; "The View from Everywhere," ms. 11; "Is There a Perennial Philosophy?," 563; "Primordial Claim," 282, 286.

52. "Two Evolutions," 47.

53. BPMM, 38-41, 49, 165; FT, 34-59; "Is There a Perennial Philosophy?," 564.

54. "Is There a Perennial Philosophy?," 564.

55. FT, 51.

56. FT, 52.

57. FT, 55, 57.

58. FT, 53.

59. Smith has later decided that his contrast between personal and trans-personal, while "not wrong," was a tactical mistake. Because "we have so much difficulty imagining anything superior to persons that, whatever is actually said, the impression that is conveyed in denying the attribute 'personal' to the God-head is that it must be subpersonal, rather than suprapersonal as the distinction intends" (BPMM, 41-42). The problem, however, is not only that we have diffi-culty *imagining* anything superior to personal qualities such as perfect knowl-edge and love; we have difficulty *conceiving* it too, and Smith has said nothing to overcome this difficulty. The mere fact that it is "actually said" by Smith and his fellow primordialists that a reality devoid of personal qualities can be supe-rior to a personal divine being does not help us conceive how this can be so.

60. "The View from Everywhere," ms. 1-2.

61. *Ibid.*, 14.

62. BPMM, 46.

63. BPMM, 120.

64. FT, 86-87.

65. FT, 87.

66. FT, 87.

67. BPMM, 165.

68. BPMM, 145.

69. BPMM, 149.

70. BPMM, 120.

71. FT, 108, 58.

72. FT, 120-21; see also 103-09.

73. "Primordial Claim," 20.

74. "Is There a Perennial Philosophy?," 562.

75. BPMM, 120, 40.

76. FT, 153.

77. BPMM, 183.

78. "Primordial Claim," 287, citing Augustine's *Confessions* VII, xiii, 19.

79. "Primordial Claim," 22.

80. FT, 28, 29, 49.

81. See my *God, Power, and Evil: A Process Theodicy* (Philadelphia: Westminster Press, 1976; Lanham, Md.: University Press of America, 1990), 92-93, 133-35, 184.

82. BPMM, 147.

83. BPMM, 148.

84. BPMM, 100-01.

85. BPMM, 104.

86. "Two Evolutions," 47-48.

87. BPMM, 104.

88. FT, 64, 67, 68.

89. FT, 75.

90. BPMM, 42.

91. BPMM, 132.

92. BPMM, 135.

93. BPMM, 165.

94. "Two Evolutions," 57.

95. BPMM, 110.

96. BPMM, 125, 121.

97. BPMM, 125.

98. "Two Evolutions," 51.

99. BPMM, 43, 67, 68, 95, 112, 113.

100. FT, 10-16; BPMM, 67, 117.

101. "Two Evolutions," 45; FT, 14; BPMM, 132, 168.

102. BPMM, 66, 111, 134.

103. BPMM, 126, 133, 166; "Another World," 56.

104. BPMM, 126, 133; "Another World," 56.

105. BPMM, 70, 113; FT, 11n.

106. "Two Evolutions," 50.

107. "Two Evolutions," 45; FT, 139.

108. BPMM, 71.

109. FT, 97.

110. BPMM, 120; FT, 107-08.

111. BPMM, 122. On David Bohm, see the contributions by Bohm, Cobb, and me in David Ray Griffin, ed., *Physics and the Ultimate Significance of Time: Bohm, Prigogine, and Process Philosophy* (Albany: State University of New York Press, 1986).

112. BPMM, 105.

113. See my "Introduction: Time and the Fallacy of Misplaced Concreteness" (1-48) and Milič Čapek's "The Unreality and Indeterminacy of the Future in the Light of Contemporary Physics" (297-308) in *Physics and the Ultimate Significance of Time.*

114. "Primordial Claim," 287.

115. BPMM, 121-22, 125-26. Smith believes that Whitehead's doctrine of actual occasions was designed to accommodate Einstein's relativity theory. Because it now seems probable that a unified field theory, integrating relativity theory and quantum mechanics, will require another paradigm change, he says, that change will leave Einstein and hence Whitehead behind (*idem.*). It is true that Whitehead was influenced by Einstein and meant his position to be adequate to the data upon which relativity theory was based. But it is not true that Whitehead based his metaphysics heavily on any particular scientific theory, or that he even accepted Einstein's relativity theory. Indeed, he was so dissatisfied with it that he wrote his own (*The Principle of Relativity, with Applications to Physical Science* [Cambridge: Cambridge University Press, 1922]). A Whitehead Relativity Group, headed by Robert Russell of the Center for Theology and the Natural Sciences at the Graduate Theological Union in Berkeley, California, and Christoph Wasserman of Germany, is now comparing Whitehead's theory with Einstein's. For a summary of the early results, see Russell's "Progress Report on Whitehead's Theory of Gravity," available from the Center for Process Studies, 1325 North College, Claremont, CA 91711. It is of interest to note that Whitehead thought his philosophical position to be compatible with both quantum and relativity theory. Whether Whitehead's position will provide help toward a unified theory remains to be seen. In any case, the anticipation of future changes in physical cosmology provides no argument against Whitehead's metaphysical theory of actual occasions. Besides the fact that it is not based on Einstein's cosmology, it does not uniquely imply any particular cosmology, even Whitehead's own cosmological conjectures. As a properly metaphysical view, it aims to describe the generic features of actuality as such, apart from the contingent features of our specific cosmos. Whitehead accordingly based his metaphysical position on a wide range of evidence, especially conscious human experience itself, as that example of actuality with which we are most intimate. Smith's

given reason for theology not to employ Whitehead's philosophy therefore reflects several misunderstandings of that philosophy.

116. BPMM, 37.

117. BPMM, 43.

118. BPMM, 43. One problem with Smith's argument here is that, a few pages earlier, he had suggested that if a reality's "locale were without bounds, it would be *omnipresent*" (40; emphasis in original). There he was arguing that size (locale) and worth are positively correlated. Is it not playing fast and loose to suggest in one context that God is infinitely large, and in another that God is infinitely small?

119. BPMM, 44.

120. FT, 142; BPMM, 170-73.

121. BPMM, 132.

122. BPMM, 122, 122n.

123. FT, 14; BPMM, 132, 166.

124. "Primordial Claim," 284-85; BPMM, 78-79, 108-09, 168.

125. BPMM, 150.

126. BPMM, 48, quoting Schuon's *Understanding Islam* (Baltimore: Penguin Books, 1972), 7.

127. BPMM, 47, 119.

128. BPMM, 45.

129. FT, 41-42.

130. FT, 42.

131. FT, 67; "The View from Everywhere," ms. 11.

132. BPMM, 152.

133. BPMM, 138-39.

134. BPMM, 166-67.

135. FT, 141.

136. FT, 141.

137. BPMM, 120.

138. BPMM, 157.

139. FT, 65.

140. FT, 28.

141. BPMM, 51.

142. I have argued this in "Introduction: Time and the Fallacy of Misplaced Concreteness," in Griffin, ed., *Physics and the Ultimate Significance of Time*.

143. See the various contributions to Griffin, ed., *Physics and the Ultimate Significance of Time*.

144. FT, 121, 122, 131.

145. BPMM, 157-58.

146. FT, 119.

147. FT, 121.

148. FT, chap. 6.

149. BPMM, 183.

150. "Another World," 62.

151. FT, 149-51.

152. FT, 125n.

153. "Primordial Claim," 288; "Is There a Perennial Philosophy?," 562.

154. See Frithjof Schuon, *The Transcendent Unity of Religions* (New York: Harper & Row, 1975), for which Smith wrote an introduction.

155. "Is There a Perennial Philosophy?," 562.

156. *Ibid.*, 10.

157. FT, 146-47.

158. BPMM, 93-93, 98, 170n-171n.

159. BPMM, 121, 125.

160. See note 115, above.

161. For this distinction, I am indebted to John B. Cobb, Jr., who has articulated it in "Buddhist Emptiness and the Christian God," *Journal of the American Academy of Religion* XLV/1 (March 1979), 11-26, and *Beyond Dialogue: Toward a Mutual Transformation of Christianity and Buddhism* (Philadelphia: Fortress Press, 1982), esp. 42-43, 86-90. It is my own wording, however, to call the metaphysical ultimate "creative experience" and to call God the "axiological ultimate."

162. Alfred North Whitehead, *Adventures of Ideas* (1933; New York: Free Press, 1967), 11.

3

THE PROCESS CRITIQUE OF PERENNIALISM: A REPLY TO DAVID GRIFFIN

Huston Smith

David Griffin has honored me with his close attention to my work. As noted in our joint Introduction to this book, we are united in more than divides us. The points on which we differ are important ones on which I hope to learn in the course of our exchange.

I. GRIFFIN'S DEPICTION OF MY POSITION

The first half of Griffin's summary of my position, entitled "The Critique of the Modern Worldview," is exemplary, as is its second half—"The Recovery of Forgotten Truth"—with one exception. To open that section with the statement, "Smith says that the best way to overcome modernity is to return to premodernity," suggests that it is the past in general, or as a whole, that we should return to, not something within it. True, Griffin gets to that distinction within two sentences by acknowledging that "more specifically, [Smith] has in mind a return to ... the 'primordial tradi-tion'," but opening sentences have a special force, and in leading off as he does he perpetuates the most common misunderstanding of peren-nialism: that its concern is with bygone truths rather than timeless ones. Griffin's earlier reference to my "program to recover ... a premodern vision of reality" (18), and his later charge that I propose "an undialectical return to a premodern vision" (23), seem likewise to encourage this con-fusion; premodern visions of reality suggest Ptolemaic astronomy and a flat earth created in 4004 B.C.E. When Griffin says that he also believes "that there are primordial truths that are in principle available to human beings in all times and places"(22), what makes his interaction with the past dialectical and mine not? We both subscribe to many things our ancestors believed; on other of their beliefs we differ. We might differ in the degree to which we see our progenitors as having been on course, and this may *look* like a difference in kind, but is it really so? I may have been imprecise in my wording at times, but careful reading of page 146 in *Forgotten Truth*, where I point out that "the issue does not concern time at all; it concerns truth of the kind that is time*less*," will show, I believe, that there is no difference between us in principle on this point.

II. GRIFFIN'S CRITIQUE OF THE PERENNIAL PHILOSOPHY

Griffin begins his critique of perennialism—the position which on bal-ance I espouse—with two characterizations of it. The first of these, that it advocates "a simple return to a premodern worldview" (35), I have already addressed, but I can be more precise about the point. A worldview is an inclusive outlook, and it is useful to distinguish its social, cosmo-logical, and metaphysical components. The social component of past worldviews included, at times, justifications for slavery and the divine right of kings, while its cosmological components described the physical universe as understood by the science of the day—Ptolemaic astronomy or whatever. The contents of those two components obviously change, so are not perennial. The perennial, unchanging philosophy is meta-physical, or more precisely, ontological. It concerns such matters as the distinction between the Absolute and the relative, and the doctrine of the degrees of reality that is consequent thereon.

As for Griffin's second introductory point, that "Advaita Vedanta seems to be normative for the premodern [note that misleading word again] vision he [Smith] advocates" (23), I do subscribe to Frithjof Schuon's view that "the Vedanta appears among explicit doctrines as one of the most direct formulations possible of that which makes the very essence of our spiritual reality,"[1] but note the qualifying phrase, "*one* of the most," in that depiction. The primordial tradition—a synonym for perennial philosophy—would not be primordial if it surfaced in one tradition only.

Still, Griffin is right in sensing that something here strikes us differently. He thinks I latch onto Vedanta as the ultimate truth and interpret other traditions in its light, whereas I see Vedanta as the initial (to me) articulation of a truth I subsequently found everywhere. For example, when St. Augustine writes, "things that are not immutable are not at all," and Meister Eckhart that "all creatures are pure nothing," I take these as Christian counterparts of the Vedantic claim that the phenomenal world is only qualifiedly real. Griffin bears me out here when, after citing my endorsement of the East's attitude that things in their entirety are as they should be, he repeats my point that Augustine says the same (28-29).

After registering these two overarching criticisms, Griffin turns to internal inconsistencies he finds in my position.

Alleged Internal Problems

1. Personal God and absolute reality. Griffin thinks that transpersonal—that is, something that is better than personal—is a meaningless concept. That which is other than personal must, by his lights, be impersonal in the pejorative sense of being sub- or infrapersonal.

Griffin has the human majority on his side in so assuming. Most Jews and Christians accept the Bible's heavily personal view of God as normative. In Hinduism, personalists (from Madhva right down to Bhaktivedanta and the Hari Krishnas of today) far outnumber the Shankarites. And in East Asia, when we include folk religion, the cult of Shang Ti the supreme ancestor, and the Shinto kamis, personalism likewise predominates. The question is whether truth has reaches that the majority has difficulty tracking.

I realize that that is an inflammatory statement, for it suggests that Griffin is incapable of following truth as far as I can. As with all evaluations, this one is awkward, for it ranks persons according to their worth. Or rather, it ranks parts of persons, that is, where they stand in certain respects—the worth of their complete and entire selves is not in question. There is something in all of us that would like to eschew judgments entirely when they relate to persons, but we know that it is impossible to do that, so it is better to evaluate forthrightly—sin boldly, as St. Paul advises. Both Griffin and I think that, on balance, on the issues at stake, we each see more than the other one does. Nothing in this dialogue is going to change either of our minds on that point. What it occasions is the opportunity to point out what, by our respective lights, the other is missing. Whether either of us has the grace to *see* what the other points out remains to be seen, but our discussion offers us the opportunity to do so.

Having introduced the matter thus, let me say outright that, from my perspective, those who stop with a process—and for present purposes personalistic—theology, do so because they stop short of broader ontological vistas. Of course, from Griffin's point of view that is because no such vistas exist—what I take to be such he sees as fairyland and fiction. In this reply, I argue the case for the reality of the more that I think I see, beginning here with the more that exceeds persons.

The word *personal* derives its meaning from persons, who (I will grant Griffin) are fearfully and wonderfully made, while being at the same time (I know he will concede) limited. Is it possible to conceive of something that possesses the virtues of persons without inheriting their limitations? This would be the Godhead—there is no reason to use Vedantic terminology. The talents of persons are in full view: it is apparent that we can experience, know, love, create, and the like. What about our limitations?

To begin with, persons always seem to be set within environments with which they interact. These environments are, by definition, other than the persons themselves, and in ways resist, while at the same time sustaining, them. This otherness with its resistence limits the person's expanse and power. But a perfect God—for perennialists there is no other—transcends all limitations, so God cannot be personal in the sense of having an environment. I am aware that Griffin thinks my notion of perfection here is incoherent, but this is just the first instance—others will follow—of his inability to rise to the ontological heights from which the perennialist views things. (Obviously I am calling the shots as they appear to me. From this point on I will simply assume this proviso and not keep repeating it.)

Again, persons, while in some ways whole, are in other ways legion; they are collections of components in precarious homeostasis. There seems to be a connection between the degree of unity in a thing and its worth. Griffin honors this connection by ranking individuated things— roughly living things in which a "dominant individual . . . gives the whole organism a unity of experience and action" (47)—above nonindividuated organizations such as rocks. Perennialists ride the momentum of this idea to claim that God is *absolutely* one—absolutely unified and whole— but in a peculiar way: as the negative theology insists, there is no way in which concepts that fit finite things map univocally onto the infinite.

The peculiarity of the divine or holy One is that it dispenses with differences—*resolves differences*, it might be better to say—without forfeiting any of the positive virtues, which at lower levels of being are parceled into separate faculties or components. Nothing is lost; only the walls of separation are removed. Are not all the colors of the rainbow included, in their wavelengths, in what we experience singly as white?

When Griffin asks, rhetorically, "if deity is devoid of attributes such as love and knowledge, how can s/he be superior to us?" (24, my paraphrase), he has in mind the positive ingredients of the attributes, whereas my mind is on their exclusivity—their bounderies and limitations. For him, the attributes are good because of what they include; for me, they are likewise good, but, because of what they exclude, they are not perfect. It is their lack of perfection, occasioned by their finitude and limitation, that I do not hold God to. Thus, I would not say (as Griffin has me saying) "that deity is ultimately *beyond* all knowing and loving." What I say is that God is beyond all knowing that is not concomitantly loving and beyond all loving that is not concomitantly knowing. According to Griffin, my claim that something can be trans- or suprapersonal is "merely verbal . . . unless some significant difference [is] specified" (24). I think I *have* specified the difference—several differences in fact. That my specifications do not help him conceive what a suprapersonal God would be (as he complains in note 59) I sincerely regret—I wish I were a better poet. For when failures in communication of this sort occur, three possibilities arise: nothing actual is being signified, the signifying is poor, or the hearer does not get it. We are back with what I have proposed as the presiding difference between us. Griffin sees the first of the three possibilities as pertaining, I the third.

2. Orientation and ineffability. Griffin does not see how an ineffable reality—specifically, the Godhead—can provide the orientation we both agree life requires. That is because he equates ineffability with ignorance, whereas I do not. Ineffability pertains to things of which we have intimations, but which are too vast and strange to fit our categories of language and thought. If a flatlander were to be taken up in a balloon, he would call his aereal view ineffable because nothing in his two-dimensional language would enable him to recount it to himself, much less report it to his fellow flatlanders. I ask for Griffin's sympathy as I try to report my theology to him, but that is in passing. The point at the moment is that, although the flatlander might find his expanded outlook disorienting at first (in the way Plato's cave dwellers found sunlight initially blinding), I suspect Griffin would agree that, in the long run, larger contexts orient us more reliably than do provincial ones. They work on us in something of the way sacred art does. Against the sermon, which indicates what must be *done* to become holy, sacred art and nobler expanses *elevate us*, naturally and almost involuntarily, *into* the world of holiness.

To expand this point only slightly, we have it from Jacques Maritain that "to penetrate into the transintelligible is the deepest desire of our intellect," and the great spiritual traditions all honor that impulse. Karl Jaspers says that the profoundest truths of Socrates, Buddha, Confucius, and Jesus "could be communicated only indirectly even to themselves." They spoke in myth or parables, and at key junctures resorted to pregnant silences.[2] A fragment from the *Nag Hammadi Library* that crosses my desk while I am writing these words reads: "I have said, O my Son, that I am Mind. I have seen! Language is not able to reveal this. . . . The angels sing a hymn in silence. And I, Mind, understand."[3]

Paul Tillich goes so far as to argue that what he calls the mystical move, "the move to lodge the Holy as the Ultimate beyond any of its embodiments," those of language included, is imperative if the Ultimate's embodiments are not to become demonic.[4]

3. Immortality and undifferentiated reality. Griffin goes beyond Whitehead's objective immortality—God's everlasting memory of our lives in their every detail—to leave open the possibility that individual awareness continues in some way after bodily death. It would be a loss, though, to his way of thinking, if at some point this awareness were to lose its individuality and phase into the consciousness of God.

To return to what I said in connection with whether God is personal, individuality connotes (along with its virtues) certain limitations, and it is the relinquishment of these that the soul's dissolution into, and identification with, the Godhead effects. India's celebrated image for this is that "the dewdrop slips into the shining seas," although again there is no need to turn to India when Teresa of Avila speaks in the same terms. If we accent the dewdrop in this analogy it can, to be sure, suggest loss because, deprived of its boundary, the dewdrop disappears. But we can just as well reverse the direction and think of the dewdrop as opening to receive the entire sea. Would this still appear to Griffin to be a loss?

Turning from dewdrops to ourselves, what I was experiencing a year ago at this moment is now gone. Am I the less because that "me" has given way to the "me" I now am? Comparably, would I in any important way be diminished if my experience were to continue to expand until eventually it included everything? Note: I am not at the moment saying what actually happens; I am thinking only of the *logic* of loss and gain. I do not see how Griffin can liken growth from the meagerest flicker of awareness to infinite awareness to the "passage from dust to dust," as if such a destination were identical with the starting point.

As for what actually happens after death, I agree with Griffin's tentativity. What I *suspect* is that at some point the Beatific Vision becomes "ecstatic" in the etymological sense of that word; which is to say, it causes us to stand outside ourselves. It does this by the simple and not-difficult-to-understand expedient of commanding our attention so completely that literally zero attention remains for self-reflection. If this were to happen, would we deplore the relinquishment of self-consciousness—our attention to ourselves as the individuals who were *having* the Beautific Vision? Most Whiteheadians think it is self-centered to want our subjectivity to continue indefinitely; it is more mature, they believe, to renounce that wish and resign our subjective experience to God's eternal memory. Griffin drops that view; he is prepared to accept the possibility that our subjective awareness continues after death. But traces of self-centeredness seem to persist in that he wants to retain his finite ego. It would not suffice for him that he be brought to the Beatific Vision. That vision must be *his* in the sense that, when it dawns on him, he must be conscious not only of its content, but of David Griffin as its observer.

Perhaps traces of such self-identity *will* persist. Perhaps, in some kind of everlasting rhythm we will be able to oscillate between total attention to God and periodic returns to the realization that it is we, we finite souls, who are so attending[5]—we skate on very thin ice when we try to conjure previews of such coming attractions. All I find myself wishing to contend here is that *if* our final destiny is a mode of being that is not differentiated from God's, I would not consider this an inferior consummation.

4a. Truth and incoherence. Griffin is right in saying that I do not deduce the truth of the perennial philosophy from its ubiquity. But neither, as he seems to assume, do I deduce that truth from its coherence, although I do believe that the position *is* coherent, even as I believe that it is ubiquitous. I do not argue its truth from its coherence because I do not believe that there are criteria (coherence, adequacy, or any other) that can be established independently—without taking into account the positions on which the criteria presume to pronounce. Abstract criteria have neither the right nor the power to rule on positions that are external to them. Claims for such criteria fall before the charge of infinite regress: what are the criteria that underwrite the criteria that are being advocated?[6] I have myself claimed that the perennial philosophy is "the view that is normal to man's station because consonant with the complete complement of human sensibilities" when these are profoundly pondered,[7] but I suspect that any criterion more precise than this will prove procrustean or be guilty of special pleading.

To Griffin, this "seems to say that no objective basis exists for deciding whether one worldview corresponds to reality more than any other" (30), and this is indeed what I wish to say. But how far apart are we here? In keeping with Whitehead's proposal, at the opening of *Process and Reality*, that the success of a speculative scheme is to be judged by its own internal consistency and coherence and by its adequacy and applicability to interpret all items of human experience, the "objective bases" Griffin favors are coherence and adequacy. Whitehead's own formulation does not sound very different from the one I proposed in the preceding paragraph, but Griffin seems to think that the criteria of coherence and adequacy can be wielded objectively. I do not recall Whitehead presenting them that way; in any case, it is not the position I hold.

To take adequacy first, a four-year-old's outlook is adequate for his experience, but not for that of a forty-year-old. The *leitmotif* of my entire response to Griffin is that I think I see some things that his worldview does not accommodate—a concrete, absolute, unsurpassable perfection, to cite perhaps the most important one. Appeals to adequacy are futile unless we first know whether such perfection exists. Griffin will invoke his second criterion here, arguing that it cannot exist because its very notion is incoherent, but can this criterion be wielded any more objectively than can adequacy? Griffin acknowledges that things "we cannot coherently conceive . . . exist" (27), but when, employing analogously the idea that matter is both wave and particle, I point to attributes of God that must appear paradoxical to our limited minds, *my* paradoxes become inadmissable. To return for a moment to Whitehead, I remember his books as larded with cautions against trying to slap logic onto life; or, to put it the other way around, to fit life into formal, logical compartments. "In formal logic, a contradiction is the signal of defeat," he notes, "but in the evolution of real knowledge . . . a mere logical contradiction cannot in itself point to more than the necessity of some readjustments, possibly of a very minor character."[8] One of Whitehead's counsels that impressed me most while I was studying him was his advice for dealing with philosophical opponents. Do not charge them with inconsistency, he admonished, for if they are worth paying attention to at all they are going to be smart enough to avoid head-on contradictions. Scan instead for their controlling presuppositions, some of which may have escaped their conscious notice; *these* are what are most likely to be vulnerable. This is the tack I am trying to take in responding to Griffin's critique.

The point in process theology that I feel needs scrutinizing is its assumption that the ontological space it works in is sufficient, or perhaps I should say here, adequate.

Sensitive to Griffin's tendency to equate perennial with premodern, I cannot resist turning the tables for a moment and asking if his confidence in the availability of objective criteria is not a bit "modern," in the dated sense of that word. Modern philosophy took off in the seventeenth century by declaring its independence from theology; Descartes set it on its course by dedicating it to the proposition that reason, its instrument, can stand on its own. An important reason for thinking that modernity has come to an end is that its faith in autonomous reason has now collapsed.[9]

4b. Material incoherence: the fact of evil. By Griffin's lights, the perennial philosophy is guilty not only of formal, logical incoherence; it is materially incoherent as well by virtue of not fitting with the facts. It "is simply not adequate to reality" (29). Elsewhere, Griffin points to time and freedom as other realities it slides over, but at this point he focuses on evil. Rightly. A position (the perennial one) that has the audacity—or temerity, or effrontery (pick your noun)—to argue that things in their final or ultimate nature are perfect in every respect must face the fact of evil as its major challenge.

There is no way that challenge can be met within Griffin's frame of reference, which hovers close to ordinary experience and the logic that governs it. There, indeed, God is either all-powerful or completely good, not both. Griffin opts for God's goodness. In doing so, he counters history, I remark in passing, because history shows people worshipping power more than virtue, but that is not the issue here. The point here is that, to Griffin's disjunctive eyes, God, being perfect, cannot be omnipotent also.

Only a wider frame of reference can allow God both attributes, and I despair of opening Griffin to its possibility, given his rejection of the notion of reality as an ontological hierarchy in which power and goodness proceed in concert. To "think in terms of degrees of being and think that these degrees are correlated with degrees of goodness," Griffin sees as "a peculiar idea" (29), but is this so? It seems altogether natural to regard dreams as less real than waking life, reflections of trees in water as less real than the trees themselves, and television dramas as of less import than those of "real life," as we revealingly say: and in all of these cases reality is suffused with notions of importance and worth. Why is it peculiar, then, to follow such intimations and, with Plato, see being itself as comparably graded? Not to do so seems a metaphysical mistake, but the immediate point is that, without such an ontological hierarchy, the perennial theodicy has no chance of coming to focus.

Can it come to focus *given* the scale?

For the perennialist, evil is clearly real at our end of the scale. "Let us seek out some desolate shade, and there/Weep our sad bosoms empty . . . Each new morn/New widows howl, new orphans cry; new sorrows/Strike heaven in the face" (*Macbeth*). And, residing as we humans do at the lesser end of the scale, the worst mistake we could possibly make is not to take that context, with the evil of which it is appreciably woven, seriously. From the moral angle, evil is here to be resisted, according to the principle: resist the devil and he becomes your friend. Not to resist him is tantamount to expecting to remain on a football team after telling the coach you do not intend to report for scrimage because scrimage is not really football—it is not a real game. To the extent that we fail to resist evil, countering it with every energy we can possibly muster, we show that we do not understand its nature, which includes its place in the entire scheme of things. By virtue of that failure, we not only fall short of the human calling; we place ourselves in line for the penalties that attend misunderstandings—ignorance before the law is no excuse. If any further points I introduce about evil compromise this initial, elemental point, one should stop reading, because unless I am being misunderstood, the compromises will be proof sufficient that what I say is wrong. This was the Dalai Lama's point when on one occasion he remarked: "If you ever feel you have to choose between śunyata [emptiness] and karma, choose karma." And Vivekananda: "The Vendantic position says that our evil is of no less value than our good. Knowing this, *you work* with patience" (my emphasis). If anything in the doctrine induces you to stop working, which here means "stop resisting evil," the doctrine is pernicious. Assuming, again, that it has been rightly understood.

Can this all-important point be kept in place while arguing that what is evil in this serious but qualified sense contributes to a whole that would be poorer without it? Arguments avail little here, so analogies are regularly invoked. Parts of a painting that are worthless—conceivably even displeasing in isolation—can contribute to the painting as a whole. Or again, villainous behavior in a play can serve the playwrite's purpose. As this second analogy makes God the supreme playwrite, it might seem to suggest that deity is cruel in using human suffering for its encompassing, divine satisfaction, but this reading would overlook other points in the analogy. Actors do not reproach playwrites or central casting when they are assigned tragic or despicable roles; they are glad to be included in the show. Comparably, although people sometimes *say* they wish they had never been born, we can wonder if they actually mean those words. This implies that creation is a generous act across the board, and that *esse qua esse bonum est*: being as being is good. To milk the analogy a final time: in the Green Room after the play is over, questions of who played which part become irrelevant as the actors consider together the performance as a whole. The perennial theodicy holds that when each soul sees "face to face," it will have the comparable opportunity to see its odyssey in cosmic review.

This is roughly the way the perennial theodicy proceeds when it rides analogies, but if we want its underlying argument, it is this. Deity would not be truly such—which is to say perfect in power and goodness *both*, the perennialist insists—if it did not create the best world possible, which world must (on pain of omission) include all the possible levels of being. This is the "principle of plenitude" in Neoplatonism's Great Chain of Being which St. Augustine gives voice to when he tells us, "I no longer wished for a better world, because I was thinking of the whole creation, and in the light of this clearer discernment I had come to see that though the higher things are better than the lower, the sum of all creation is better than the higher things alone."[10]

Only if Augustine's "sum of all creation" is in clear view can what is emphatically evil on our plane be affirmed as appropriate in the total scheme of things. An anecdote from the great Sufi saint Rabi'a conveys the spirit of this affirmation:

> One day Hasan of Basra and Malik son of Dinar and Shakik of Balkh came to see Rabi'a when she was ill. Hasan said, 'None is sincere in his claim [to love God] unless he patiently endure the blows of his Lord.' Rabi'a said, 'This smells of egoism.' Shakik said, 'None is sincere in his claim unless he give thanks for the blows of his Lord.' Rabi'a said, 'This must be bettered.' Malik son of Dinar said, 'None is sincere in his claim unless he delight in the blows of his Lord.' Rabi'a said, 'This still needs to be improved.' They said, 'Do thou speak.' She said, 'None is sincere in his claim unless he forget the blows in beholding his Lord.'[11]

Process theologians argue that if God's beatitude is unalloyed, God is either oblivious of our woes (is ignorant) or does not care (is calloused). But is this so? We have all heard friends say of a movie, "It was wonderful. I cried all the way through it, " and Shelly in his *Skylark* argues that "the sweetest songs are those that tell of saddest thought." The evening I saw Judith Anderson in *Oedipus Rex*, tradegy if there ever was one, I left the theater exalted. Process philosophy's own notion of value as "the experience of strong contrasts harmoniously integrated and intensely felt" seems almost to set things up for a God who feels our sorrows but takes them in stride, if one may put the matter thus. Without the strong contrasts that evil introduces, would God's feeling be as intense?

5. *Dualism or nondualism.* Griffin is right in seeing me as "of two minds on the question of dualism" (30), but this again illustrates the futility of calling upon abstract, out-of-context criteria. I distinguish sharply between the Absolute and the relative. Call that dualism if one pleases, but is it more so than Whitehead's distinction between abstract and concrete entities—eternal objects and actual occasions? Metaphysical systems simply—and necessarily—cut their pies in different places.

When Griffin quotes me as saying that "dualism is the great 'schizomorphic' structure of Western intelligence" (30), it is the modern, scientistic West I have in mind. That West sees sentience as restricted to biological organisms that are set in a sea of dead matter. Whitehead's panpsychism is one effective way of countering that dualism, but it is not the only way. For an icon to be spiritual, neither its pigments nor their atoms need possess feeling. Comparably, the presence of dead matter in the world—if matter *be* dead; I consider that question negotiable, which accounts for the different ways I bounce off of it—need not affect the world's significance. For that significance to remain intact, all that is required is that matter be intentionally created and put to good use, in the way furniture is built and pressed into the services of a home. A successful home throws its warmth *over* the wood in the dinner table, so to speak, drawing it into the ambiance of the home as a whole. To the extent that we feel genuinely at home with things, we do not have to commit what some consider the "pathetic fallacy" of imputing feelings to what may be inanimate objects. We feel akin to them without that imputation, in the way we feel comfortable with old shoes.

6. *Science and theology.* "Smith clearly rejects an accommodation of religious thought to the materialistic worldview with which modern science has been associated," Griffin notes (32). "What is not clear," he continues, "is whether he sees the possibility for a relation of mutual support between theology and certain developments in recent scientific thought."

Science and theology can support each other through mutual respect, each honoring the right of the other to be listened to in its region of competence. In addition, scientific findings can have *symbolic* import for theology, but they can prove nothing in its domain.

The relation between the two is one of part to whole. Being objective and empirical, science deals with visible, material nature and has developed near-perfect methods for understanding it pragmatically. This nature is part of the larger whole which concerns the theologian. Theology must include a theology of nature, but it obviously does not get into the interstices of nature the way science can.

Nothing that science discovers about those interstices tells us anything directly about what lies beyond them. Science can, however, *suggest* what lies beyond. For example, its demonstration that nature, as part, is more awesome than we had supposed—awesome, not just in size but in its strangeness as well—suggests that the whole is more awesome as well. The same holds for its finding that unity runs deeper in nature than we had suspected. If the part is well integrated, it seems reasonable to suppose that the whole is as well, although (to repeat) there is no way that science, confined in its competence to the part, can prove that this is the case. Griffin has this exactly right when he says that I seem to think of "the positive significance of science as merely symbolic" (34). This is all I intended to claim in the scientific "clues" to reality that Griffin lists (33-34).

My reasoning on this point is vectored, as Griffin perceives, by my belief that the physical or exact sciences provide, and should provide, the model of what science should do and be. Because we live in an age that looks to science for truth, we feel a constant pressure to expand its sphere. I see Griffin as prey to that pressure. What those who give in to it do not see is that with every step science takes beyond the objective, palpable domain of nature, its revelatory power declines, because that power resides in the controlled experiment. We have the choice, therefore, of (a) a science that possesses great truth-discovering power in a restricted region—physical nature—or (b) one that grows flabby as it moves into outlying provinces. It confuses matters, I think, to use the word *science* in the second of these ways. I like my science limited but compelling.

Does all this leave "the scientific and the religious viewpoints . . . diametrically opposed" (32)? Only if both purport to pronounce on the whole of things. If the part/whole relationship is honored, there need be no conflict. I do not "reject . . . a theistic account of evolution, according to which we could say that we are the products of both God and evolution" (32). Only when the theory of evolution is put forward (as Darwin himself presented it) as explanatory without God do I marshal evidence to show the hollowness of that claim.

Although he introduces material considerations in places, Griffin has been primarily concerned up to this point with what appear to him to be internal inconsistencies in perennialism. From this point forward, he turns to its failure to map the world that actually exists.

Alleged Incongruence with the Way Things Are

    1. Premodern versus postmodern. I have already dealt with Griffin's charge that perennialism advocates "a simple return to a premodern worldview" (35). We talk past each other on this point because, in what I have written about the modern world, I have not always been careful to distinguish the three things I mentioned on page 62 which here translate into: (a) modernity in general, (b) the modern worldview, which includes its cosmology, and (c) modern metaphysics and ontology *per se*. Only the third of these, most specifically modernity's claim to have improved upon the perennial philosophy, do I reject categorically. With these distinctions in place, Griffin's assertion that I seem "to think that the modern world has nothing to contribute at the level of basic truths" and that "premodern thought needs to be corrected and supplemented [only] with regard to details" (35), should—if it is to be faithful to my intent—be emended to read "basic *ontological* truths," and "*metaphysical* details," and his assertion that I "reject . . . modernity *in toto*" (36) is best dropped. I have no quarrel with $E = MC^2$ as a basic *scientific* truth, and the modern concern for human rights is not a detail. Whether that concern is modern or instead modernly conceived, I am not sure—the Stoics and Prophets were fairly good on the subject. But we cannot have enough of the concern itself and, to the extent that it is new, I applaud it wholeheartedly.

On the constructive side, Griffin makes a good point when he asks, "if . . . science cannot be completely separated from an encompassing metaphysic, how can we say that science can make progress while metaphysics cannot" (36)? I agree with the first half of that rhetorical question; I doubt that anything can be completely separated from metaphysics. However, what is the nature of the correlation? Not such, I would say, that progress is the one spells, or waits on, progress in the other. (Griffin seems to concur, for he says in note 115 that "Whitehead's metaphysical theory . . . does not uniquely imply any particular cosmology.) A good part of the pressure that brought Cartesianism into being was the wish to provide science with a worldview in which it could progress freely, unhampered by what it took for such irrelevancies as final causes. Are we to take science's progress under the mandate of Descartes as evidence that Cartesianism is a better metaphysics than Platonism or mysticism?

2. Causation: downward and upward. Both Griffin and I reject "modern reductionism, according to which all causation goes upward from elementary particles, and the evolution of complex organisms is due entirely to material interactions" (36-37)—I like his wording here. He thinks, however, that I advocate an "inverse reductionism" wherein "all causation is seemingly downward, from mind to body, from God to the world" (37). This is true in the ultimate, ontological sense; in keeping with the doctrine of creation or emanation, I do not think there would be anything without God or the One. Once finite entities are brought into being, though, each has its sphere of influence which must—and should—be respected. Some of their influences obviously extend upward, whence the "body-mind interaction" Griffin acknowledges that I affirm. At this secondary stage, causation is exactly as Griffin reports: "upward and sideways as well as downward" (37).

3. Gnostic dualism. Having earlier voiced his concern about dualism in general, Griffin here zeros in on a specific variety: the view that, in contrast to eternity and spirit, which are good, time is "wasted motion" and matter likewise a "waste." He sees the perennialist as party to this gnostic view, but he is mistaken in this. To perennialist eyes, nothing is wasted. How could it be, for waste is an evil, and in perennialism (as we have seen) there is ultimately no such thing.

We are back with the same kinds of issues that arose in connection with evil. There I quoted St. Augustine's verdict that although higher things are better than lower, the sum of both is better than the higher things alone. The same principle applies here—the principle of plenitude. We have to realize that Reality is infinite, and that, *being such* it has to actualize within itself every coherent possibility, because if it excluded any, it would not be infinite. So far from being wastes, matter and time are indispensible. They make it possible for the Infinite to be truly such.

4. The unimportance of time. This charge was just addressed. Time is ontologically important in perennialism, because if it did not exist there would be a Swiss cheese hole in God's infinity. And because "being as being is good" (*esse qua esse bonum est*), this lack—this gaping hole—would compromise the divine perfection. So the word *not* should be stricken from Griffin's assertion that in perennialism "the temporal process is not needed for the divine realization of value" (38). It *is* needed, while figuring in God differently from the way it figures in us. God experiences time timelessly. It is not easy to imagine what this would be like. Perhaps being caught up in a movie we have seen before, so that we know the outcome, provides a feeble hint. Or going through the steps of a problem with a child while to us its answer is self-evident.

To this fact that time is *ontologically* important in perennialism, it is hardly necessary at this stage of the discussion (I hope) to add that *humanly* it is decisive. Humanly our lives are *woven* of time, so that not to take time seriously comes down to not taking our lives seriously—it involves fancying ourselves to be beings we are not. Because no move could be more disastrous, I repeat the Dalai Lama's admonition: If anything in perennialism keeps us from taking serioulsy the temporal decisions that are our current lot, we should expunge that philosophy from our minds at once.

5. *No social progress.* Is historical progress "an illusion," as Griffin has me saying (39)? When I asked Reinhold Niebuhr that question in an interview for the Public Broadcasting System in its early days, he conceded progress in restricted areas—"in plumbing," he proposed when pressed for an example. No amount of pressure, however could get him to affirm *net* historical progress—an average increase in either virtue or happiness. I resisted his conclusion at the time—I was a young man then—but have since come virtually to accept it. I do not say that social progress *cannot* occur; it *has* occurred on certain fronts, in certain locales—I mentioned civil rights a few paragraphs back. To what extent these pockets of progress will enlarge, I do not know, but we should certainly give them every chance and every assist we can possibly manage. I do not even rule out the possibility that the pockets may expand to the point where they affect the "balance of trade" between good and evil and raise the "gross national (or rather global) product" of human well being. I merely confess that the formula Dr. Coue inscribed on his faith-cure sanitarium—"every day in every way I am getting better and better"—is not part of my creed. I am sure that even Griffin disavows the implied inevitability in that superficial slogan, but we seem to differ in that I am not even sure that if we all put our shoulders to the wheel things will get better; or—what comes to the same thing—that it is probable that we all will put our shoulders to the wheel. This usually elicits the charge that doubt about progress cuts the nerve of social action—"If you don't believe there's a good chance that things can get better, why try to improve them?" is the regularly asked rhetorical question. When I asked Niebuhr that question, he asked *me* one in return. "Need a doctor believe that he is eliminating disease, or even reducing its ratio to health, to take his duties seriously?" His point impressed me. In the days that followed our interview, I had to admit to myself that Niebuhr's doubts about progress had clearly not cut *his* nerve for social action. It was as if his faith, which did not lean on the seventeenth-century faith in progress—did not *need* to lean on it—left him not unmoved by the cry of the oppressed, but unshaken by it.

6. *The essential identity of all religions.* Unimpressed by my argument from revelation—what kind of a god would God be if he or she played favorites with his or her children?—Griffin finds it implausible "to think of the various great religions as equally embodying revelations of the same divine reality" (41). This seems to be because he sees personal and transpersonal—not "impersonal" as he again repeats—imagery as pointing to alternative Gods between which we must choose, whereas

I see them as aspects of a single deity, or (as one might equally say) complementing approximations in our understandings thereof. The issues here seem to me to be these:

a. Are the great enduring religions, while different, equals? By characterizing as "unilluminating" my claim that they are "equally adequate for salvation" (42), Griffin seems to imply that they are not on all fours.

b. Both Griffin and I recognize that religions are not carbon copies of one another, so the question is whether there are also respects in which they are alike. As everything both resembles and differs from everything else—resembles it minimally in that both exist; differs from it in that they are at least numerically distinct—the various religions *have to* be alike in some ways; we would not refer to them collectively as religions if they had nothing in common. Whether we are more impressed by their similarities or their differences is something of a fielder's choice. I am more interested in their similarities (which is to say that those are their aspects that strike me as being most important) for two related reasons. First, my ruling interest is in salvific truth—truth about ultimate reality, the knowledge of which conduces to maximum human fulfillment. Second, I resist the prospect of whole segments of humanity having been excluded from this truth for the bulk of human history. If we think of the truth in question as entering through revelation, I do not like the thought of God's withholding it from the human majority—this was the point with which this section opened. But if we prefer the alternative aetiology and think of truth as surfacing through the deepest intuitions of religious geniuses, it seems equally unlikely to me that genius is unequally sprinkled around the world. If Griffin's top priority is social justice and he sees this as the most important feature of religion, I can see how the differences between the religions would outweigh their similarities and how they would not seem equal in worth, for this feature *is* stressed in Western religions more than in the others. Otherwise, I am not sure where he stands on what I see as the basic issues in this section.

c. To say that the ontological unity that informs the great religions—the One that inspires them all and gives them their basic trajectory—is transcendent is merely to acknowledge that it cannot be adequately articulated. Articulation is always affected by language, culture, and temperament from which it proceeds. On the level of their creedal affirmations, the religions obviously differ.

7. Premodern worldview in a modern world. Griffin opens this section with the thesis that prompts his whole critique of perennialism, namely, that "an advance to a postmodern worldview would be better than a simple return to a premodern outlook" (42). He notes that I do not want a premodern world but only its worldview, but then asks how I can have one without the other unless I disavow the power of ideas.

A good point. It forces me again to see that, when I speak of worldview—or outlook, or sense of reality—my eye is on the ontology or metaphysics of the position, not its cosmology or social philosophy. If these three ingredients are not distinguished, there obviously is no perennial philosophy, for cosmologies (as I have noted) change constantly, and the social structures of India, China, and Christendom have been dramatically different. Let me say again that I am indebted to Griffin for prompting me to make this point explicitly. With it in place, I do not see us differing as to whether ideas have consequences. The consuming question is: which consequential ideas of our predecessors merit our continued allegiance, and which should be retired?

III. GRIFFIN'S VISION FOR A POSTMODERN WORLD

Griffin closes his statement with his own vision of a philosophy to serve the postmodern world, and while I find that vision inspiring in its own right, I naturally cannot agree that it provides "a more coherent, adequate, and illuminating account of reality than any of its rivals" (46). I give it good marks for coherence, but to my eyes it sacrifices adequacy and illumination in order to preserve what—again by my lights—lies in the direction of Emerson's "foolish consistency that is the hobgoblin of little minds." I despair of substantiating that judgment by reacting to specific features of Griffin's vision, the few that I would want to question.[12] The ways in which he sees it as improving on the perennial outlook were implied, where not explicitly stated, in his preceding critique of my position, and I have responded to them there. As for my criticizing specific features of his position, I shall not begin that way because (as I noted earlier) I am so impressed by the extent to which preprogramed patterns of perception influence the way their constituent elements *appear* that I despair of getting a tight grip on those elements by addressing them *ad seriatim*. (I think Griffin's critique of specific points in my position bears this out. The items he targets are not the items as they appear to me.) So, I begin by responding to Griffin's outlook as a whole, after which I explain why I find some of its ingredient features constricting.

A recent letter from a professor in India contains a slip which is as illuminating as it is delightful. In requesting a copy of my *Beyond the*

Post-Modern Mind, he inadvertently changed *post-modern* to *post-mortem*. This chances to be precisely the way Griffin and I see the metaphysics of modernism; we think it has had its day. Vectored by the cosmology of the then-new physics, that metaphysics was essentially Newtonian. It presented life as precariously perched on a universe of matter that was preponderantly dead. Its atoms were as isolated and self-contained as billiard balls. And they were inflexibly governed by natural laws.

It was Whitehead's genius to reverse all three features of that appalling vision.[13] Our world is alive, not dead. We humans are intimately and integrally related to the entire past. And we are free, not determined.

I continue to remember vividly the exhilaration I felt when Whitehead turned that metaphysical page for me. It was akin to breathing after someone had been holding my head under water for almost a decade. Of course, the relief depended on my accepting the truth of what Whitehead said, but his scientific credentials enabled me to do that. I was then under the spell of scientism, and could not have believed anything that did not carry its imprimatur.

Whitehead did more than correct Newton. On the isolation issue, he went on to argue that not only are we rooted in the past, indeed literally *constituted* by it; we are understood, *completely understood*, by a God who shares our every experience. And who preserves those experiences forever in her never-to-be-eroded memory. With this single stroke, Whitehead solves both the problem of loneliness and the problem of time, the perpetual perishing of experience, which, if unrelieved, would constitute life's deepest tragedy. Moreover, God is provident. As "the Divine Eros of the universe" (50), she avails herself of her omniscience to incline (but not require) us to choose at every juncture the best outcome circumstances allow.

I said that this God solves the problem of time, but not quite, for Whitehead stopped with objective immortality. After we die, God remembers every detail of our lives as if it had just occurred, but our own consciousness ends. Griffin thinks Whitehead was unduly constrained by modern conventions here and argues that his metaphysics allows for subjective immortality as well.

So majestic is this view of life and reality that understanding why Griffin could wonder how there could be an alternative that tops it is easy. In the next several paragraphs, I indicate why, for me, such an alternative exists.

I take the alternative to be superior because it satisfies me more. This may sound like wishful thinking, as if I simply believe what I want to believe, but I do not see it this way. I am speaking of intellectual satisfaction, not the satisfaction of personal whims. Philosophers who worry about the concept of explanation have yet to offer a clearer criterion for why and when an explanation works than that it leaves the inquirer satisfied. When we try to account for why anything produced intentionally is the way it is and not some other way, the account (to succeed) must take the form of that being the best way it could be. Why inventors build better mousetraps needs no further explanation; their "better" is reason enough. But if someone set out to build a worse mousetrap, we might feel a psychiatrist was needed to ferret out the reason.

This bears on the present discussion as follows: When asked why the perennialist's view is more accurate than Whitehead's, the controlling reason I sense is that it appears as the better world of the two. After all the ways in which Whitehead has God covering for our mistakes, the residual fact is that it would be better if those mistakes did not occur, which concedes that things would have been better had they been otherwise. Comparably with time. The God of process theologians improves by amassing more experience. But improvement implies an initial lack (read, a defect); the divine reality is subject to something other than itself, in this case to time as deployed by the metaphysical ultimate. Defects in the ultimate nature of things the perennialist resists, for they amount to metaphysical surds.

I am aware of the restiveness this tack incites in process theologians; the objections it evokes are familiar terrain. To address those objections, however, would retrace the route we have come, so I content myself here with remarking that what Charles Hartshorne sees as "theological mistakes" in classical theism,[14] I do not take to be such. Believing that little would be accomplished by pecking at specific points in Griffin's postmodern vision—once again, the few points with which I would *want* to take issue—I have gone directly to what seems to be the underlying, controlling difference between us, the big difference that vectors all the lesser ones. Having indicated what I think that basic difference to be, however, I will mention some specifics in the process view of things that would feel constricting to me if I had to live with them.

1. Whitehead contended that God should not be an exception to metaphysical first principles, which seems to be a carryover from the modern, scientistically derived prejudice against supernaturalism.[15] My impulse is to argue the opposite: a God who does not exceed the categories that govern nature does not deserve our worship. To absolutize those categories is a category mistake, similar to trying to explain biology in terms of physics or chemistry. Whitehead's categories are demanding, but they *do* in the end fit into our three-dimen-

sional reason, from which it follows that to fit God into them is to position her inside our limited understanding. This translates into putting God in a cage. Religion must, to be sure, be intelligible in certain ways, but to try to make it *rationally* intelligible, fully so, is to sound its death knell. (In keeping with perennialists generally, I draw a sharp distinction between *ratio* and *intellectus* inasmuch as the latter operates intuitively and directly.) It is to squeeze the *pneuma*—a word usually translated as *spirit*, but etymologically deriving from *breath* or *air*—out of it, leaving us with what someone has called "flat-tire" theology. I realize that my rejection of Whitehead's "ontological principle" here will sound like mystery-mongering to process theologians, but, apart from the pejorative in the word *mongering*, I welcome the charge. *Vis-à-vis* most modern and postmodern theology, I side with Sir Thomas Browne, who complained in his *Religio Medici* that the religion he typically heard preached did not contain sufficient impossibilities, adding that it is "no vulger part of faith" to believe things not only above but contrary to reason and against the evidence proper to our senses.[16] Process theology accommodates the quantitative awe of Pascal's spaces and Kant's starry skies, but not the qualitative awe of quantum mechanics and relativity theory. We can imagine "actual occasions," they being extrapolations from what we are ourselves, but matter that is both wave and particle is beyond imaging. It is from paralleling postmodern science in its counterintuitive respects that perennialism's paradoxes arise, the ones Griffin sees as making hash of the position. Time and evil are as real as Griffin insists they are, and moral evil as repugnant and deserving of combat,[17] yet in the transmuted light by which God sees them, and by which eventually we will see them too, they have their place, possessing which their limitations withdraw. (We are back with my principle of perfection: if Griffin is going to deny that it would be *better* if there were no evil, I am going to charge *him* with not taking evil seriously. If, as William James tells us, religion claims that the best things are the most enduring things, perennialism is that white-hot brand of religion that claims that ultimately they are the only things.) Griffin wants me to come down on one side or the other of my paradoxes, but I want to keep both sides in sharp tension. As Niels Bohr noted in a famed remark: the opposite of a small truth is a small error, but the opposite of a great truth is another great truth.

2. Griffin's two ultimates, creative experience and God, sound provisional to me. Whitehead had a third ultimate, the structure of actual occasions, but, be they two or three—or four if we add eternal objects—, I find multiple ultimates unsatisfying; they have (for me) the

feel of metaphysical polytheism. My hunger for wholeness prods me to push past them. Why don't the process theologians make one of their ultimates *really* ultimate and productive of the others?, I keep asking myself. I do not think my tropism toward unity here is exceptional; on the contrary (and with apologies for the offense), it strikes me as an important mark of a philosopher. A sentence in a recent issue of a scientific journal tells us that "the aim of philosophy is to see the world as a unity [which process philosophy does]; to understand it in terms of a single, all-encompassing principle [which process philosophy does not]."

3. The singularity that philosophy seeks is needed because the essence of ultimacy is not primordiality or ubiquity, as process philosophers would have it, but rather the possession of ultimate power. *Shared* power is never ultimate because, unless its division is fixed from the start (in which case who or what did the apportioning?), it must be negotiated with a rival, as Manichaeism clearly perceived. Process philosophers shift the weight of ultimacy from power to ubiquity[18] because they do not try to press the explanation of why the world is the way it is to its logical limit. Beginning with the world as we experience it, they trace it to the fewest number of agents that are needed to account for that world, and there rest their case. Why the world and its agents are as *they* are, and why there is something rather than nothing, are not considered fruitful questions. I see things differently. Not to pursue such questions feels to me like stunting the philosophical quest. "*Some* world of finite beings must exist," Griffin says (45), but unless one accepts the fact that some such world does exist as the reason that it must exist, I do not find him saying why. For me, this is too close to Bertrand Russell's positivistic pronouncement on a radio program that "the world is simply *there*, and that's all there is to it."

4. It would not take much to convert Griffin's two ultimates, metaphysical and axiological, into my ultimate (the Absolute) and its first expression (the Logos). Distracted for a moment in writing this very paragraph, my eye falls on the following epitomization of perennialism: "The first discernment necessary is that between the Absolute and the relative; the second is that between the Divine Essence, Beyond-Being, and the Divine Person, Being—Being is the 'form' of the Essence." This sounds strikingly similar to Griffin's assertion that creative experience "is ineffable, in that it has no characteristics by which it could be described," while "God is the *primordial characterization* of creative experience" (45). The difference seems to be that my Absolute is actual in the absolute sense of containing within itself all the possibilities that will issue from it; in this respect it is similar to

the metaphysical counterpart of matter's pre-big-bang super-pellet which, in exploding (astro-physicists currently tell us), produced our universe. What makes the Absolute ineffable is that we cannot imagine how All-Possibility (its synonym) is compacted concretely within it, its latent distinctions retained in the absence of differences that would violate the divine simplicity. By comparison, Griffin's "creative experience" seems abstract and dependent, like Aristotle's forms that cannot exist apart from the substances that embody them. The Neoplatonic, Brahmanic, Taoist One seems so much richer to me; by an account drawn from Romantic Platonism, it is "a unity intrinsically manifold; a *pleroma* or fullness that cannot but 'flame out' beyond its own most proper limits into the being of every existing thing, the manifestation of all that it was already." Emanation and radiation are the operative principles here. Emergence, their alternative, is unintelligible, given the fact that from nothing, nothing can derive.

Griffin concludes his statement with a prophetic call for a new, postmodern science that will support rather than oppose theology. It is a bracing summons, but it rides a crucial oversight. To the extent that science moves in the direction Griffin wants it to, it will relax its effort to control and will content itself with trying to describe, because most of the things Griffin wants it to add to its repertoire—the immaterial, qualities, final causes, freedom, downward and divine causation—cannot be manipulated. There is nothing wrong with describing, of course, or anything sacrosanct about control. Quite the contrary; the most valuable aspect of Heidegger's entire corpus is his analysis of the way Western civilization has drifted toward calculative reason and the disaster portended by that drift. The question is not whether we should correct this drift, as Griffin and I are both convinced we should; the question concerns division of labor and what Confucius called "the rectification of names." I see Griffin as still wedded to the modern conviction that science is the privileged mode of knowledge. If this conviction be true, it stands to reason that all knowing should enter its camp. And so Griffin would have it: "science . . . means knowledge," he tells us, so "even the modern boundary between science and theology will . . . be overcome" (49).

We can, to be sure, define words as we wish and make them mean what we want them to mean. We can even go so far as to revert to the vocabulary in which theology was "the queen of the sciences," if we so choose. But all this seems to breed confusion. Why do we want science to do everything respecting knowledge? But more is at stake here than a fielder's choice regarding the way we define words. However much Griffin may wish to enrich the definition of science, it currently *has* in the

English-speaking West a very solid, weighty, operational referent—roughly the one that guides the National Science Foundation in its appropriation of funds. No amount of protest on Griffin's part is (in the foreseeable future, which is to say *our* postmodern world) going to disengage "science" from its heavy—indeed, decisive and appropriate—involvement with the controlled experiment, hence with upward causation. That is what modern science has been and, because that is the direction from which its power derives, that (by the test of where we put our public money) is what we are going to ask it to continue to be. To hire science as a consultant for the higher reaches of life is, therefore, willy-nilly to invite those regions to be seen in inferior ways. It invites reductionism. Much cleaner and safer is the route that portions out the noetic field, respectfully assigning its visible, material regions to science while remaining clear-eyed and very stern about the incompetence of the methods that work superbly there to say explicitly anything of the slightest importance about other domains.

Griffin's allusion to evolution—the point in science where he takes perennialists to task—is too laconic to say much about. That a soul in the Aristotelian sense (analogous to the structure of Whitehead's dominant individual?) does not "emerge," as Griffin would say—I prefer "descend as a Platonic archetype"—until a corporeal receptacle of a certain complexity has appeared to properly host it, is no problem for the perennialist. I actually see the perennial account as fitting the punctuational equilibrium hypothesis (which the fossil record now points toward) better than does the Whiteheadian version, which seems naturally keyed to Darwinian gradualism. Generally, process philosophy inclines toward continuity, which may explain Griffin's tendency to see "gnostic dualism" lurking behind what for others are merely categorial differences. Perennialism, on the other hand, wants to make sure that we do not overlook differences that are not merely ones of degree, but of kind.

NOTES

1. Frithjof Schuon, *Language of the Self* (Madras: Ganesh & Co., 1959), 15.

2. Karl Jaspers, *The Great Philosophers* (New York: Harcourt, Brace and World, 1962), 104.

3. *The Nag Hammadi Library*, ed. James M. Robinson (New York: Harper and Row, 1977), 295. From among any number of mystics I could just as well have quoted Dionysius, who writes in his treatise *On the Divine Names*: "It is impossible to utter this truly wondrous name, the name that is set above every name that is named either in the present world or in the world to come."

4. Paul Tillich, *The Future of Religions* (New York: Harper and Row, 1965), 87.

5. See St. Teresa's account on 173.

6. Whitehead himself says that "there is not a sentence or a word which has a meaning which is independent of the circumstances under which it is uttered." Quoted by Hartshorne in *Whitehead's Philosophy: Selected Essays, 1935-1970* (University of Nebraska Press, 1972), 226-27.

7. Huston Smith, *Forgotten Truth* (New York: Harper and Row, 1976), 18.

8. Quoted in A.H. Johnson, ed., *Whitehead's Interpretation of Science* (Indianapolis: Liberal Arts Press, 1961), 174.

9. I argue this in "The Crisis in Philosophy," *Behavior* 16/1 (Spring 1988).

10. St. Augustine, *Confessions*, VII, xiii, 19, tr. R.S. Pine-Coffin (Baltimore: Penguin Books, 1961), 149.

11. Quoted in R.A. Nicholson, *Translations of Eastern Poetry and Prose* (London: Cambridge University Press, 1922), 134.

12. Let me reemphasize: far more unites than separates us. Paraphrasing the commonalities that Griffin lists (43): we both believe that finite existence is anchored in God; that values, qualities, and purposes extend to (or better, proceed from) the very foundations of existence; that the more influences the less; that our physical senses are not the only faculties we have for receiving messages from the world (we have direct access to the experiences of others, for example); and that the human self is nobly made and is immortal. Griffin extends this list (48) by noting that we both subscribe to the existence of an external world, causation, partial freedom, objective values, the correspondence theory of truth, and a holy reality.

13. In note 115, Griffin argues that although Whitehead's metaphysics accommodates twentieth-century physics, it was not tailored to that accommodation. I am not fully persuaded of this—I suspect that the question is a matter of degree. I do, however, see clearly (now that Griffin has pointed it out) that in the passages of mine to which he refers I should have cited field rather than relativity theory. Griffin knows Whitehead better than I do, of course, but I would need to hear more from him to be persuaded that Whitehead's philosophy of organism would have been only incidentally, not structurally, different had he not been as thoroughly conversant with the physics that was falling into place as he wrote.

14. As in Hartshorne's *Omnipotence and Other Theological Mistakes* (Albany: State University of New York Press, 1984), for example.

15. Cf. Griffin, 47: "No appeal to supernatural aid is . . . necessary."

16. In a book of fiction that I happen to be reading at the moment, the author notes that "theology must always contain a strong dose of the inexplicable and incomprehensible" (Milan Kundera, *The Unbearable Lightness of Being* [New York: Harper and Row, 1985], 126).

17. As Gary Snyder, speaking for what perennialists consider the Buddhist version of this point, said in a recent interview for *Inquiring Mind* (4/2 [Winter 1988], 5):

> The large scale view of things that often comes with Buddhist practice doesn't take us off the hook from responsibility to respond to events. To use that larger perspective as an excuse for not being concerned in the moment is cheating. That would be the exercise of wisdom without compassion. Larger scale views do not excuse us from the necessity of acting in our lives, in our moment, taking pain, taking oppression, taking confusion, taking destruction as it presents itself to us and seriously working on it, if only because we are very small, conditioned beings and that is our responsibility and our territory."

18. Creative experience is called "agency itself" (45), but that is not what makes it ultimate for Griffin or God would not also be ultimate.

4

PERFECTION, UNITY, AND PRIMORDIAL TRUTHS: A COUNTERREPLY

David Ray Griffin

I began my critique of Smith's position by emphasizing the points we have in common, then devoted most of my attention to our differences. Smith does the same in his response. This is proper, because the overriding intellectual question of our time is: Given the perceived inadequacy of the modern worldview, with what view should it be replaced? We want a view that is more adequate to and illuminating of the various facts of experience than is the modern worldview, and that also provides a more adequate basis for human living. Smith and I both believe that the other's view is better than the modern worldview in these respects; but we each believe that our own is better yet. Because our respective reasons for holding this latter belief inevitably dominate our dialogue with each other, it is easy for the former belief, which is more fundamental, to get lost. By analogy, two candidates for their political party's nomination inevitably spend most of their time pointing out why their program is better than that of their rival; and yet they are united on the deeper conviction that either of their programs would be far better than that of the other party. Accordingly, before plunging into my counterreply, I again call attention to our common conviction that the incumbent party's platform, the modern worldview, must be overcome for the sake of our individual and collective health and even survival.

In this chapter, I seek to bring more focus to our dialogue by reducing the number of issues. I had organized my original critique of Smith's position in terms of thirteen issues, with two underlying ones. Smith appropriately responded to each issue, although he expressed discomfort with the *ad seriatim* approach and helpfully devoted attention to what he considers the major, underlying difference between us. I have organized my counterreply in terms of seven headings: (1) divine perfection and worldly evil; (2) truth and coherence; (3) personal God, transpersonal absolute, and the religions; (4) time, social progress, gnostic dualism, and immortality; (5) primordial, premodern, and postmodern; (6) science and theology; and (7) dualism, supernaturalism, and philosophical unity.

Even with fewer issues before us, the *ad seriatim* approach tends to obscure a fundamental point, which I want to emphasize: the inextricable connection between substantive and formal issues. I try to keep that point in mind by mentioning it occasionally, and also by alternating somewhat between substantive issues (1, 3, 4) and formal ones (2, 5, 6, 7). Our different substantive convictions condition, and are in turn conditioned by, differing convictions on formal issues.

I indicate with the title what I consider to be the major issues. Smith and I have different visions of what constitutes divine perfection and of the sense in which our world can be considered perfect. This substantive difference supports, and is supported by, different ideas of the kind of unity a philosophical theory should seek. These differences support, and are in turn supported by, a different criterion for, and a different list of, the primordial truths to which any acceptable philosophy or theology must be adequate.

I. DIVINE PERFECTION AND WORLDY EVIL

Smith correctly points out the "big difference," the "underlying, controlling difference" (80) between us with regard to our substantive visions: my vision of divine perfection must be compatible with the conviction that genuinely evil events occur, while Smith's vision entails the ultimate denial of any genuine evil. (In Smith's discussion of the "big difference," this substantive point is conjoined, appropriately, with a formal difference involving the kind of explanation that is found satisfying; I come to this dimension of the difference under the second heading, "Truth and Coherence.")

Smith's portrayal of my position on this issue is a little misleading in two respects. First, he suggests that I, believing that God must be "either all-powerful or completely good," opt for divine goodness. He suggests further that my position will be psychologically ineffectual, because "history shows people worshipping power more than virtue" (69). I do not disagree with this historical point; indeed, I *define* religion in terms of the universal desire to be in harmony with the ultimate power of the universe. In my own position, accordingly, I emphasize and seek to portray convincingly the persuasive power of God as the supreme power of the universe.[1]

Furthermore, going beyond this historical or psychological insight to the theological point that only perfection is *worthy* of worship in the strongest sense, I emphasize that God is *perfect* in power (as well as goodness), which means that God has the greatest power it is possible for any one being to have. The test of possibility here is the Anselmian test of *genuine conceivability: God has the greatest power it is consistently conceivable for a creator of a universe to have.* The defense of this claim, which is provided at length elsewhere,[2] cannot and need not be repeated here. The relevant point for now is that Smith and I do not disagree on the equation of divinity with perfection, and on the inclusion of perfect power within the divine perfection. We differ only on the proper understanding of perfect power. We differ on whether omnipotence in the traditional sense is consistently conceivable. (Or, perhaps more accurately, we disagree on the importance of consistent conceivability, as will be discussed in the next point.) I do not deny that God is "all-powerful" if this means that God has all the power it is possible for a creator of a universe to have; I only deny that God is "all-powerful" if that is taken to mean omnipotence in the traditional sense, which means that God *essentially* has *all* the power, period, so that any power possessed by finite beings is wholly derivative and can therefore be cancelled or overridden at will. I accordingly said: "Perfect power cannot mean omnipotence, if that means the power to override the creative power of the creatures or the effects thereof"(46).

Smith is also slightly misleading in saying that "to Griffin's disjunctive eyes, God, being perfect, cannot be omnipotent also" (69). This is true (assuming omnipotence in the traditional sense is meant) in the same way that, to my disjunctive eyes, a ball, being round, cannot also be triangular. The similarity of these two impossibilities is brought out by the traditional "problem of evil," which can be formulated thus:

1. If God exists and is perfectly good, God would want to prevent all genuine evil.
2. If God exists and is omnipotent (in the traditional sense), God could unilaterally prevent all evil.
3. Genuine evil does occur.
4. Therefore, God (so defined) does not exist.

What is misleading about Smith's statement is its suggestion that my eyes are any more disjunctive (at least on this issue) than his own. Smith considers this argument formally valid, and would therefore accept its conclusion if he considered all the premises true. But he rejects the third premise; he denies that genuine evil occurs.

In my book on the problem of evil, I defined *genuine evil* as "anything, all things considered, without which the universe would have been better."[3] Smith denies the reality of genuine evil in this sense, indicating that he cannot accept any view that says that "things would have been better had they been otherwise" (80). I stated this definition in other words by saying that "some event is genuinely evil if its occurrence prevents the occurrence of some other event which would have made the universe better, all things considered, i.e., from an all-inclusive, impartial perspective." Smith explicitly denies genuine evil thus defined, saying that, although in one sense evil is "real . . . repugnant and deserving of combat," the events thus considered evil are not evil "in the transmuted light by which God sees them, and by which eventually we will see them" (81). He says that that which is regarded as evil from our perspective should also be seen as contributing to "a whole that would be poorer without it" (70). Any possible doubt as to Smith's position is removed by his statement that I rightly focus on this issue in his position, because any position that argues "that things in their final or ultimate nature are perfect in every respect must face the fact of evil as its major challenge" (69). How does Smith respond to this challenge?

Smith refers to the statement in which I say that his position, in holding that "no genuine evil of any kind exists," is "simply not adequate to reality" (29, 69). What lies behind my claim is the assertion that the denial of genuine evil is counterintuitive in the strong sense (29), because the reality of genuine evil belongs to that core set of ideas the truth of which "can be verified through the fact that no one can consistently deny them" (48). These ideas are what I mean by *primordial truths*. I have elsewhere referred to them as hard-core common sense ideas.

What I mean by *hard-core commonsense ideas* can be indicated in three points: (1) They must be universal, therefore truly *common* to all humanity. Many ideas that are carelessly referred to as "common sense" are parochial ideas, not being shared by all human beings; these "soft-core commonsense ideas" are not in view here. (2) Saying that these ideas are universal does not necessarily mean that they belong to every-one's repertoire of explicit, consciously held beliefs. Indeed, many peo-ple may consciously *deny* them. All that is necessary is that they be held implicitly, in the sense of being *presupposed in practice*. (3) They must be *inevitably* presupposed in practice, so that no one can live without giving implicit testimony to their truth. In fact, the very attempt to deny a hard-core commonsense idea will give implicit witness to its truth. For example, belief in an "external world" beyond my present experience is such a belief; a solipsist could not announce his nonbelief in an external world without presupposing the existence of the beings to whom he made the announcement. Likewise, we all presuppose the power of things to exert causal influence upon other things; I could not try to cause others to give up their belief in the reality of causal influence without thereby contradicting myself.

Because such beliefs cannot be consistently denied, it makes no sense to deny them. We must presuppose that they are true. Because they fit Smith's description of primordial truths as those that are believed at all times and all places, we should equate these hard-core commonsense ideas and primordial truths. The primordial truths of which we are con-scious should be taken as the ultimate criteria in terms of which to judge all other beliefs. We should accept no philosophy or theology that is inconsistent with any of these truths.

I maintain that the reality of genuine evil belongs to this set of pri-mordial truths. Every human society has moral and legal codes which are based on the presupposition that a distinction between good and evil exists. The denial of genuine evil implies that that distinction is not ultimately valid. Our feelings of conscience and guilt presuppose that our actions or thoughts have not been as good as they might have been; but if even our foulest deed is to be seen as "contributing to a whole that would be poorer without it," our guilt-feelings are inappropriate—neither Hitler nor the child molester should feel any remorse. Furthermore, we cannot teach the absence of a distinction between good and evil without presupposing it. Smith's teaching that everything is ultimately perfect, for example, presupposes that it is better for people to believe this than the opposite, and that it is worse if they believe as I do. The distinction between good and evil, and therefore the belief in the reality of genuine evil, shows every sign of being a hard-core commonsense idea, a primordial truth. It is on this basis that I say that Smith's theology is "not adequate to reality."

Incidentally, although Smith regards my criticism here to be the claim that his position is "materially incoherent . . . by virtue of not fitting with the facts" (69), I included this point under "internal criticisms" on the grounds that Smith himself implies his own belief in the reality of genuine evil in his criticism of the modern worldview (29). Indeed, in his reply he refers to the modern worldview as an "appalling vision" (79). Has he not thereby contradicted his statement that the world is "perfect in every respect"?

Smith attempts to reconcile this apparent contradiction by means of his doctrine of various levels of reality, the central point of which is the distinction between the *absolute* and the *relative* levels. While the evil of evil disappears at the absolute level, it is said to be real at the relative level, where we are. We are therefore to resist it, "countering it with every energy we can possibly muster" (70), while at the same time knowing that it is not evil from the absolute point of view—that reality is perfect down to the tiniest detail, and that the evil we are resisting some- how contributes to this absolute perfection. Has Smith thereby avoided contradicting the reality of genuine evil and thereby a primordial truth? I cannot say so. He is saying that evil appears to be real to us but that it really is not real. In fact, as I pointed out (23), Smith also calls the distinction between the absolute and the relative levels the distinction between *reality* and *appearance*. To say that "evil is clearly real at our end of the scale" (70), therefore, is simply to say that it *appears* to be real. To say that nothing is evil from the divine perspective is to say that nothing is *really* evil.

Another question to ask about Smith's treatment of evil is whether he has given us any good reason for believing that evil is unreal from the ultimate perspective. His main argument is a deductive one, based on God's omnipotent goodness plus the "principle of plenitude" inherent in the idea of the "great chain of being." The argument would, along with other premises, contain the following:

1. The best possible world would be one that includes all the possible levels of being.
2. Because degree of goodness and degree of being are correlative, the lower degrees of being have less goodness, thereby more evil.
3. The best possible world would contain evil, and would be perfect and thereby devoid of evil precisely by containing evil (relatively).

The remainder of the argument is that God, being perfect in goodness and power, would necessarily create the best possible world, and there- fore one with all the possible levels of being.

One part of my critique that Smith ignored was my criticism of this argument. This argument, I complained, trades on an ambiguity in the notion of evil. The type of evil justified by the argument is what some have called "metaphysical evil." Within the metaphysics of the great chain of being, finite things are said to be evil (metaphysically) simply be virtue of being finite, by not being God, or the absolute. A perfect statue (say, Michelangelo's *David*), a perfect dog (say, a Samoyed), and a perfect human being (say, Jesus or Gautama) would all be metaphysically evil simply by virtue of being finite. A perfect dog, being lower on the scale of being, would be more evil than a perfect human being, and a perfect statue would be more evil yet, metaphysically speaking. This argument seems only to explain why every *kind* of possible being must exist (from, say, angels to quarks); it does not seem to explain why there must be such imperfect examples of each kind (fallen angels and quirky quarks). Why must there be human beings who are *morally* evil as well as *metaphysically* evil? Granted that the world, to fulfill the principle of plenitude, must have cells, why must some cells be cancerous? Granted that it is good that the world have cows, why must most milking cows nowadays live a miserable existence indoors, fastened to a milking machine? Granted that it is good to have babies, why must some of them be born deformed?

Smith evidently did not respond to this point because of a failure of understanding.[4] But once its significance is grasped, it confronts him with a dilemma. On the one hand, he *could* say that moral and physical evil are contained within metaphysical evil. In this case, the principle of plenitude would explain not only why the world must contain every possible species, but also why, within each species, every form of evil that is possible for that species must be actualized. But if Smith grasps that horn of the dilemma, the implausibility of the principle of plenitude becomes all too obvious. Why should we accept the paradoxical notion that the most perfect world is by definition one that contains every possible evil? On the other hand, if Smith says that the principle of plenitude does not apply within each species of being, then this principle provides no explanation for the presence of moral and physical evil in a world created by omnipotent goodness.

Yet another question to raise about Smith's treatment of evil is whether it makes the goodness of God plausible. In trying to explain the way what seems evil to us might contribute "to a whole that would be poorer without it," he says: "Villainous behavior in a play can serve the playwrite's purpose" (70). He realizes that this analogy seems to suggest that the creator cruelly uses creaturely suffering for its "own divine satisfaction." He seeks to counter that charge by pointing out the way we are often "exalted" by a tragic movie, play, or song. But this analogy is not the best one, because no actual suffering is being witnessed; we know that the play is merely "play." The question is: Could we regard someone as good who was exalted by seeing people die of AIDS, watching a bloody battle, or observing the remains of thousands of people who were killed in death camps? I hope not. (Smith even suggests that the Whiteheadian vision of God behind my own position implies that the world's evils contribute positively to the value of the divine experience; I have elsewhere explained why that suggestion reflects a serious misunderstanding.)[5]

Besides the fact that Smith's denial that evil is real from the divine perspective impugns God's goodness, and is not really believable because it contradicts a primordial truth, it is problematic in a third way. Smith himself says that if anything about his doctrine—assuming "that it has been rightly understood"—would lead one to resist evil less strenuously, this consequence would by itself prove his doctrine to be "pernicious" and "wrong" (70). It seems to me that this consequence would quite often be the case. If seeking to overcome some form of evil requires that we risk our lives or even give up our Saturday evenings (Oscar Wilde declared the trouble with socialism to be that it takes too many evenings), would not the thought that the evil in question really, in some mysterious way, contributes to the overall good of the universe incline us to be less likely to make the sacrifice—at least some of us, some of the time? Although we cannot, I have argued, consistently and therefore wholeheartedly believe the doctrine, people can believe it partly or half-heartedly, and this halfhearted belief can affect their behavior, especially in cases where the belief is convenient, allowing them to rationalize their sloth or selfishness. Smith's response would probably be that, if the doctrine had this effect, then the doctrine had not been "rightly understood." But the slackening of effort cannot *ipso facto* be taken as proof that the doctrine has been misunderstood, or else Smith's offer to take such a consequence as proof of his doctrine's falsehood is vacuous.

In thinking that the doctrine, rightly understood, would never contribute to a lack of moral seriousness, I suspect that Smith has been misled by the case of his own life and that of people like him, who have come to this belief somewhat late in life, long after their moral character and habits had been largely molded. Even if Smith had been able (*per impossibile*) to convince Reinhold Niebuhr in his forties that all is perfect in the eyes of God, I doubt that the pace of Niebuhr's battle for good against evil would have slackened a whit. But what about people who had accepted this doctrine from earliest childhood? Would not at least some of these people be less concerned to overcome various forms of evil throughout their lives than they would have otherwise been? After all, the doctrine logically implies that, whatever happens, the greatest possible good is ensured; if we decide to ignore or even to participate in forms of evil, that decision and its consequence will contribute to the perfection of the universe. And at least some people, some of the time, *are* influenced by the logic of their beliefs. I do hold, therefore, that Smith's doctrine, rightly understood, would have pernicious effects. My saying this will doubtless upset Smith, because he is very passionate about this idea; his entire worldview hinges upon it. But he must realize that I am equally passionate about rejecting this idea; my entire worldview hinges upon it.

Does this conclusion mean that we are at an impasse, so that the best we can do is agree to disagree? Perhaps. But perhaps not. While I believe that my affirmation of the reality of genuine evil is based upon a primordial truth, I also believe that Smith's position is based upon a true intuition. That true intuition is reflected in the Christian and Hindu doctrines of the divine bliss (*ananda*) and the Buddhist doctrine that wisdom brings serenity or equanimity. The true intuition is exaggerated into a falsehood when one says that the divine bliss is impassible, unalloyed with suffering of any sort, or that true wisdom knows the ultimate unreality of the suffering sentient beings to whom one's compassion is directed. The true intuition I have in mind is this: that the evils of the world, while truly and ultimately evil, are part of a process that is very good on the whole; that the good in the process is not possible without the possibility and virtual inevitability of the evil; that the distinctively human evils are occurring in a long process that will eventually lead to such great and universal good that all the participants in the process will agree that the sufferings endured *en route* were worth while; and that one with a truly adequate perspective on the process—namely God—can experience the evil as evil (even feeling the sufferings of the creatures in a way analogous to our feeling of the pain in our bodily members) with serenity. In this sense, I can accept Smith's statement about "a God who feels our sorrows but takes them in stride" (71). If Smith would agree that this formulation expresses his intuition, then we could agree, presenting a unified front against the late modern denial that reality is perfect in any sense.

Smith's deepest conviction, I think it is safe to say, is that reality is perfect. Not just divinity, but reality as a whole. My own vision also is that reality as a whole is perfect, in a very strong sense. I believe that the divine reality is perfect, being perfect both in creative love or power and in responsive love or compassion, and that the *structure* of the world is perfect, being one of the best of all possible worlds. The only difference from Smith's view, if I have correctly understood him, is that I hold that in the concrete, contingent details of the world (as distinct from its abstract, necessary structure), genuinely evil events do occur, events without which God's own experience, and therefore the universe as a whole, would have been better. But it is not evil that genuine evil can occur, and its occurrence is not in vain and therefore not simply a waste. If Smith could formulate his intuition to allow genuine evil in the concrete, contingent details of the world, his intuition about the perfection of reality would be compatible with the human unanimity about the occurrence of genuine evil, which is universally presupposed in practice even though not consistently affirmed in theory.

My proposal implies the importance of finding a way to reconcile all our fundamental intuitions in a coherent philosophical or theological position. I turn now to deal directly with this formal issue.

II. TRUTH AND COHERENCE

Smith's statement about the big, underlying difference between us comes in the midst of his account of the type of explanation he finds satisfying. He believes his perennialist vision to be more accurate than my Whiteheadian vision because its world is a better world. Anticipating the charge that such reasoning is merely wishful thinking, he says: "When we try to account for why anything produced intentionally is the way it is and not some other way, the account (to succeed) must take the form of that being the best way it could be" (80). Although with regard to the products of finite and rather self-centered creatures this statement would generate much debate, it does voice a widespread intuition about the kind of explanation that is found satisfying with regard to the basic structure of reality. To have a religious vision of reality, in fact, is to believe that, in some fundamental sense, the world *is* the way it *ought* to be, that the "rational is the real," that this is (at least *one* of) the "best of all possible worlds."

Among those of us who agree on this point, the question then becomes: What is the best *possible*? That question is implicit in Smith's formulation, as he speaks of "the best way it could be." That ontological question raises the epistemological question: How do we decide what is possible with regard to such fundamental issues? My view, which is a widespread view, is that possibility should be closely connected with conceivability. If some verbal phrase does not evoke a coherently conceivable idea in our minds, we should not say that the phrase points to a possible truth. This criterion does not mean that nothing beyond what we can coherently conceive can exist; to say that would be the height of foolish arrogance. This was my point on page 27, not, as Smith would have it, that I acknowledge that "things we cannot coherently conceive ... exist" (68). We do not know whether such things exist. My point is that we have no good reason to affirm that they do exist. Furthermore, even if we assume that there are extant things whose defining characteristics would forever exceed the grasp of earthly minds, so that we could not understand how some of their attributes are compatible with others, we have no reason, when we read some verbal phrase that evokes attributes that seem incompatible to us, to assume that that phrase refers to one of those extant things. That is, there is an indefinite number of verbal phrases that would evoke apparently incompatible attributes in our minds; even if we assume that a few such phrases actually refer to extant realities, we would have no good reason to assume that any particular phrase was one of the lucky ones—one of those one-in-a-billion-or-so seemingly nonsense phrases that does actually have a referent. By tying possibility closely to conceivability, then, I mean that we should not assume that a set of words describes a really possible world if that so-called world is not consistently conceivable. In our philosophies and theologies—which are human creations, after all—we must limit our assertions about the best possible world to the best conceivable world—until someone comes up with a better world that seems, to our best understanding, to be genuinely conceivable.

I cannot accept the world as described by Smith as a better possible world than the one portrayed in my own account because I cannot accept his as a possible world. I cannot see how some of the *prima facie* evils of the world can be genuine evils, so that we should battle against them, and yet not be genuine evils. Accepting partial freedom as another primordial truth, as does Smith, I cannot understand how we can be genuinely free and yet wholly determined by downward causation from the absolute as Smith's account seems to imply. (If all things were not wholly determined by the absolute, how could the absolute perfection of all things be guaranteed?) I cannot understand in general how something can be actual, which for me means having some activity of its own, and yet be fully determined by God. For these and other reasons, I believe that the best possible world is necessarily a world in which genuine evil is possible and virtually inevitable. We can *speak* of a world in which this is not the case, but we cannot coherently conceive of such a world.

Smith saves some of his strongest words for this feature of my position. While giving my vision good marks for coherence, he finds this coherence more of a weakness than a strength, because it moves toward that "foolish consistency that is the hobgoblin of little minds" against which Emerson warned us (78) (although, in reality, Emerson's statement has nothing to do with the type of consistency that is at issue here[6]). To some extent, my consistency betokens small-mindedness because, Smith believes, it is achieved at the expense of adequacy and illumination. But to some extent Smith regards this coherence as inherently problematic: he does not hesitate to side with those who claim that a satisfactory religious vision must preach "impossibilities." And by *impossibilities* he means things that are inconceivable not only in the weak sense of being "above reason," but also in the strong sense of being "contrary to reason." To make religion "rationally intelligible," he says, "is to sound its death knell" (81). He emphasizes his defiance of rational consistency by repeating his favorite saying from Niels Bohr— that "the opposite of a great truth is another great truth" (81).

If I follow Smith's meaning, the opposite of the great truth that the world is absolutely perfect, down to the most minute detail, is the great truth that genuine evil exists, and that we should resist it with all our might. The opposite of the great truth that we are partially free, and therefore partly responsible for how we respond to evil, is the great truth that our feelings, thoughts, and outer actions are fully determined by downward causation from the absolute.

Smith's position thereby seems invulnerable. To my claim that we should judge a theological position on the basis of its coherence as well as its adequacy and illuminating power, Smith replies that we should accept a religious vision only if it is incoherent. To my question, why should we accept Smith's incoherent position rather than some other incoherent position (28), he replies that his is better. To my claim that it is not a better *possible* position, because not coherently conceivable, he replies that this is a strength, not a weakness, that we should not take coherent conceivability by our small minds to be a criterion of possibility, and that in fact incoherence is a *conditio sine qua non* of an adequate and illuminating vision. We thus seem to be caught in a vicious cycle. By my formal criteria, my substantive position is superior, but by Smith's formal criteria, his own substantive vision is superior. We seem to have reached a relativistic impasse. To see if this is really so, we need to look more closely at Smith's position.

Smith indeed claims invulnerability to criticism in terms of the criteria of adequacy, illuminating power, and self-consistency—especially the latter. He says:

> I do not believe that there are criteria (coherence, adequacy, or any other) that can be established independently—without taking into account the positions on which the criteria presume to pronounce. Abstract criteria have neither the right nor the power to rule on positions that are external to them. (67)

Does Smith mean that the formal criteria of adequacy and self-consistency (or noncontradiction) are not neutral, universally applicable criteria, but are only applicable to those positions that hold reality itself to be self-consistent? Smith does seem to invoke the criterion of adequacy in a vague way, saying that the perennial philosophy is "the view that is normal to man's station because consonant with the complete complement of human sensibilities" (67-68). The absence of the criterion of coherence, noncontradiction, or self-consistency in this statement is striking, given the fact that this statement occurs in Smith's section on "Truth and Incoherence." The principle of noncontradiction does, to be sure, need to be stated very precisely to be universally applicable, but if we give it up altogether, what basis remains for rational discussion of anything? Smith says that any criterion more precise than the one he offered would probably be "guilty of special pleading" (68). But special pleading seems to be Smith's own crime. As I pointed out (26), he uses the criterion of self-consistency against his opponents. Having thereby recognized its validity, what right does he have to exempt his own position from it? Of course, once one has renounced the need for self-consistency, I suppose that one can excuse one's own position from this criterion while rejecting other positions because they violate it, thereby being consistent with one's announced intention to be inconsistent. But I doubt that Smith wants to adopt such an extreme position. Assuming not, it would be good to know how he justifies using the principle of noncontradiction against his intellectual opponents if he does not intend to hold himself to it.

What Smith means by saying that formal criteria such as adequacy and self-consistency cannot be established apart from the substantive position they are to judge seems to be indicated by his belief that he sees something that my worldview does not accommodate—"a concrete, absolute, unsurpassable perfection" (68). It would not be to the point for me to discuss again the fact that I also affirm an unsurpassable perfection, and that we diverge only on how to explicate the meaning of such. What is to the point here is to question whether Smith's belief in such a perfection, however interpreted, is relevant to the question of the universal applicability of the principles of adequacy and self-consistency. He continues: "Appeals to adequacy are futile unless we first know whether such perfection exists" (68). This is a surprising statement. The principle of adequacy is generally taken to mean "adequacy to the rather obvious facts of immediate experience." (I have lifted up "the hard-core commonsense ideas" as those facts of immediate experience to which adequacy is most important.) One tests an interpretive theory about the nature of reality in terms of whether it is adequate to those rather obvious facts of immediate experience. But Smith here seems to say that the principle of adequacy must apply to "a concrete, absolute, unsurpassable perfection," assuming that such exists. In other words, an account fails the test of "adequacy to the facts" unless it affirms the reality of such a perfection! But surely the idea that such a perfect reality exists is not the result of a fairly straightforward description of data that belong to the immediate experience of all human beings. The idea is rather an *interpretation* that goes far beyond any phenomenological reportage. (Although Smith says that he *sees* such a perfection, he should surely say that he *believes in* such a perfection.) Whitehead has a statement bearing directly on this point.

> In our cosmological construction, we are . . . left with the final opposites, joy and sorrow, good and evil, disjunction and conjunction . . . flux and permanence, greatness and triviality, freedom and necessity, God and the World. In this list, the pairs of opposites are in experience with a certain ultimate directness of intuition, except in the case of the last pair. God and the World introduce the note of interpretation.[7]

Whitehead would say that his interpretive theory of God and the World had to be adequate to the other pairs of opposites. He would *not* say that his description of, say, good and evil had to be adequate to his account of God and the World, as if this latter pair were given with more or even equal "directness of intuition." If we are to accept Smith's statement, by contrast, then the believer in phlogiston could claim that appeals to adequacy are futile unless we first know whether phlogiston exists. The atheist could say the same about the nonexistence of God; the doctrinaire Marxist could say the same about the dialectical process of history. I do not see, in sum, how the validity of the formal criterion of adequacy to the facts of experience is contingent upon any substantive interpretation of the nature of reality.

Smith rejects the idea that the criteria of adequacy and coherence can be "wielded objectively" (68). That is a quite different issue. Because of finitude and sin, none of us can wield them objectively, especially by ourselves. That is one reason why we have a community of inquiry, and publish our ideas, so that one person's areas of ignorance and bias can be corrected by other perspectives, in which different mixtures of partiality and partial knowledge are found, and in which the ignorance and bias of one group (say, white males in the so-called First World) can be corrected by the knowledge and perspectives of others (say, black people, women, and people from the so-called Second and Third Worlds). The assumption behind this process is that an interpretation that takes into account the perspectives of informed people with a wide diversity of partial perspectives will come closer to that impartial perspective which only God has and which constitutes the very meaning of truth. Formulating such an interpretation is not easy, and any attempt will itself reflect the partiality of the interpreter. *But to point out the difficulty of wielding the criteria objectively is not the same thing as questioning the objectivity, in the sense of the universal applicability, of the criteria themselves.* To give up their objectivity in this latter sense would be to give up the only basis in terms of which the ignorance and bias of one individual or group can be even partially overcome through criticism in terms of the perspectives of others. Indeed, to give up the reality of such formal criteria would be to succumb to that complete relativism of which Smith is rightly so critical.[8]

To hold to these criteria is not, as Smith suggests, to adhere implicitly to modernity's "faith in autonomous reason." I do not, as I have stated elsewhere, believe that reason alone, apart from a substantive religious vision, can create a satisfactory worldview. Apart from some substantive vision based on nonrational sources, reasoning cannot, in fact, generate any worldview at all. Any worldview presupposes a nonrational (that is, prerational) vision of reality.[9] I also reject the distinctively modern idea, expressed in the idea that the so-called naturalistic fallacy is a fallacy, that an ethical theory about how we *ought* to live can be formulated apart from a substantive vision about what *is*. But to say that reason and therefore philosophy cannot be independent from a religious vision and therefore theology is not to say that any substantive theological ideas allegedly derived from revelation or deep intuition should be allowed to override reason's purely formal criteria of self-consistency and adequacy to the facts of experience.

Smith appeals elsewhere for a division of labor (83); this is one place it should hold. Experience—including religious, aesthetic, and moral intuitions as well as sensory perception—provides the substantive content for our worldview; reason, as a purely formal dimension of experience, checks our worldview for adequacy and self-consistency. Although experience must be consulted to see if our arguments are sound, reason must first tell us whether they are valid. Just as we should not pretend that reason alone can generate a worldview, we should not claim that experience alone—that is, experience undisciplined by the formal principles of rationality—can produce a sound worldview.

Smith seeks to show that experience can override reason's concern for self-consistency, saying that "matter is both wave and particle" (68). But we do not know that. We know at most that matter exhibits wave-like properties in some experiments and particle-like properties in other experiments. The Bohr or Copenhagen interpretation of quantum physics is not a theory of what matter in itself is at all; it restricts itself to formulae to correlate and predict instrument readings. The central controversy regarding the Copenhagen theory is indeed whether it is the best that we can do or whether we can press beyond it to understand the realities of subatomic nature behind the observational phenomena. As I mentioned in my critique, David Bohm, a physicist to whom Smith generally appeals with approval, is one who seeks to move beyond the Copenhagen theory to a self-consistent description of the behavior of light and matter that would explain why they produce wave-like phenomena in some experimental contexts and particle-like phenomena in others. Whitehead before him had sought an explanation that "conciliates Newton's corpuscular theory of light with the wave theory."[10] What is germane to the point at hand is not the viability of the suggestions of Bohm and Whitehead on this issue but only the fact that they sought a theory of what light really is that would reconcile the apparently contradictory phenomena. Smith could reply that Bohm and Whitehead are in a distinct minority here, and that most physicists and philosophers of science follow Bohr's view. But then Smith would run up against his own cautions about uncritically following the majority view (63), and about hitching one's philosophy to some current scientific theory that is likely to change (33).

Niels Bohr himself, *qua* amateur philosopher, did develop the principle of complementarity into a general epistemology, and his authority has been invoked by some theologians to justify incompatible principles. Hans Küng, for example, appeals to Bohr's principle to reconcile causal determinism and ethical freedom, and the impersonal deity of Einstein with the personal God of the Bible.[11] I can only regard this practice as pernicious. It is a way to avoid hard thought. Most intellectual breakthroughs, including those in the natural sciences, have come about through the attempt to overcome apparent contradictions by finding a deeper truth that reconciled seemingly contradictory truths. Had our forebears simply chanted "complementarity" every time they faced an apparent contradiction, human thought would not have far surpassed that of the other primates. To whatever extent Smith's program is a call to return to the past, he clearly would not want to go *that far* back!

The difficulties that would follow from accepting complementarity in Bohr's sense as a general truth, even for some issues, can be seen by reflecting upon his statement that, while the opposite of a small truth is a small error, the opposite of a great truth is another great truth. Smith believes that the existence of divine perfection is a great truth. Should we then believe that atheism, in the sense of a denial of the existence of any divine reality, is an equally great truth? Smith believes that the perennial philosophy is a great truth, in fact, a summary of all the great truths, and he presents it as the opposite of the modern worldview. Should we believe that the modern worldview, with its "appalling vision" (79), is an equally great truth? Bohr's paradox, like most paradoxes, is fun to quote, and it has value insofar as it shakes us free from conventional habits of thought. But if taken literally and used as a general principle, it will stifle creative thought, not promote it.

Smith does not deny that religion should be intellectually intelligible, but he does deny that it should be *rationally* intelligible (81). His point here depends, he tells us, upon a sharp distinction, generally made by perennialists, "between *ratio* and *intellectus*." The intellect, he says, "operates intuitively and directly" (81). This terminological distinction is somewhat confusing, given the fact that philosophers in recent times are more likely, with Bergson, to distinguish radically between intuition and intellect rather than equating them. In any case, given *Smith's* meanings, when he speaks of an explanation as "intellectually satisfying" he means intuitively satisfying, as distinct from rationally satisfying. (Unfortunately, he then speaks of paradoxes that we should accept, such as the idea of matter as both particle and wave, as "counterintuitive" (81); but that can be passed over as a mere terminological slip.) He believes that religion should be intuitively but not rationally intelligible. He says that "to try to make it *rationally* intelligible, fully so, is to sound its death knell. . . . It is to squeeze the *pneuma*—a word usually translated as *spirit*, but etymologically deriving from *breath* or *air*—out of it, leaving us with what someone has called 'flat-tire' theology" (81).

Smith usually portrays himself as a defender of classical Christian theism. But this antithesis between *ratio* and *pneuma*—even with his etymological definition of the latter—seems to be a rejection of one of the most important insights contained in the traditional doctrine of the trinity. This is the insight that the cosmic *Logos*, which is the source of human rationality as well as all other forms of order and measure, and the *Holy Spirit* of the universe, which is the source of all vitality, enthusiasm and inspiration, are inseparable aspects of one and the same divine creative and saving power. The insistence upon rationality does often quench the spirit, and responsiveness to the Holy Spirit has often taken an antirational form; that there is no denying. Liberal, rational churches are often unspirited, and charismatic churches are often unreasonable. But the doctrine of the divine trinity points toward an ideal synthesis of rationality and enthusiasm which religion at its best has approximated.

Smith justifies his disjunction between intuitively and rationally satisfying explanations, and his preference for the former to the neglect of the latter, by reference to intimations we have of things that are "too vast and strange to fit our categories of language and thought" (65). I agree, along with Whitehead, that we have intimations or intuitions that exceed our current categories. Whitehead remarks that "mothers can ponder many things in their hearts which their lips cannot express." This is not a sexist remark but a poetic rendering, making use of a biblical allusion, of his conviction that "we know more than can be formulated in one finite systematized scheme of abstractions."[12] The question is: What do we do when we find that we have intuitions that seem to outstrip our present categories? I say that we should not assume that our present categories are the best that "rational thought" can produce but try to find more adequate categories. I agree neither with Smith, that we ought to reject rationality in the name of mystical intuitions, nor with modern thought, that we ought to reject mystical intuitions in the name of rationality, but with Whitehead, that the task of philosophy is to "rationalize mysticism."[13] It can do this only by enlarging its categories of rational understanding.

What should we do when one intuition seems to contradict another? We should not simply reject one (such as freedom) in the name of another one (such as determinism); nor should we simply say that the two are in some mysterious way compatible. Rather, we should, knowing that infallibility has incarnated itself in neither us nor our ancestors, assume that our own or inherited *formulations* of one or the other or both of the intuitions are faulty. As Whitehead says, "the chief error in philosophy is overstatement."[14] That is, we should assume that "earlier statements will be not so much wrong, as obscured by trivial limitations, and as thereby implying an exclusion of complementary truths."[15] The task, then, is to restate one or both of the two intuitions so that the statements no longer contradict each other. "Progress in truth" is made by "evolving notions which strike more deeply into the root of reality."[16] The goal is to reformulate all inherited formulations of fundamental intuitions "so as to absorb into one system all sources of experience."[17] Smith believes that this concern for consistency is a sign of a small mind. But which program is more likely to encourage the unending expansion of the mind, the Whiteheadian program of continual deepening and broadening, or the thought-stopping process of taking apparent contradictions at face value and "reconciling" them by deriding the importance of rational consistency?

Smith wrongly suggests that Whitehead is on his side, speaking of Whitehead's refusal to try "to slap logic onto life." Smith quotes Whitehead's statement: "In formal logic, a contradiction is the signal of defeat: but in the evolution of real knowledge . . . a mere logical contradiction cannot in itself point to more than the necessity of some readjustments, possibly of a very minor character" (68).[18] "But that is just the point: Whitehead does not rest content with contradiction, but insists on "the necessity of some readjustments." Smith describes the ninth widespread assumption that is rejected by Whitehead in the Preface to *Process and*

Reality as "the belief that logical inconsistencies are evidence of ante-cedent errors." But Smith has misread: What Whitehead rejects is the belief "that logical inconsistencies can indicate *anything else than* some antecedent errors."[19] One of the beliefs that Whitehead thereby rejects is precisely the view that logical contradictions in our thought should be taken as signs of something in the nature of things. Smith also portrays Whitehead as saying that any philosophical opponents "worth paying attention to at all . . . are going to be smart enough to avoid head-on contradictions" (68). But there is no thinker to whom Whitehead devotes more space in *Process and Reality* than John Locke, and Whitehead's main point about Locke is the inconsistency of his epistemology—the inconsistency that David Hume sought to overcome.[20] Hume is the other philosopher to whom Whitehead devotes the most attention, and Hume also is criticized for inconsistency.[21]

Smith is right to stress the importance of controlling assumptions. But that issue is not disconnected, in Whitehead's criticisms of Locke and Hume, from their inconsistencies. Whitehead looks for those con-trolling assumptions that, insofar as they are carried out consistently, lead to "negations of what in practice is presupposed."[22] He speaks par-ticularly of those controlling assumptions based on the fact that the words and phrases of an "old established metaphysical system" have gained "a false air of adequate precision."[23] In the cases of Locke and Hume, the controlling assumption was the idea, based upon the subject-predicate mode of thought, that a substance has "private ideas" and is never quali-fied by another substance.[24] This assumption, carried through partly by Locke, and more consistently by Hume, led to the solipsistic idea that we never perceive another actual thing but only ideas or qualities. This epistemology leads to the negation of "what in practice is presupposed," that is, that we are actual beings interacting with other equally actual beings.[25] Even Hume cannot consistently deny his knowledge of this fact. As Whitehead points out, when Hume is honoring his philosophical assumptions, he says that impressions of sensation arise in the soul "from unknown causes." But then "the heat of argument elicits his real convic-tion—everybody's real conviction—that visual sensations arise '*by* the eyes.'" In other words, as Whitehead says: "The causes are not a bit 'unknown,' and among them there is usually to be found the efficacy of the eyes."[26]

Whitehead's major criticism of Hume is for his antirationalism. Rationalism for Whitehead is not contrary to empiricism but is based on it. It begins from "the metaphysical rule of evidence: that we must bow to those presumptions, which, in despite of criticism, we still employ for the regulation of our lives."[27] These are what I have called the *primor-*

dial truths, the *hard-core commonsense ideas.* "Rationalism," says Whitehead, "is the search for the coherence of such presumptions."[28] Hume's antirationalism is manifested in his contentment with "two uncoordinated sets of beliefs,"[29] one labeled philosophical "theory," the other labeled "practice." That is, Hume admitted that, in practice, in his ordinary life, he presupposed the reality of an external world and of causal influence between actual things, but he did not feel compelled to coordinate those presuppositions with his theoretical epistemology. Whitehead believes that Hume should have used the inevitable presuppositions of practice "in criticism of his premises," not "in supplement to his conclusions." The inconsistencies within Hume's discussion are, in other words, an important indicator of inadequate controlling premises which need to be challenged.

My criticism of Smith is similar. I see that he presupposes the importance of consistency when criticizing other philosophers, even though he denies that his own position needs to be self-consistent. He presupposes that bad things really happen, such as the rise to dominance of the modern worldview, even though his philosophical theology says that every detail of the world process is ultimately perfect. I note that Smith's solution to this inconsistency is even similar to Hume's. Hume's two levels of "theory" and "practice" are paralleled by Smith's two levels of "reality" (or "absolute truth") and "appearance" (or "relative truth"). Smith says that, because evil has a relative reality, appearing to be real at the level where we now live, we are to resist it with all our energy, even though we already know that, in reality, from the perspective of absolute truth, it is not evil. My claim is that we cannot live with that type of bifurcation, any more than we can live with a Humean bifurcation between theory and practice, or with a Kantian bifurcation between theoretical reason and practical reason. Those bifurcations, furthermore, reconcile the inconsistencies inherited from the old metaphysical systems too superficially, preventing us from searching for that larger truth through which divergent presuppositions of practice can truly be coordinated with each other.

I have thus far been using the terms *self-consistency* (in the sense of avoiding self-contradictions) and *coherence* as virtual synonyms, whereas Whitehead, at least in some places, distinguishes between them. When he makes this distinction, *incoherence* means "the arbitrary disconnection of first principles."[31] An example is provided by the Cartesian treatment of mental and physical substances. As defined by Descartes, neither mental nor physical substances require the existence of the other type. There is, accordingly, "no reason why there should not be a one-substance world," with only physical or only mental substances.[32] Because these finite mental and physical substances depend upon God for their existence, God is for Descartes the only true substance, the only one that truly requires nothing but itself in order to exist.[33] The existence of the world is thus held to be an arbitrary fact; God's existence does not require it, but it must be affirmed to connect the philosophy to experienced fact.

Much of my criticism of Smith's position is because of its incoherence in this strict sense. He holds, with classical theists generally, that the world's existence is not necessary for God in any sense—not necessary for God to exist, and not needed to contribute value to God. The divine reality is said to be absolutely perfect and complete in every respect in itself; the world with its (apparently) temporal process adds no value to deity that was not there from the beginning. Why then, given the assumption that only God exists necessarily, should the world exist? Smith's answer is that every level of being must exist, by the principle of plenitude, for the best possible world to exist. But why should *any* world exist, if its existence adds not a whit to the sum total of reality and value? This doctrine of the relation between God and the world seems to be an extreme example of incoherence.

My questions about dualism press in the same direction. If mental and physical substances are different in kind, they not only would seem not to *need* relations to each other, they also would seem *incapable* of relating to each other. Smith, recognizing this dualistic difficulty, seems to call upon God, as did Descartes and his follower Malebranche, to mediate between these otherwise unrelatable opposites, as I pointed out (31). This *ad hoc* solution is needed because of the incoherence of the basic assumptions. My question about gnostic dualism was even more pointedly focused on this issue. Smith's reply (75) missed the main point of the question, which is whether entities as complex as human souls could be created by God directly, without the mediation of a physical body developed through an evolutionary process. The question is not simply, as Smith's response seems to presuppose, whether the soul *in fact* does not emerge (or, as Smith prefers, descend) "until a corporeal receptable of a certain complexity has appeared to properly host it" (84). The question is whether Smith supposes that this order reflected necessity, or whether he supposes that a human soul, or something like it, capable of enjoying such rich experiences and actualizing such high values, *could* be created apart from an organism something like a human body. Given Smith's insistence upon divine omnipotence and downward causation (and his preference for speaking of "descent" rather than "emergence"), it would seem that he would have to say the latter. And if so, we have another case of strong incoherence, in Whitehead's sense of the arbitrary disconnection of fundamental elements. The recognition that we have bodies appears to be a purely *ad hoc* concession to empirical fact; the perennial philosophy provides no illumination as to why we *should* have bodies. (My own position, by contrast, says that, although the human soul may now be able to survive apart from that specialized environment provided by a human body, it could not have originally been created without such an environment.)

Having discussed the primary formal issue between us, that of the importance of coherence in the sense of self-consistency, and now the importance of coherence in the strong, peculiarly Whiteheadian sense, I turn back to substantive matters, beginning with the relation between God and the absolute, in which the issues of self-consistency and coherence (in the strong sense) are of central importance.

III. PERSONAL GOD, TRANSPERSONAL ABSOLUTE, AND THE RELIGIONS

In my critique, I suggested that the key substantive issue between us is the nature of the metaphysical absolute and its relation to God and to the finite world. This is an alternative way of getting at the issue that Smith described as the controlling substantive difference between us, the nature of divine perfection. Whereas I distinguish between two ultimates—God as the axiological ultimate and creative experience as the metaphysical ultimate—which are equally primordial, Smith believes that only one of them can be truly ultimate, and that to be such it must be productive of the other (82). He thinks of the transpersonal absolute as truly ultimate, in comparison with which the personal God is only relatively real, being a derivation or emanation.

Smith rejects my characterization of the absolute as impersonal, which seems to imply that it is *sub*personal. He insists that, for those with eyes to see, a transpersonal reality can be superior to a personal deity (64-65). I think of the metaphysical absolute with Whitehead not as a concrete reality but as "abstract creativity."[34] As abstract, it is not an agent and is not a being with experience. Creative experience as such is an abstraction from all the creative experiences of the universe, including the divine creative experience; it is not an additional experience or agent distinct from all of them. Smith, by contrast, thinks of the absolute as concrete (he believes in a "concrete, absolute, unsurpassable perfection" [68]), even though it is transpersonal. I cannot understand how it can be concrete if it is not a unified experience; and if it *is* an experience (or a series of such), I would call it personal, not transpersonal. If it is personal, there would be no need to distinguish between the absolute and the personal God, regarding the latter as a secondary, derivative reality. If it is not an experience, on the other hand, then I do not see how we can intelligibly call it transpersonal, or suprapersonal, as if it were somehow superior to a personal being of cosmic proportions.

Smith, by contrast, believes that he can have it both ways. He asks whether it is "possible to conceive of something that possesses the virtues of persons without their limitations" (64), and implies that an affirmative answer can be given. But can we consistently conceive this? That is what I had questioned. Pointing out that we normally correlate superiority positively with the capacity to know and love, I asked how a deity that is "ultimately *beyond* all knowing and loving" can be thought to be superior to us in every respect (24). Smith replies: "I would not say (as Griffin has me saying) 'that deity is ultimately *beyond* all knowing and loving'" (65). But I did not make that up. I quoted Smith as saying that theism, which speaks of the God who "knows and loves his creatures," is "not the final truth," and that humans must realize that "in the last analysis God is not the kind of God who loves them" (23). I have no desire to hold Smith to his previous formulations (that *would* be to insist on the "foolish consistency that is the hobgoblin of little minds"); in fact, I would be delighted if he would renounce his earlier statement that everything ultimately derives from a nonpersonal absolute. But if he is rejecting that doctrine, then much of what he says in his reply is unnecessary.

The question of the conceivability of Smith's absolute, which is supposed to have the positive ingredients of personhood without its limitations, is also raised by some remarks in his reply. Smith says that God (evidently meaning the Godhead or the absolute), being perfect, "cannot be personal in the sense of having an environment" (64). The reason is that an environment is something other than a person which *resists* the person. What positive ingredient of "knowledge" is left if we say there is nothing other than God for God to know? What praise is contained in the attribute "all-knowing" if there is nothing to know? The notion of divine love without an environment is even more problematic. What positive ingredient of "love" is left if there are no others to love? Conceiving of some positive residue from the notions of action, providence, and will is equally problematic.

Smith himself points out the problem of conceivability in his discussion of God as "absolutely one—absolutely unified and whole" by adding: "but in a peculiar way; as the negative theology insists, there is no way in which concepts that fit finite things map univocally onto the infinite" (64). But in this denial of univocal language, does any shred of analogy remain, or do we pass into complete equivocation, where the words when applied to God contain nothing in common with their ordinary meanings? The notion that God is absolutely unified is usually referred to as divine "simplicity." That doctrine has always been in strong tension not only with the doctrine of the trinity but also with the notion that all possibilities (Platonic ideas, Aristotelian forms) are contained within God. Smith's reaffirmation of this latter doctrine raises another problem of conceivability. He says: "What makes the Absolute ineffable is that we cannot imagine how All-Possibility (its synonym) is compacted concretely within it, its latent distinctions retained in the absence of differences that would violate the divine simplicity" (83). It seems, in short, that Smith's question about the conceivability of a transpersonal absolute must be answered in the negative.

It may be, however, that the inconsistencies in Smith's position on this point result from his oscillation between two quite different understandings of *transpersonal* and *simplicity*. In an understanding different from the one just mentioned, God does have personal attributes, but they are not distinct from one another, as they are in us. Smith says:

> The peculiarity of the divine or holy One is that it dispenses with differences . . . without forfeiting any of the positive virtues, which at lower levels of being are parceled into separate faculties or components. Nothing is lost; only the walls of separation are removed . . . . I would not say . . . "that deity is ultimately *beyond* all knowing and loving." What I say is that God is beyond all knowing that is not concomitantly loving, and beyond all loving that is not concomitantly knowing. (65)

If this is what divine simplicity and transpersonality mean, then we can completely agree. Hartshorne makes the same point as does Smith:

> The "simplicity" of God has here its true meaning, that there can be no duality of understanding and motivation in a being in which either understanding or motivation is perfect. Both come down to love pure and simple and indivisible. To fully sympathize with and to fully know the feelings of others are the same relationship, separable in our human case only because there the "fully" never applies, and we never know the feelings of others but only have knowledge about them . . . .[35]

We can also say that God is one or unified in many other ways in which the unity of persons is only partial. God's love and power are one, in the sense that God does not exert power on any beings with whom God does not fully sympathize, and in the sense that God's exertion of power on finite beings is nothing other than God's creative love flowing into them. God should be thought, furthermore, to be devoid of anything analogous to a split personality (contrary to Carl Jung and E. S. Brightman), and of any tension between conscious and unconscious dimensions of experience.

Thus understood, Smith's insistence that God is transpersonal would not mean that God is wholly devoid of personal attributes, but only that God is not one finite personal being among others. Smith's view of the personal and transpersonal as "aspects of a single deity" (77) would be similar to that of Whitehead, who attempted to reconcile "the doctrine of God as the impersonal order of the universe and the doctrine of God as the one person creating the universe" as a wholly external thing through an act of will.[36] The universe is not simply a derivative, external product, but is more of an emanation, in which the infinite realm of possibilities within God are being unfolded. We should look at the world about us not as an external creation of a separate divine being but as a manifestation of its divine ground and center which is dialectically identical with it. That is, God both is and is not identical with the world. The world is "other" than God, but not in the way a table is other than the carpenter who built it, or even as a child is other than its mother. It is other than God more in the way my body is other than me: I feel its feelings so intimately, and it expresses my thoughts and feelings so directly, that I and others often think of it as me. And yet it is a case of "I, but not I" (to use St. Paul's phrase). The analogy would be even closer if we thought, as do some people, of the soul as having gradually formed its body as an expression of itself. (Room must be made in the analogy, of course, for the great extent to which the world, especially at the human level, does *not* express the divine feelings and thoughts. Only so can this "panentheism" be compatible with the fact of evil.)

If the divine simplicity and transpersonality were consistently understood by Smith in this manner, the ineffability of God would not prevent belief in God from providing orientation for human life. God *is* ineffable in that we cannot begin to imagine or describe what the divine experience is like concretely. Nor can we with any adequacy describe those special experiences of the Holy Reality which sometimes overwhelm people; we mutter such things as "numinous," "incredible bliss," "time seemed to stand still," and "the peace that passes understanding," but we finally give up, saying that the experience is ineffable, beyond description. But ineffability in these senses does not prevent us from thinking of God as one whose perfect knowledge is nothing other than all-inclusive, responsive love, and whose perfect power is nothing other than outflowing, creative love. And such a conception provides a basic orientation.

We can form a contextual but nonrelativistic definition of the *good* and the *right* as "that which God prefers in this situation." (Many ethicists, including atheistic ones, agree that these terms can best be defined in terms of what an omniscient, perfectly sympathetic being would prefer.[37]) And, as Hartshorne has said, this view of God provides a good model for us to imitate, insofar as the *imitatio dei* is possible. It will lead us to imitate God's sympathy for the feelings and desires of all sentient beings; to imitate God's respect for old values while creating new ones; and to achieve integration by approximating that unity of love, knowledge, and power which only God can perfectly embody.[38]

I like Smith's statement that "in the long run, larger contexts orient us more reliably than do provincial ones," even though they at first may be disorienting. The idea that the Holy Reality of the universe loves our enemies as much as us, and forgives both our enemies and us for our worst failings (even though those failings hurt God most of all, because of God's love for all of us), is a terribly disorienting idea. Contemporary interpreters of the parables of Jesus stress their initially disorienting function. And most of the human race, including that portion that calls Jesus "Lord," does not really live by this vision of God. And yet this larger vision, which is implicit in the confession of the divine simplicity, would provide us with a better orientation, if we would accept it.

This understanding of divine simplicity, with its initially disorienting-but-finally-truly-orienting vision, does stand in tension with some of Smith's comments. If he is going to hold consistently to this view, according to which God is not *beyond* all attributes such as love and knowledge but only beyond that finite mode of personhood in which these virtues "are parceled into separate faculties," then he should not use some of the expressions I cited in my critique. That is, he should not use the term *nirguna Brahman*, which indicates that God is wholly without qualities; nor should he say that in our conception of God "the attributes themselves must be transcended" (23). Otherwise, his statement that the infinite "is undifferentiated" will inevitably be taken to mean not simply that "God is beyond all knowing that is not concomitantly loving, and beyond all loving that is not concomitantly knowing," but that God is ultimately beyond all knowing and loving whatsoever. Likewise, Smith should not endorse Tillich's mystical "move to lodge the Holy as the Ultimate beyond any of its embodiments" (66). If God embodies love and knowledge in an undifferentiated way, then God is the primordial embodiment of being itself, or creativity itself, or experience itself, or creative experience itself. Tillich's disjunction—either being itself or a being—is wrong. God can be understood as both a creative being and creativity itself, by virtue of being the primordial embodiment of creativity, the one individual who embodies it eternally and necessarily.

We need to look critically, furthermore, at Tillich's claim that his version of the mystical move is, in Smith's words, "imperative if the Ultimate's embodiments are not to become demonic" (66). As Tillich knew, and Hans Jonas pointed out, even the conception of the holy as being itself can become demonic, as evidenced by Heidegger's notorious proclamation that to follow Hitler as the Führer was to follow the call of being.[39] Tillich's own doctrine of God, I argued in my first book, finally provides no basis for religious or ethical orientation, in spite of Tillich's valiant "search for absolutes."[40] The Smith-Hartshorne conception of the divine simplicity would be far superior, providing not only universal norms but also the inspiration to approximate those norms by incarnating and imitating the Holy Reality.

Much of Smith's response to my position comes, however, from the other side of his thought, in which the personal and transpersonal aspects of deity are not equal; the personal God is instead derivative from the transpersonal absolute. Smith thinks I should say the same. Finding "multiple metaphysical ultimates unsatisfying," he wonders why Whiteheadian theologians do not "make one of their ultimates *really* ultimate and productive of the others" (77). I had provided an answer to this query. On the one hand, "God does not create creative experience, "I pointed out, "because that would imply a self-contradiction" (45). How can creativity be created? Creativity must eternally exist if anything ever is to be created. On the other hand, "creative experience does not create God, because it is not an agent which can create." As Whitehead says, in explaining why he came to affirm the existence of God as a primordial actuality: "Unlimited possibility and abstract creativity can procure nothing."[41] And as Whitehead says elsewhere: "The creativity is not an external agency with its own ulterior purposes."[42] Just as Aristotelian prime matter cannot by itself account for the existence of material things, because it is not a concrete entity which can exist apart from and hence prior to material things, neither can creativity account for the existence of creative beings. Creativity cannot create God any more than God can create creativity. Each presupposes the other. This is one example of coherence, in the strong, peculiarly Whiteheadian sense. This ideal of coherence requires two or more eternally existent types of realities.

Smith points out that, besides God and creativity, finite actual entities exist with equal necessity for Whiteheadian thought (81). This idea does not mean that any particular finite actualities, such as Huston Smith or the molecules in my typewriter, exist necessarily; that would imply a determinism and necessitarianism that would contradict the reality of creativity. But it means that some plurality of finite events or other, some world or other, has always existed. For example, even if the big bang theory is correct, we would not need to say, as some have, that the big bang involved a *creatio ex nihilo*, taking the *nihil* to mean a complete absence of finite things. The more plausible position is that the material for the big bang was congealed out of a chaos of energy events. In turn, this chaos would have been the residue from a previous cosmic epoch, which may have originated from an earlier big bang, and so on back, as much Hindu and Buddhist thought has speculated. In any case, God, creativity, and finite actual beings all mutually presuppose the existence of the others. As Whitehead says, "there is no meaning to 'creativity' apart from its 'creatures,' and no meaning to 'God' apart from the 'creativity' and the 'temporal creatures,' and no meaning to the 'temporal creatures' apart from 'creativity' and 'God.' "[44] Because there is no meaning to any of these categories of existence apart from the others, it would be nonsensical to speak of one of them as producing the others, as if it could have existed prior to them.

The principle of coherence, or mutual presupposition, extends also to a fourth category of existence, that of the ideal forms, or "eternal objects" (mentioned by Smith [81] and in the quotation above from Whitehead as "unlimited possibility"). These are the *pure possibilities* inherent in the nature of things, that is, primordially subsistent in the "primordial nature of God." These are possibilities which finite actual things can in principle actualize; they thereby presuppose the existence of finite actual entities. They are likewise presupposed by actual entities, because an actual entity is an actualization of possibilities. It would be nonsense to speak of the creation of possibilities, in the absolute sense, because to create something presupposes that it was not impossible. We do, of course, speak of "creating the possibility of such and such," but what we mean is that we have turned a *pure* (or *abstract*) possibility, such as going to the moon, into a *real* (or *present*) possibility. Such space travel could become a real possibility for earthlings in the twentieth century only because it had been an abstract possibility all along. Abstract possibility cannot be created; it must exist eternally (which is what Whitehead means by calling pure possibilities "eternal objects"). But likewise it could never have been the only form of existence, from which the others derived, because possibility as such cannot do anything. It is efficacious only insofar as it is embodied in actual beings. It is *primordially* efficacious through its primordial embodiment in God, who, as the Divine Eros of the universe, proffers novel possibilities as lures for feeling to finite beings, calling them beyond their prior realization of possibilities.

Smith and I seem to be at one on this point, as he says that his absolute "is actual in the absolute sense of containing within itself all the possibilities that will issue from it" (82). He seems to agree, thereby, that we have two realities, the absolute and all possibilities, that are distinguishable but not separable, because they are mutually presupposing. In my position, this coherence includes four categories rather than simply two, but the principle is the same.

Smith claims that a satisfactory philosophy can have only one ultimate because "the essence of ultimacy is not primordiality or ubiquity —but rather the possession of ultimate power" (82). But the word *ultimate* refers to the *furthest*. Surely that which is everlasting, existing as far back and as far into the future as one can imagine, qualifies as ultimate. Surely that which is not only temporally but also spatially ultimate, extending to every place, qualifies. It seems arbitrary, even counteretymological, to deny that primordiality and ubiquity belong to the essence of ultimacy. Omnipotence has seldom if ever been taken to be the sufficient condition of divine ultimacy, but has taken its place as a necessary condition along with such attributes as necessary existence, eternity, omniscience, and omnipresence.

I agree that the possession of ultimate power is a necessary characteristic of the type of ultimacy to be ascribed to God, the object of theistic worship. Worship is evoked by that which we conceive or imagine to be the supreme power of the universe, that which is finally most effective, especially with regard to matters of ultimate value. That is one meaning of the ultimacy of God's power. This power is also ultimate in the sense of being perfect power, the greatest power a single being could possibly have. There is no need, however, to think of divine power as ultimate in the sense of being ultimately the *only* power, especially if that is not conceivable. (What is power that is not power *in relation* to something else? If the creation of finite beings as such was the origin of time, how can we talk about the absolute existing *before* the world? How can God be perfectly good if God alone is unilaterally responsible for a world such as ours? How can we conceive the apparent mutiplicity of the world to be really an illusion, so that ultimately only one being exists? How can our freedom be real if ultimately all power belongs to the one absolute being? These and other problems suggest that the perennialist's view is not possible as well as not necessary.)

Smith objects that a situation with shared power could not be ultimate. He presents a dilemma. If "its division is fixed from the start," we have to ask "who or what did the apportioning" (82), in which case that agent would be ultimate. But the point is that there is no "start." The situation described is thought to be primordial or eternal, and, as Aristotle recognized long ago, the necessary and the eternal are equatable. The eternal, by being necessary, is precisely that which requires no agent to explain why it is. Smith does not believe that the absolute started to exist, and would consider it nonsensical to ask who created the absolute. My position is that God and a plurality of finite actualities eternally and hence necessarily exist, along with the creativity and the pure possibilities they presuppose. It would be nonsensical to ask who created this situation, or who decided how to apportion the creativity between God and the world.

The other horn of his alleged dilemma is that the sharing of power would have to be "negotiated with a rival, as Manichaenism clearly perceived" (82). Besides the fact, as I have already said, that eternal things are not negotiable, the allusion to Manichaenism is inappropriate. Manichaenism is the doctrine of (1) a unified agent of cosmic scope, which is (2) inherently evil and (3) equal or almost equal in power to (the good) God. None of these features applies. Creativity is not an actual being, therefore not an agent; nor is it inherently evil. No finite being is cosmic in scope, even remotely rivaling God in power or in temporal or spatial unlimitedness. The position for which I speak cannot be discredited by association with Manichaenism.

Smith believes that the view of multiple ultimates represents a refusal "to press the explanation of why the world is the way it is to its logical limit." Rather than simply beginning with "the world as we experience it," then tracing it back to "the fewest number of agents that are needed to account for that world," we should ask why "the world and its agents are as *they* are, and why there is something rather than nothing" (82). Smith finds positivistic inclinations lurking in this refusal. But does Smith ask why there is something, that is the absolute, rather than nothing? Does he ask why the absolute, or the Godhead, is as *it* is? No, except to say that it exists necessarily. Smith might add that it is as it is because it is better to be as it is than any other way; but this explanation does not involve tracing the existence of the Godhead back to some yet more ultimate agent which produced it. It is generally recognized that the principle of causality cannot properly be formulated to say that "everything requires a cause," or else an infinite regress results. If the cosmological argument is so stated, the sophomore replies triumphantly: "Then who created God?" The proper formulation is: "every contingent thing has a cause." (Although stated in the singular, this "cause" might be comprised of all the causal influences from the entire past plus the self-causation of the event in question.) With this formulation, we do not ask why necessary things exist, or why they are as they are. Smith does not ask this question of the eternal Godhead (and evidently the eternal possibilities which are included in it). I hold that that which exists eternally and therefore necessarily is not simply God, but God-and-a world (including the eternal possibilities envisaged by God and the eternal creativity embodied in both God and worldly actualities).

This answer is no more positivistic than Smith's; it simply differs about what must be posited—a plurality of actualities rather than a solitary One. Having accepted Whitehead's suggestion that the "category of the ultimate" is comprised of "creativity," "many," and "one,"[45] I hold that a one (as an actuality) can exist only as a unification of a many. The idea of a solitary One, a God existing all alone without a world, therefore makes no sense. The idea that God has always existed but that a world of finite actualities came into existence once upon a time makes no more sense, from this perspective, than the idea that a world has always existed but that God came into existence once upon a time. God is essentially, not accidentally, the soul of the universe. The eternally existing reality is God-and-a-world. It makes no sense to try to go behind this.

The fact that people differ about the proper stopping point, because of differing intuitions about satisfactory explanations, can be illustrated by considering what Nicholas Rescher would say about Smith's stopping point. Rescher, in *The Riddle of Existence*,[46] argues that a satisfactory explanation must explain the existence of actuality as such.[47] He believes the sophomore's question, "Then who created God?," is a good one, because even God's existence cannot be taken as self-explanatory. Rescher rejects the "hoary dogma" that *ex nihilo nihil fit*, according to which all reasons must be grounded in actual things.[48] The only way to avoid an infinite regress, he says, is to explain the existence of actual things by reference to value; it alone provides a satisfactory stopping point.[49] By value he does not mean the purpose of some actual being, for that would, he holds, beg the question of where that actual being came from. It is value, not purpose, that Rescher regards as self-explanatory.[50] The reason the actual world exists, Rescher posits, is that it is better that it exists. And it has the structure it has because this structure is better than any other possible structure. These axiological principles brought the actual world out of a merely possible one.[51] How can values by themselves have an explanatory role? Because that also is for the best, he says.

Accepting, as I do, the hoary dogma, as Rescher calls it, that "from nothing [actual], nothing [actual] can derive" (83), Smith would reject Rescher's answer to "the riddle of existence," and I would agree with him. And Smith would reject Rescher's claim that his (Smith's) stopping point is arbitrary, that it, in Smith's words, involves a refusal "to press explanation . . . to its logical limit." I would agree with Smith again. But I would likewise reject Smith's characterization of my position in these terms. To say that worldly actualities necessarily exist, and to provide a reason for thinking this, is to press explanation as far as it can go. Just as Smith would think that Rescher's attempt to go behind the existence of actuality as such is to press explanation beyond a reasonable limit, I think the same thing about Smith's attempt to go behind God-and-a-world to God alone.

My doctrine of emergence, incidently, does not violate the doctrine that "from nothing, nothing can derive," as Smith intimates (83). Each instance of emergence involves the creative influence of the past, the influence of God, which is based upon God's appetitive envisagement of all possibilities, and the self-creativity of the finite events in question. Far from coming out of nothing, emergent experiences and structures come out of a plurality of things. The only issue between Smith and me on this point is whether the actualization of novel forms is best understood as the work of a single source, thereby as "emanation,' as Smith prefers, or as the product of the cocreativity of many, thereby as "emergence," as I prefer. I have suggested several reasons for preferring this view, not least among which is that it allows us to take seriously the contingency and imperfection which seem, to varying degrees, to pervade the world.

The final topic in this section is the relation between these two ways of understanding God and the absolute and a theology of the religions. As a preliminary point, I do not know why Smith thinks it justifiable to say that I speak of "alternative Gods" (76). That misrepresents my position at least as much as Smith's is misrepresented by the use of the word *impersonal* for what he calls *transpersonal*. Creativity, or creative experience, is not an agent, is not an individual, is not concrete, does not know, does not love, and is never referred to by me as "God" or "a God." I did refer to "the divine reality to which Shankara and Nagarjuna were oriented" (42), but I was there speaking from their standpoint: whatever they regarded as divine is the divine reality for them. It may be that, in Smith's world of discourse, anything called *ultimate* or *the absolute* is *ipso facto* a God, but that is not my world. Some people may well regard creativity as the (or a) divine reality, and I do believe that creative experience is the ontological reality that is described by Shankara as nirguna Brahman and especially by Nagarjuna as Emptiness (although each of their descriptions differs somewhat from Whitehead's description of creativity); but that is a different matter.

Coming now to the issues: Smith says that I seem to imply that the "great enduring religions" are not equal in worth (77). But when I call *unilluminating* his claim that all religions are equal for salvation, what I am rejecting is the idea that the devotees of all the great religions "are *really* worshipping the 'same God,' " and that "the salvation sought by, say, Moslems and Mahayana Buddhists is the same" (42). To say that the various religions are different is not to say that they are unequal in worth; they could be different but equal.

While agreeing that the various religions differ in many respects, Smith believes that they are essentially similar if one focuses on "salvific truth—truth about ultimate reality, the knowledge of which conduces to maximum human fulfillment" (77). But there are different "saving truths," I hold, which bring different kinds of wholeness and fulfillment, which may be equal in spite of their differences. These different saving truths reflect different aspects of the total "truth about ultimate reality." The total truth, I have suggested, includes (among other things) the truth about creative experience as the ultimate reality, and the truth about our personal creator. Truths about the former bring one general type of salvation (with variations) as shown by centuries of Buddhist meditation upon Emptiness and Hindu meditation upon nirguna Brahman; truths about the latter bring a quite different type of salvation, as shown by saints of Judaism, Christianity, Islam, Pure Land Buddhism, and bhakti devotion in Hinduism, for example. If people were to devote equal attention to both creative experience and God, regarding truths about each as saving, a more complete type of salvation might be realized. That is one reason it is important not to blur the differences between the various religions; only if their differences are clearly perceived will each have the chance to make an equal contribution to a more satisfactory religion of the future. If we think of all people as "anonymous Christians," or as "anonymous Advaita Vedantists," we will be unlikely to allow each religion to contribute its most distinctive insights. The emphasis on differences, therefore, is made not to deny equality, but to protect it (as well as to be adequate to the facts).

Thinking instead of a single saving truth, Smith resists "the prospect of whole segments of humanity having been excluded from this truth." Using the language of revelation, Smith does not like "the thought of God's withholding it from the human majority" (77). But that depiction presupposes that the revealed message is not essentially colored by the medium through which it is refracted. In other words, it presupposes divine omnipotence in the traditional sense, according to which God essentially has all the power; it presupposes Smith's position according to which God is identical with the metaphysical absolute, understood as creative power, or is at least the first derivation from it. But Smith's conclusions do not follow if we distinguish God and creative power, and regard the latter as embodied in worldly beings as well as in God. As I said: "Because downward causation from deity cannot override human freedom, including the freedom to err, we have no deductive reason to assume that all religions essentially reflect the same truths" (52). That is, it does not follow from God's goodness, which would include God's desire for the best type of salvation for all people, that all the great religions ultimately teach the same thing. Each one may have gotten a different portion of that which, were it known, would be *the* (complete) saving truth. That is my assumption, and it seems to fit the empirical realities better than does the perennialist's assumption. Speaking of the great religions, Smith refers to "the One that inspires them all and gives them their basic trajectory" (77). I do believe that God inspires all the religions; but I also believe that the "basic trajectory" of each is shaped not only by God but also by the cocreativity of the members of that religion, and that a minor divergence between two trajectories at an early stage can lead to increasingly greater divergences in successive centuries.

For those who prefer to speak of religious truth as arising not from divine revelation but from "the deepest intuitions of religious geniuses," Smith says that it seems unlikely "that genius is unequally sprinkled around the world" (77). That seems unlikely to me also, especially in the light of empirical realities. Artistic and scientific genius, for example, seems to arise wherever the conditions permit. China and Japan have produced painting that is as superb as any in Europe in comparable periods. And, as Joseph Needham has shown in his monumental *Science and Civilization in China*, the Chinese not only have exhibited an equal capacity for scientific insight but they did it much earlier than the Europeans. As these examples show, however, comparable genius does not necessarily produce the same results. Japanese and Chinese painting is very different from European painting. Science in China was very different from European science, and the Chinese worldview evidently lacked those presuppositions that would have led to the kind of breakthroughs and cumulative tradition that have appeared in European science during the past four centuries.

By analogy, there is no reason to suspect that equal religious genius would express itself in the same way in different traditions. Empirical realities suggest that it does not. The chief symbols of Christianity and Buddhism—Jesus in agony on a cross and the Buddha serenely sitting in meditation—suggest that the basic message of these two great traditions is fundamentally different. Smith agrees that the religions differ on "the level of their creedal affirmations" (77), but thinks that a common core lies beneath these creedal differences. I do not consider the difference between calling Jesus the Christ and calling Gautama the Buddha to be so superficial. I believe that the creedal differences reflect quite different underlying visions of the holy reality and of human salvation.

IV. TIME, SOCIAL PROGRESS, GNOSTIC DUALISM, AND IMMORTALITY

The status of time in the nature of things is as fundamental as the previous substantive issues. This issue is, in fact, only another side of those previous issues. To ask whether the temporal process can contribute anything of ultimate value to the divine reality is the reverse side of asking whether evil in the process detracts from the ultimate value. This question is also another way of posing the question of the relation between the personal God and the timeless absolute: if the former is derivative from the latter, then time is derivative from timelessness and ultimately has no reality and therefore no importance. The issues of social progress, gnostic dualism, and immortality are all variants of the issue of time, as will be seen.

Smith's position on time is parallel to his position on evil. On the one hand, he insists that time is ultimately unreal, and that what occurs in the temporal process neither adds to nor detracts from the divine perfection. On the other hand, he insists that time is real, and that what he says about time's ultimate unreality should not lead us to take our temporal decisions less seriously. The question is whether he can have it both ways.

Smith has clearly said that time is derivative and ultimately unreal, and that the temporal process does not contribute anything to the divine absolute, which is alone ultimately real. I quoted in my critique his statements that "time derives from nontime" and that "nothing turns on time, for the limitless landscape is there from the start," and his description of deity as "concrete, timeless perfection" (38). I also cited his argument that time is shown to be illusory by physics. Because Smith did not comment upon my dual challenge to this argument (that it involves the type of appeal to contemporary science that he elsewhere decries, and that physics in fact, as some recent physicists are recognizing, does not support the illusoriness of time [39]), he is perhaps dropping this support for his view. In any case, his reply reiterates his earlier views. While saying that time is, like evil, to be regarded as real at our level, its limitations, like those of evil, *withdraw* "in the transmuted light by which God sees [it], and by which eventually we will see [it] too" (81). With regard to evil, this statement that its "limitations withdraw" means that it loses its character of being evil; to say that time's limitations withdraw evidently means that it loses its character of being time, with its distinction between past, present, and future. (How can we speak meaningfully of "eventually" coming to see that time is unreal? This is evidently one of those paradoxes that Smith's position forces him to defend.)

Smith puts his denial of time in the midst of his discussion of the controlling difference between us. After saying that a world in which no evil occurs is a better world, he says: "Comparably with time. The God of process theologians improves by amassing more experience. But improvement implies an initial lack (read, a defect)" (80). The implication is that the temporal process adds nothing of value to God, which it could not, of course, if God is "concrete, timeless perfection."

It is interesting, then, to see that Smith challenges my conclusion that, for him, time or the temporal process is ultimately unimportant for the realization of value and therefore wasted motion. He replies:

> Time is ontologically important in perennialism, because if it did not exist there would be a Swiss cheese hole in God's infinity. And because "being as being is good ... this lack ... would compromise the divine perfection. So the word *not* should be stricken from Griffin's assertion that in perennialism "the temporal process is not needed for the divine realization of value." It *is* needed. (75)

Smith's argument here is a purely deductive, *a priori* argument: the world, to be perfect, must have everything; time is something; therefore the world must have time. There is nothing wrong with this type of argument as such. But it becomes problematic if its conclusion, that "the temporal process is needed for the divine realization of value," is contradicted by Smith's other deductive argument, mentioned above. This argument, if spelled out, might run: To declare the temporal process necessary for the realization of value from the divine viewpoint would imply an initial defect in God; God can have no defect; therefore the temporal process is not necessary for the realization of value from the divine viewpoint.

One might think that the apparent inconsistency could be overcome by noting that, when Smith denies the importance of time, what he denies is that God improves through the temporal process. The idea that God is morally and ontologically perfect is compatible, surely, with the idea that God's experience is enriched by the values realized in the temporal process. Smith, one might think, is denying only that God improves morally (becoming more loving and more concerned for the good of the whole) and ontologically (becoming more omniscient and more powerful); if so, Smith would be at one with process theologians such as myself.

But Smith knows this form of theology too well to be thus interpreted. He knows that we affirm a dipolar theism, according to which God's abstract essence, which includes God's moral and ontological attributes, is unchanging, while God's concrete experience is continually enriched (and pained) by the positive (and negative) values realized in the world. Smith rejects this distinction between the timeless essence and a temporal concrete experience by speaking of deity as "concrete, timeless perfection," and by insisting upon divine simplicity in the traditional sense. In denying that God is improved by experiencing the temporal process, Smith rules out not only moral and ontological improvement but also what Hartshorne calls *aesthetic improvement*, which means being enriched emotionally and experientially by sympathetically enjoying the enjoyments of the creatures (analogously to the way we enjoy the enjoyments of our bodily members during physical exercise, eating and drinking, and sexual ecstacy). The moral, religious, and aesthetic experiences and achievements of human beings, and the delight in existence felt by all the other species, are not allowed to contribute anything to God's perfection, which has to be timeless. All possible values had to be there from the beginning, or timelessly. Neither Jesus, nor Gautama, nor Mozart, nor a dolphin has enriched the divine life. I hope that this is not what Smith finally wants to say, but it seems to be the implication of many of his statements. At best, Smith seems to be saying both things: that the temporal process is and is not necessary for the divine realization of value. Perhaps he can overcome the appearance of contradiction.

His statement that the temporal process is necessary for the divine realization of value, quoted above, is also problematic, because he seems to take it back in the immediately following sentences, in which he says: "It *is* needed, while figuring in God differently from the way it figures in us. God experiences time timelessly. It is not easy to imagine what this would be like" (75). One question: Why should we think this? On what basis should we think that God experiences time timelessly? Does some infallible revelation tell us this? Does reason lead inexorably to this conclusion? Do mystical experiences of apparent timelessness necessitate this conclusion? Do so-called precognitive experiences prove it? What basis do we have for accepting a conclusion that is so momentous and so paradoxical? I deny that we have any such basis. But at least if we knew what this purported basis is, we could debate it.

A second question is: What does it *mean* to say that "God experiences time timelessly?" How can we conceive of such a thing? Is not time something that can, by definition, only be experienced temporally? If time involves a distinction between past, present, and future, how could an experience devoid of such distinctions know what time is?

Furthermore, apart from the problem of experiencing *time* timelessly, is not experience as such necessarily temporal? *Our* experience is certainly temporal: the distinction between what has happened (memory), what is now happening (perception), and what may happen (anticipation) is of the essence of our experience. What basis do we have for thinking that "timeless experience" is not self-contradictory? Is it not in the same category as "round square?" Smith admits that it is "not easy to imagine what this would be like." But can we even consistently *conceive* it? Is this problem another reason that Smith denies the importance of consistently conceivable ideas?

In trying to help us imagine what it might be like, Smith suggests: "Perhaps being caught up in a movie we have seen before, so that we know the outcome, provides a feeble hint" (75). That hint suggests heavenly bliss less than hellish torment. What could be worse than being condemned to watch reruns of Cecille B. Demille biblical epics for all eternity? Smith's analogy should lead us to scrutinize more critically his claim that it would be a defect if God were "subject" to time (80). Smith believes it is always a defect if something is "subject to something other than itself." But do we consider it a defect that we are "subject to" love? Some of us, in any case, agree with the song that says "people who need people are the luckiest people in the world." Likewise, while some people speak of "time, the devouring tyrant," others write of "time, the refreshing river."[52] Can we imagine experience to be good apart from anticipation, novelty, and surprise? Even if experience apart from these characteristics were possible, would any of us desire it? Would not being *subject to timelessness* make the problems inherent in being "subject to time" pale in significance? Being subject to timelessness, unable to experience curiosity, hope, anticipation, resolution, and novelty, sounds less like Blake's "eternal delight" than like *eternal ennui*. For experience to be temporal is not only a necessity, so far as we can conceive; it is also a blessing, as Smith's movie-analogy unwittingly reveals

To be sure, the temporality of the divine experience should not be thought to involve those limitations inherent in our temporality that are true defects. Our memory is selective and subject to fading; the divine experience should be thought to include all that has occurred, and to retain the remote past as vividly as the immediate past. In *that* sense, the divine experience is timeless, not subject to the ravages of time. Also, our uncertainty about the future is often a source of distracting anxiety, due to ego involvement in particular outcomes and to worries, often warranted, about survival. The divine anticipation of the future, even with its genuine uncertainties due to the freedom of the creatures, should be thought to be free of all such anxiety. Buddhist serenity is a real clue here. In *that* sense, God is not subject to time. In sum, just as the divine love is free from the imperfections of our loving which are due to finitude and sin, while yet being genuinely analogous to our love, so the divine temporality is free from the imperfections of our temporality (which again are due to finitude and sin, while being genuinely analogous to our temporality. Our analogical language does not pass over into equivocation upon close examination. The divine temporality belongs among the divine perfections. Temporality, like love and knowledge, is capable of perfect and imperfect embodiments. God as concrete exemplifies perfect temporality, while the abstract essence of God exemplifies perfect timelessness.

I like Smith's view, mentioned above, that the perfection of the universe requires time, and his more general view that the perfection of the universe requires the realization of all possible values (at least if one stipulates *positive* values). A stronger reason can be given, however, for the necessity of time than simply the argument that it, being a possibility, must be actualized. This reason is that not all possible values are compatible—some are "incompossibles." For example, the values realizable while listening to Mozart cannot be enjoyed while listening to Stravinsky; the pleasures of reading Huston Smith are incompossible with those of playing tennis. But in each case I can enjoy the one *after* the other. As I said earlier, "Time is, as it were, the universe's way of getting around the fact that not everything can happen at once" (50).

The denial that anything turns on time provides an example of the real differences, mentioned in the previous section, between the visions of reality underlying the creedal differences of the various religions. The Hebrew-Christian scriptures generally presuppose that something does turn on time, that not everything was present at the beginning, that reality as a whole is enriched by the historical process. In later Christian thought, to be sure, this biblical vision was combined with Greek visions of timeless divine perfection, which brought Christian theology into closer accord with those Indian traditions in which time is unessential, even illusory. Because of the normative role the Hebrew-Christian scriptures have had in the West, however, the Western world has had a particularly keen sense of the importance of the temporal process, and of historical decisions. Smith reflects this sense when he says, "Humanly our lives are *woven* of time, so that not to take time seriously comes down to not taking our lives seriously. . . . If anything in perennialism keeps us from taking seriously the temporal decisions that are our current lot, we should expunge that philosophy from our minds at once" (75). Smith's distinction between the phenomenal level, where we live, and the ultimate level, where time loses its importance, is an attempt to keep the biblically inspired sense of time's importance while rejecting the vision of reality that nourished that sense of importance. I resist the call to return to a vision of timeless divine perfection, then, not only because I believe that vision false, but also because I believe it would undermine one of the most valuable themes of the biblical vision of reality, especially now that the Hebrew-Christian scriptures no longer have the widespread normative status they enjoyed in earlier centuries.

The question of time and that of social progress are closely related. Social progress can be understood in the widest possible sense, to include progress not only in human society but in the evolution of the cosmic society as a whole. I presented Smith as denying that such progress occurs. Smith begins his reply on this point by asking, "Is historical progress 'an illusion,' as Griffin has me saying?", and then asserting: "I do not say that social progress *cannot* occur; it *has* occurred on certain fronts" (76). But my comment referred to the following passage from Smith:

> we are going to say that progress is an illusion; not only future progress but past progress as well. The last part of that statement will have to be qualified, but in essence it will stand. Utopia is a dream, evolution a myth.[53]

Again, I have no wish to hold Smith to any of his past assertions— especially those with which I disagree. But if he now says things that seem to contradict previous assertions, we need to know if he is speaking at two different levels, if he is cheerfully living with self-contradiction, or if he has simply changed his mind.

I am puzzled as to why Smith brings Coue's slogan, "every day in every way I am getting better and better" (76), into this discussion of social progress. That is a very individualistic idea of progress. I also do not know why Smith says that probably "even Griffin disavows the implied inevitability in that superficial slogan"; I talked about the possibility and desirability of progress, not its inevitability. In any case, exactly what Smith is saying is not clear. He says that he is not "sure" that things will get better, that he has some "doubt about progress" (76). I can say the same. But then he seems to indicate that this is the same as not believing that "there's a good chance that things can get better." I am puzzled as to how that statement coheres with the assertion of the goodness and omnipotence of God and the priority of downward causation. Even I, with my belief that God's power is merely the greatest possible, and that this means persuasive power, believe that there is a "good chance" of social progress.

Smith seeks with a reference to Reinhold Niebuhr to allay doubts that scepticism about social progress, if widely shared, "cuts the nerve of social action." As Smith correctly points out, Niebuhr's own doubts did not cut his own nerve for social action. However, Niebuhr's own religious life was oriented much more around the holiness of the *ought*, whereas Smith, as we have seen, elevates the holiness of the *is* (40). In the early years of Niebuhr's professional life, moreover, he was heavily influenced by the "social gospel" interpretation of Christian faith. Had he become so sceptical about the possibilities of social progress at, say, age eighteen, we do not know that his commitment would not have slackened. Even if these facts were not true, furthermore, a general rule is not disproved by a few exceptions unless it is supposed to be a universal rule. Those who say that social pessimism cuts the nerve of social action generally mean that it does so in the main, with a large percentage of those involved. Reinhold Niebuhr's life, for these reasons, does not provide significant evidence against the belief that Smith's view, if widely shared, would have deleterious effects.

The deeper issue between us here, I believe, involves the contrast between what I call Smith's individualism and the social or ecological viewpoint informing my own vision (52). Smith's position seems to presuppose the individualistic view of the self that is expressed in the Cartesian doctrine of the soul, according to which it is a mental substance requiring nothing but itself (and God) in order to exist, and in the Hindu doctrine of the *atman*, which is essentially independent of all relations (except to Brahman, which might or might not be a relation of identity). The Buddhist doctrine of no-soul (*anatman*), based on the more general doctrine of the co-dependent arising of all things, was a protest against this doctrine of the substantial *atman*. The Buddhist doctrine, in most general terms (there are many varieties), is that what we call the soul is comprised of events, each of which arises out of dependence upon other events. Whitehead's doctrine, in rejecting the Cartesian doctrine, is similar. The world in general is comprised of events that arise out of *constitutive* relations to prior events, and the soul in particular is a serially ordered society of high-grade events; calling the soul a *society* emphasizes that its endurance is based on *social relations*. Far from requiring nothing but itself to exist, each soul-event requires its predecessors and, ultimately, the whole past universe, as well as God.

Human souls in various times and places do have much in common, on this Whiteheadian view, because they all share in the same creativity with its metaphysical structure, are influenced by the same God (even if they do not have the same conscious beliefs about deity), have a similar physical body, and in more general terms relate to the same earth and universe. But these commonalities do not exhaust the soul's constitutive relations. Equally constitutive of its very essence are its relations with more local, contingent features of its environment, especially its relations with other human beings. A human soul will tend to be graced, or polluted, by its relations to its parents and those other human beings who are most significant for it, especially in its formative years. Given this view, a human being's opportunity for attaining spiritual health is heavily conditioned (even if not wholly determined) by the nature of the society in which he or she grows up. Individual health and social health are closely connected. Because this conditioning is not total determination, exceptions will always be found; no virgin birth or other miraculous intervention is needed to explain how outstanding individuals can rise far above the general level of spiritual wholeness. But in the main, what one is will largely reflect the society in which one's formative years were spent. Accordingly, to deny the possibility of social progress is, for the most part, to deny the possibility of the improvement of individuals in successive generations.

I suspect that Smith rejects this view, thinking instead of individual salvation more as a matter of "coming to one's self," that is, getting below the levels of false selfhood to that underlying true self which has been present and perfect all along. If so, it is no surprise that we differ radically on the issues of time, progress, and evolution.

Using the phrase *gnostic dualism* to characterize Smith's position was a way of stating, with regard to the human soul, that the evolutionary process does not seem necessary, from Smith's perspective, for the production of the highest forms of finite value. Could the types of values realizable by human souls have been realized apart from a long evolutionary process? In other words, could human-like souls have been created apart from human-like physical bodies? Smith's position seems to be that, as a matter of fact, souls did not emerge (or better, descend) until appropriate bodies were ready, but that such souls *could* be directly created (or emanated) apart from such bodies. While I discussed this issue earlier under the topic of coherence, I now stress its connection with the issues of time and progress. If Smith does espouse gnostic dualism (as just defined), this doctrine provides a good illustration of the unessential status of temporality in his system, in the sense that time is not necessary for the realization of the highest forms of value.

Regarding evolution in general, I was pleased to see Smith indicating that it is important to have a philosophy that is consistent with the apparent facts of the evolutionary process (84). The only other point that requires a response is Smith's suggestion that the Whiteheadian view of the God-world relation seems to be keyed to Darwinian gradualism, therefore not fully consistent with the theory of "punctuated equilibrium," for which good evidence seems to exist. I have written about this issue elsewhere, seeking to show that Whitehead's doctrine can account for discontinuity in effects without returning to a supernaturalistic affirmation of discontinuity in divine causation.[54] I will not repeat that discussion here, except to cite a couple of passages suggesting that Whitehead himself thought of evolution, both biological and cultural, more in discontinuous than gradualistic terms. Stephen Jay Gould, one of the chief proponents of punctuated equilibrium, has described evolution as "a series of occasional pulses, driving recalcitrant systems from one stable state to the next."[55] Whitehead refers to the notion of perfection, or deity, as "the notion of that power in history which implants into the form of process, belonging to each historic epoch, the character of a drive towards some ideal, to be realized within that period."[56] Against the idea of slow, steady progress, he says: "Mere static survival seems to be the general rule, accompanied by a slow decay. The instances of the upward trend are represented by a sprinkling of exceptional cases."[57]

The final topic of this section is human immortality. It belongs in this section, because the question of our immortality is the question of whether the evolutionary process, in bringing us forth after several billion years, has thereby brought forth something that adds permanent value to the universe. Has time meant progress in this sense? If we are not immortal in any real sense, it would seem to follow that nothing finite is, and thereby that, when all is said and done, nothing of permanent value will have been said and done. The cosmic process will have been ultimately meaningless unless something of everlasting value has been attained. I believe that Smith and I agree on this. What we seem to disagree on is how to conceive immortality, although we both know that any light we have on this topic is extremely dim.

My critical comments about Smith's position were closely connected to my assumption that by speaking of the Godhead or the absolute as *undifferentiated* he meant nirguna Brahman, being without attributes. But, if he means *simplicity* in the sense discussed earlier—that the various attributes, such as knowing and loving, are not separated in the divine experience—then the notion that we are destined to become identical with the absolute suggests something quite different than I had imagined. What Smith has in mind may be best suggested by his reversal of the old image of the drop and the ocean for understanding the merger of the self and the Godhead. We can "think of the dewdrop as opening to receive the entire sea." Our journey, then, might be understood as "growth from the meagerest flicker of awareness to infinite awareness" (67).

This is not an expectation I can share (that is, that my finite subjectivity will ever become infinite; we could, for example, know far more than we now know and still be categorically removed from omniscience). But it is clearly a vision of progress in the temporal process. I think

Smith's position would be much more consistent and attractive if he would emphasize this side of his vision, while dropping those doctrines that belittle the importance of time and the possibility of real progress.

Smith's presentation of my own view on this topic—insofar as I can call it a view—distorts it somewhat. I distinguish between life after death and immortality. On immortality, meaning thereby *everlasting* significance, I still hold the Whiteheadian-Hartshornean view of "objective immortality," according to which our immortality is our enrichment of the divine life. I do now, in addition, believe with some (although not total) confidence that our finite lives, with their subjectivity, will continue their journey after their sojourn in their present bodies. And I suspect that this continued journey will involve growth in grace, involving real enlargement of the self, toward a far less ego-bound form of existence. I like Smith's suspicion that at some point a Beatific Vision will produce "ecstacy" in us, a standing outside ourselves (67).

I do not, however, expect that this enlargement and postegoistic existence would involve becoming literally identical with God. Nor would I expect this journey to continue forever—after all, a million billion years is just a drop in the bucket (or a dewdrop in the ocean) in relation to forever! Nor can I conceive a form of experience that would be eternal (instead of everlasting), that is, timeless. Accordingly, my own suspicion is that, if our journey does continue beyond the present life, it will be finite in duration, even if quite extended. I suspect that it will come to an end when we are ready for it to do so—when we feel perfectly fulfilled—so that the anticipated end of subjectivity would in no way be a source of anxiety. There may be truth, in other words, in the doctrine that finite existence is perpetuated by *karmic* actions, those expressing a desire for continued existence.

In any case, this doctrine of continued life after biological death makes the prospect of objective immortality in the divine subjectivity much more appealing. It provides a basis for hope that we will all eventually become the kinds of persons for whom the prospect of being remembered everlastingly will be more of a promise than a threat. We will all have the opportunity to make contributions to each other, and thereby to God, of which we can be pleased. Life after death, thereby, without being another form of immortality in the strict sense, can enable our true immortality to be much more enriching of the universe.

V. PRIMORDIAL, PREMODERN, AND POSTMODERN

Having considered several substantive issues, we are now in position to return to the basic formal issue with which our dialogue began: the difference between premodern and postmodern ways to recover primordial truths. Smith believes that it is unfair to characterize his position as "premodern," and that the difference between his program and mine, which I call "postmodern," is at most a difference in degree (62). I maintain that there is a real difference between the two visions, and that to contrast them as premodern and postmodern is not inaccurate.

To clarify his claim that his program is concerned with timeless truths, not bygone ones (62), Smith distinguishes between the social, the cosmological, and the metaphysical or ontological components of a worldview. With reference to the social and the cosmological, he says that "the contents of these two components obviously change, so are not perennial" (62). Only the metaphysical or ontological component is unchanging and therefore perennial, he says. Only it deals with "truth of the kind that is timeless."

This set of distinctions reflects an important truth. Social and cosmological theories refer to contingent, changing features of reality. It is a false ideal to strive for *the* correct sociological theory that would be equally adequate for human societies of all times and places. The sociological laws or generalizations refer to the widespread habits of a society, and the habits of people in twentieth-century America, say, differ greatly from the habits of the Native Americans we supplanted. Any universally applicable sociological theory would be very abstract. Likewise, cosmology deals with contingent, historical truths. Cosmogonic theories, such as those of the big bang, seek to explain the way our particular world came into existence. The sciences of physics, chemistry, and biology seek to describe the habits of the types of entities comprising our particular world. The so-called laws of nature are descriptions of the most widespread habits, those of, for example, electrons, protons, neutrons, photons, atoms and molecules of various sorts, and prokaryotic and eukaryotic cells. The natural sciences studying these habits do not deal with universal, unchanging truths, but with truths that apply for limited portions of time. Because electrons, neutrons, protons, and photons last much longer than human societies, or even the human race, we are tempted to think of physics and sociology as different in kind, but they are finally only different in degree. Just as human societies come into existence at a particular time and, sooner or later, pass out of existence, getting only partial conformity from their members in the meantime, so the cosmic society involving electrons, neutrons, protons, and photons (among other things) has come into existence at a particular time and will pass out of existence at some time in the future, in the meantime obtaining only statistical conformity from its various members. Metaphysics, by contrast with sociology and cosmology, deals with those features of reality that are eternal, features that characterize not only our particular cosmos but any possible cosmos. Whereas sociology and cosmology deal with the contingent and changing, metaphysics deals with the necessary and unchanging.

But Smith's argument involves a confusion between (1) the kinds of truths metaphysicians seek and (2) the attempts of metaphysicians to formulate these truths. Metaphysicians indeed seek timeless truths, truths about those features of reality that are eternal. Principles dubbed *metaphysical* or *ontological* are *intended* to be formulations about necessary, unchanging aspects of the world as a whole. But these formulations themselves are far from unchanging; metaphysicians differ considerably about what the unchanging aspects of the world are. The metaphysical categories of Aristotle, Descartes, Leibniz, Whitehead, Shankara, Nagarjuna, and Aurobindo all differ. The history of metaphysics is a history of changing attempts to formulate the unchanging. The various metaphysical theories probably do have more in common than the various cosmological and sociological theories. But the difference is one of degree, not kind; we cannot say that metaphysics, because it seeks timeless truths, is itself timeless.

My difference from Smith on this issue lies behind my description of his philosophy as premodern and his program as a call to an undialectical return to the past. He believes that the basic metaphysical truths, the primordial truths, have already been adequately stated in premodern metaphysical systems, such as Shankara's Advaita Vedanta. I believe that an adequate formulation is a task for the future. I do believe that the metaphysics of modernity denied several primordial truths that had been stated with relative adequacy by one or more premodern systems of thought; I call, accordingly, for a recovery of premodern truths and values. But I also believe, as indicated in my discussion of the various religions, that some primordial truths are somewhat clearly reflected in some premodern systems, that other primordial truths are somewhat clearly reflected in other premodern systems, and that no premodern system gave a balanced presentation of all the primordial truths. I also believe that that tradition we call modernity was based upon some primordial truths. Accordingly, I do not call for a simple return to some particular premodern system, even at the level of metaphysics, but for a dialectical return, a "return forward," in which we seek an unprecedented synthesis of primordial truths.

Another basic difference between us involves the criterion for identifying primordial truths. I am not sure what Smith's criterion is. In saying that "Advaita Vedanta seems to be normative for the premodern vision he advocates" (23), I suggested that the criterion was perhaps conformity to that system. But Smith says no, that that system is just one of many formulations of the primordial truths. What then *is* the criterion for deciding which ideas in these various systems should be considered primordial truths?

I provided my own criterion earlier: we identify ideas as primordial truths by seeing that they are hard-core commonsense ideas, meaning ideas that are inevitably presupposed in practice, even if denied verbally. These truths are primordial in that they are presupposed by people in all times and all places, and are therefore in principle available to be known consciously and formulated verbally. Some of the ideas that pass this test are: causal influence (each event is influenced by other events, and influences other events), freedom (while influenced by things beyond ourselves we are not totally determined by them), time (that there is a difference between the past, which is settled, the present, which is being settled, and the future, which is still in part to be settled), ontological realism (other real things beyond my present experience exist), axiological realism (some things are better than other things), evil (some things happen that are worse than other things that could have happened), and ultimate meaning (somehow what happens is ultimately meaningful). We could not deny any of these ideas without presupposing them.

I do not find, however, that all the ideas considered primordial truths by Smith pass this test. For example, he quotes Augustine's doctrine that "things that are not immutable are not at all" (63). The process philosophy of Whitehead and Hartshorne is based on the explicit denial of that principle, maintaining instead that all fully actual things are processes of becoming, and that all immutable things are abstractions from the fully actual things. I do not see that this affirmation on their part necessarily contradicts some presupposition of our practice, which it would if the Augustinian principle were a primordial truth. Their denial of this principle, in fact, seems to have resulted in a philosophy that is *more* consonant with the presuppositions of human practice.

For another example, Smith mentions "the distinction between the Absolute and the relative, and the doctrine of the degrees of reality that is consequent thereon" (62). I would agree that a distinction between appearance and reality, the way things seem to be and the way they really are, is a primordial truth, which could not be consistently denied. But I cannot agree that Smith's way of formulating this distinction is a primordial truth. He speaks of "the Vedantic claim that the phenomenal world is only qualifiedly real" (63). I can accept that claim under a particular interpretation. I distinguish, for example, between the way a rock appears to our visual perception—a passive, inert colored shape—and what it really is—a society of active molecules, which are composed of even more active subatomic events. I distinguish between the way I appear to others, and am described by the phenomenologist or behaviorist psychologist, on the one hand, and the way I really am, as a feeling, thinking, acting subject, and am known by myself and even more fully by God, on the other. In this sense, I agree that the assertion that "the phenomenal world is only qualifiedly real" expresses a primordial truth.[58] But in Smith's way of understanding this assertion, what I and the rock are in ourselves—as well as what we appear to be to the sensory perception of others, belongs to the phenomenal world, which is said to be only relatively real. I can deny that formulation of the doctrine without thereby being led into self-contradiction; it is therefore not a hard-core commonsense truth.

The difference between us on this point might, incidentally, lay behind our difference on the importance of coherence, and of hard-core commonsense ideas themselves. Because I take our human experiences to be actual entities, no less actual than the divine experiences (although inferior in every other way), I take with utmost seriousness those ideas that we all seem to share in common, and that we cannot consistently deny. I believe that progress in truth lies in the direction of (1) identifying more and more of these truths and (2) finding ways to understand how they cohere with each other. If Smith does not accept this program, or at least takes it less seriously, it may be because he believes our present existence to be phenomenal and only relatively real through and through. The fact that some ideas cannot consistently be denied by us, in our present mode of existence, would not confer any ultimate authority upon those ideas. They would ultimately be in the same boat as other ideas that more obviously do not express ultimate truths about the nature of things. This would explain why Smith feels free to suggest as primordial truths not only ideas that are not hard-core commonsense ideas, but even ideas that contradict certain hard-core commonsense ideas (for example, his denials that time and evil are ultimately real). Our difference on this issue is perhaps the ultimate example of how our respective substantive positions are intertwined with our respective formal positions.

In any case, I hold that the formulation of the true metaphysical position is still a task for the future, that we cannot find it ready-made in the past. To be sure, we will, *contra* modernity, find many of our best clues in the premodern past. But we will find some clues in one tradition, others in a second, and still others in a third, and so on. And we will generally find that the clues provided most clearly by the first tradition were formulated there in such a way as to exclude complementary truths from other traditions. Accordingly, we will have to reformulate the clues that we do find, so as to make them mutually compatible, not simply take them over as expressed. Furthermore, I assume that there are many important clues to be found in the modern tradition. Some of these, such as the ultimate reality and importance of time and freedom, were reassertions of truths reflected in the biblical tradition that had been partially denied by medieval theology. Other clues have been provided by that effort in cosmological discovery called *modern science.*

Metaphysics, which seeks to discover primordial, necessary truths, is distinguishable from scientific cosmology, insofar as the latter focuses upon contingent truths primarily (or exclusively, if we accept Popper's falsification principle as the criterion for demarcating scientific from metaphysical truths). The cosmological insights of science can nevertheless be a big help in discovering metaphysical truths. Our task, in fact, is not simply to develop a metaphysics in abstraction from cosmology, but to develop a postmodern cosmology in which the postmodern metaphysics is embodied. Cosmology is important in itself and also as a way of testing the mutual compatibility of our formulations of primordial truths and the correspondence of these formulations to well-attested empirical truths. I turn now to this question of the role of science in the quest for a truly ecumenical metaphysical theology.

VI. Science and Theology

Smith's program for relating science and theology involves a division of labor based on a division of dominions. Theology deals with the whole, science with a part (72). Science's domain is that part of the world we call physical nature—the "objective, palpable domain of mature," the "visible, material regions" which can be manipulated and thereby controlled (72, 83-84). Through this division of labor, Smith believes, we can keep the good features of modern science while overcoming its deleterious cultural effects. I believe that this program is neither theoretically defensible nor practically realistic.

One theoretical problem is where the line between that which science can and cannot study should be drawn. Smith clearly thinks of physics as a paradigmatic science ("the physical or exact sciences provide, and should provide, the model of what science should do and be" [73]). But the objects of elementary particle physics are hardly "palpable" and "visible"; no one has touched or seen an electron, let alone a quark or a neutrino. If visibility and tangibility do not even provide the criteria for the domain of the physical sciences, why should they be used to exclude anything from the domain of *science as such?* The problem of the most elementary level of nature aside, where does one draw the line above which science dare not tread without growing "flabby" (73)? Can science deal with macromolecules and viruses but not with living cells, so that molecular biology is the only scientific form of biology? Or can it deal with cells, and those organisms of cells we call plants, but not with multicelled animals? Or if it can deal with low-grade multicelled animals, where do we draw the line above which the study is no longer real science? Is the psychology of rats real science, while human psychology is not? Or if human psychology is genuinely scientific, what about parapsychology? But have we not long since left behind the visible and the palpable? The life of the cell is not visible or palpable any more than is the psyche or mind of the rat. Any attempt to draw an ontological line of demarcation around the proper domain of science would be arbitrary.

The same is true of Smith's attempt to indicate a methodological line of demarcation by reference to the controlled experiment. As I have pointed out in the first volume in this series, many philosophers of science say that, while science requires open demonstration, it does not require the controlled, laboratory experiment.[59] As I mentioned in my initial critique, Smith accepts Darwinian evolutionary theory as scientific (32); and yet most of this theory is not based upon repeatable, laboratory experiments. Some laboratory experiments are used, to be sure, to support particular features of the theory, especially Mendelian genetics; but the theory itself is based much more upon observation (of fossil remains) and imaginative reconstruction than upon controlled experimentation. The same is true of geology and astronomy.

With regard to Smith's attempt to demarcate science from theology ontologically and methodologically, it is interesting to note the position of Ken Wilber, who accepts "the basic ontology of the perennial philosophy; specifically, as summarized by [Arthur] Lovejoy, Huston Smith, . . . Frithjof Schuon, et al."[60] Wilber defines scientific method in terms of hypotheses that are testable by reference to data that are potentially public or open to repetition by peers. He denies that this delimits science by reference to a particular domain, such as that of sensory or physical objects. That restriction would exclude not only psychology and sociology, but also logic and mathematics.[61] Having listed five domains of reality (matter, life, mind, soul, and spirit), he says that all domains "contain certain features or deep structures that are open to scientific investigation."[62] There is evidently nothing in Smith's hierarchical view of reality, then, that necessitates his restrictive view of science. This restrictive view seems to follow less from the hierarchical metaphysics than from the acceptance of the modern prejudice that has equated the science of the simple and the inert with science as such.

A third theoretical problem in Smith's program involves his proposal that we should understand the relation of science to theology as that of a part to the whole. The problem is that this part/whole relationship is not intelligible if the categories used by science and theology are different in kind. Theology for Smith speaks in terms of downward causation, purposes, and qualities, while science for him speaks exclusively in terms of upward causes, mechanical causes, and quantities. How then can science be part of theology, or the domain studied by science understood as part of reality as a whole? Smith correctly says that we need a theology of nature (73); but how can a purely mechanistic, reductionistic account of nature contribute to a *theology* of nature in which all causation ultimately flows from higher to lower orders of existence? This problem is illustrated by Smith's own treatment of evolution. He says that he does not, contrary to my interpretation of his position, reject "a theistic account of evolution, according to which we could say that we are the products of both God and evolution," but that he only rejects evolutionary theory when it is put forward as "explanatory without God" (73). But is that view reconcilable with the following passage?

> To his children's question, "Who made us, God or evolution?" a British theologian, Don Cupitt, found himself answering, "Both" .... On reflection, though, Cupitt tells us, he concluded that his answer was "diplomatic, orthodox, and shallow." Darwinism does not purport to describe the instrumentalities through which God works. It is the scientific account for how we and other creatures got here, and as such it must, on pain of begging the question, proceed without recourse to anything remotely resembling divine intention or design. ... Darwinism qualifies as being scientific because its working principles are strictly nonteleological: natural selection is purely mechanical, and mutations on which it works arrive solely by chance.[62]

How can this be read other than as an endorsement and explanation of Cupitt's conclusion that to say that we were created by both God and evolution is shallow? The problematic nature of Smith's position is revealed by his next sentence: "By the same token, if Darwinism is accepted as true, the Great Origins hypothesis is replaced by the Small Origins one."[64] (The Great Origins hypothesis is the view that we were created by God; the Small Origins hypothesis is the reductionistic view that the greater has arisen from the lesser, ultimately from subatomic particles.) Smith is saying, in other words, that the Darwinian, reductionistic account is the only one that counts as scientific, and yet that if it is accepted, then the theological view is excluded. This does not portray a part/whole relation between science and theology; it implies instead that, to accept the theological view, we have to reject the scientific view.

Besides these theoretical problems which arise if Smith's proposal for a division of domains is examined closely, Smith's program also seems practically unrealistic. With regard to the question of whether science and religion are in opposition, he says; "Only if both purport to pronounce on the whole of things. If the part-whole relationship is honored, there need be no conflict" (73). But is it not naive to think that this relationship is going to be honored? There is nothing new about this proposal; it has been with us at least since Kant and Hegel, and to some extent since Descartes. But it has for the most part gone unheeded, both by scientists and by the culture at large. The drive to understand reality in terms of one set of categories has overridden all attempts by philosophers and theologians to place a "no trespassing sign" beyond which scientists with their method were not to proceed. As long as "science" is understood to involve explanation or description in exclusively mechanistic, reductionistic, quantitative terms, there will be a drive to understand everything that exists in these terms. Those things that cannot be thus described will be said not to exist.

Smith believes that his own proposal is more realistic than the attempt to create a postmodern science. He holds that science will forever, or at least indefinitely, remain *modern*, reductionistic science, and that no protests will change this—alternative proposals by theologians or philosophers are not "going to disengage 'science' from its heavy . . . involvement with the controlled experiment, hence with upward causation" (84).[65] Much better, he says, is

> the route that portions out the noetic field, respectfully assigning its visible, material regions to science while remaining clear-eyed and very stern about the incompetence of the methods that work superbly there to say explicitly anything of the slightest importance about other domains. (84)

But who is it that "portions out the noetic field" in this way? The philosopher or the theologian, of course. If scientists and others will not listen to alternative proposals by theologians or philosophers about how to understand science, why does Smith think they will allow philosophers or theologians to portion out the noetic field, and especially to assign themselves the prestigious task of dealing with the whole, while assigning to science the task of merely treating a part? In a passage in which he is rejecting the idea of altering the relation between science and religion through a new understanding of science, he refers to science as the "top dog" in the relation.[66] What understanding of human (or canine) nature leads him to expect the top dog to allow the defeated rival to arrogate to itself the lion's share of the territory? Smith's proposal seems to be much less likely to succeed than a program to change the dominant image of what science is.

One reason why the idea of a postmodern science, even if proposed by philosophers and theologians, might succeed is that it has a precedent: as recent studies have shown, the mechanistic paradigm of modern science was originally adopted more for philosophical and theological motives than because of empirical evidence.[67] Another reason for possible success is that the movement for a postmodern science is already well underway. This is a movement, incidentally, that includes not only philosophers and theologians, but also historians and sociologists of science, as well as some practicing scientists.[68] One reason for this movement is the growing awareness that the reductionistic program for a "unity of the sciences" has failed, while the desire for a unified understanding of reality has not been stilled.

Smith believes that the desire for a postmodern science, in which the divisions between the physical sciences, the biological sciences, the social sciences, and philosophy and theology are overcome, reflects "the modern conviction that science is the privileged mode of knowledge" (83). He thinks he detects that same assumption in my observation that the word *science* means *knowledge*. But those comments reflect Smith's own acceptance of the late modern identification of *science* with *modern science*, and his acceptance of physics as paradigmatic for it. The same is true of his statement that my proposal reflects the conviction that "all knowing should enter its [science's] camp." That would be objectionable only on the assumption that the "science" in question were unreformed, reductionistic, modern science. But the vision of a postmodern science that I adumbrated (48-49) could with equal accuracy (and inaccuracy) be said to reflect the conviction that all knowing should enter theology's camp, or philosophy's camp.

We have for so long accepted the term *science* for one method of knowing, applicable only to a limited range of objects, that it is difficult at first to imagine using it in an inclusive way to cover all our forms of knowing and their results. But this change is essential. Because the term *science* does mean simply knowing, or knowledge, any methods and results not labeled scientific will continue not to be counted as knowledge.

To say that the modern disciplinary divisions will be broken down does not mean that no distinctions whatsoever will remain. A major distinction will remain between knowledge of *ideal* entities (logic, mathematics, ethics, aesthetics) and knowledge of *actual* entities (which we have called, for example, physics, chemistry, geology, biology, psychology, and theology). Within the study of actual things, an essential distinction must then be made between nonindividuated aggregates, such as rocks, and true individuals, such as electrons, cells, and animals, because only the behavior of the former can be completely manipulated, controlled, and predicted. All true individuals will be recognized to have some degree of spontaneity, which cannot be controlled or predicted absolutely. Another distinction will be between higher-level individuals, which have a higher degree of spontaneity, and lower-level individuals, which have less. The ability to predict and control individuals will therefore be recognized to be a matter of degree. The further the individuals are below us in the hierarchy of individuals, the more their behavior can be predicted and controlled. Our ability to predict and control the behavior of individuals at our own level is much less, although not wholly nonexistent. The concrete behavior of any individuals superior to us would be assumed to be even less amenable to prediction and control. In the light of these distinctions, we might, with apologies to Reinhold Niebuhr, propose the following Prayer for Postmodern Scientists:

> Oh God, give us the knowledge to control safely those things that can and should be controlled, the ability to co-exist harmoniously with those things that cannot or should not be controlled, and the wisdom to know the difference.

To incorporate this type of wisdom within science itself will be much more effective in curbing the drift of our culture toward calculative reason, the need for which Smith remarks (83), than the attempt to insist, after accepting the equation of science with controlling knowledge, that a higher form of knowledge exists to which science must subordinate itself. Once knowledge based on control and sought for the sake of control is no longer the inclusive ideal within science itself, the insatiable desire to control which has possessed our culture can be exorcised. The attitude of "letting be" could then come to pervade our male-female relations, our parent-child relations, our international relations, and our relations with the rest of nature.

As with most of the other issues explored here, my position is quite close to one side of Smith's position. As I pointed out in my critique, he does, in spite of all his protestations to the contrary, use evidence from science to support his theological position. Although he reiterates in his reply that the positive significance of science for theology is "merely symbolic" (73), the difference between this and a more integral role is hard to see. And indeed, if the relation between science and theology is supposed to be that of part to whole, that more integral role is what we should expect.

I had listed eight ways in which Smith sees science as supporting philosophical theology (33-34); I would accept five of these: science reveals unexpected unity in nature, a hierarchical view of reality, downward causation, the presence of experience throughout the biosphere, and evidence for a non-Darwinian theory of evolution. To this list I would add many more, including the following. Physics shows nature most fundamentally to be a complex of interdependent events, not of independent enduring substances.[69] It shows time and space to be inseparable (thereby supporting the view that nothing is independent of temporality). Ecology supports this picture of interdependence. Chemistry and biology show the difference between so-called living and nonliving things to be a difference of degree, not of kind. Physics, chemistry, and biology provide evidence against determinism (both in quantum physics, and by showing those things that are fully determinable not to be individuals but aggregates of millions or billions of individuals). The mechanistic view of nature is further undermined by evidence for action at a distance in physics as well as in parapsychology. And parapsychology provides important evidence for many other ideas important to theology, such as the reality of nonsensory perception, the power of the human soul (against epiphenomenalism), and the capacity of the soul to exist, perceive, and act apart from its biological body. By showing extrasensory perception, psychokinesis, and psychic healing to be natural albeit extraordinary capacities of human beings, so that "miracles" need not be interpreted as supernatural interventions, parapsychology has also undermined one of the main bases for that supernaturalistic idea of divine action that put theology and natural science at such loggerheads in the late modern period. By developing a picture of the creation of our world through a very long, slow, evolutionary process, geology, astronomy, and biology have undermined another reason for thinking of divine action supernaturalistically, namely, the idea that the present shape of our world was created all at once. Divine action can thereby be thought of as "persuasion from above," in Smith's phrase. In these and other ways, science has helped theological thinking move beyond not only premodern and early modern supernaturalism but also late modern atheism.

As this statement shows, I agree with Smith that philosophical theology must try to understand reality as a whole, and that theology must include the truths of those domains studied by what we have called the natural sciences as a part of the whole. But I believe that this is only possible if we reformulate our understandings of both science and theology, so that they share a common set of principles. This means, among other things, that science must not exclude divine influence from the explanatory principles applicable to all things, and that theism must be naturalistic, not affirming any interruptions of the universal causal patterns.

VII. DUALISM, SUPERNATURALISM, AND PHILOSOPHICAL UNITY

The most surprising and, from my perspective, most ironic statement made by Smith involves the drive for unity. After asking why process theologians do not "make one of their ultimates *really* ultimate" in the sense of "productive of the others" (which I answered earlier), Smith says:

> I do not think my tropism toward unity here is exceptional; on the contrary (and with apologies for the offense), it strikes me as an important mark of a philosopher. A sentence in a recent issue of a scientific journal tells us that "the aim of philosophy is to see the world as a unity [which process philosophy does]; to understand it in terms of a single, all-encompassing principle [which process philosophy does not]." (82)

What is ironic is that almost all my criticisms of Smith's position are due to what I see as a lack of unity in it. Lack of self-consistency is a lack of unity among one's various assertions. Lack of coherence (in the strict, Whiteheadian sense) is lack of mutual implication among the basic elements: minds that do not need bodies (gnostic dualism), physical things that do not need mentality (a mechanistic view of nature), a God who does not need a world (supernaturalism). Ordinary mind-body dualism says that mechanistic principles apply to one part of the world, while final causation applies to another part. If Smith says that the world contains not just two but four ontologically different types of things, then the absence of a unity of principles is even more extreme. This lack of unity is exemplified also in the God-world relation. Smith rejects my view that "God should not be an exception to metaphysical first principles," saying instead that "a god who does not exceed the categories that govern nature does not deserve our worship" (80). The most extreme lack of unity is perhaps the dualism between the absolute and the relative levels, according to which even those principles that we inevitably presuppose in practice, such as the reality of time and evil, do not apply at the absolute level. My concerns for consistency, coherence, panexperientialism, pantemporalism, and naturalistic theism are various manifestations of the concern for unity. It is very surprising to learn that Smith thinks his position more true to the philosophic drive for unity than mine.

Charles Hartshorne, upon whom I am heavily dependent, agrees strongly with the statement quoted by Smith that the aim of philosophy is to understand the world in terms of a single, all-encompassing principle. And he believes that this drive, which philosophy and science share (science simply being a development out of that part of philosophy that used to be called natural philosophy), will eventually lead scientists to adopt the panexperientialist view. The reason for this expectation is that science can never rest content with an ultimate dualism, which prevents a conceptual unification, and that materialism is simply dualism in disguise.[70] As the only truly nondualistic view, Hartshorne argues, panexperientialism allows for an unprecedented conceptual unity, in which nine apparently quite different relations are understood to be variants of one fundamental relation. That relation is what Whitehead called "prehension," which is the *nonsensory sympathetic perception of antecedent experiences.* (The fact that only *antecedent* experiences are prehended is one reason for emphasizing that temporal relations are ultimately real, and that time exists even for a single atom.) Whitehead, Hartshorne points out, showed (sensory) perception, causation, memory, time, space, enduring individuality (or substantiality), the mind-body relation, the subject-object relation in general, and the God-world relation all to be explainable in terms of prehension. Hartshorne calls this result "the most powerful metaphysical generalization ever accomplished" and "a feat comparable to Einstein's."[71] He says that those who cannot see the importance of it (I quote this with apologies for the offense) "can never have understood what generalization means in science."[72]

We have two quite different intuitions about the type of unity that philosophic thought seeks. We might have to accept an ultimate relativism on this point, concluding that one philosopher's unity of origin is a second's incoherence, and that the second's unity of principle is smallness of mind. But is this so? Or is the unity of principle celebrated by Hartshorne not a better exemplification of the type of unity sought by science and philosophy alike—the desire to understand the world "in terms of a single, all-encompassing principle"—than Smith's desire to see all things as derivative from a single, self-sufficient origin? It certainly seems so to me, especially considering that Smith's positing of a single origin for all things leads him into a host of dualisms, formal and substantive, which prevent understanding the world in terms of any single principle. Good philosophers have always, to be sure, sought to understand the world in terms of the fewest possible types of primordial entities—three or four, say, rather than ninety, or even ten. But this effort has always been part and parcel of the desire to have the fewest possible basic principles. If the move from three or four types of primordial entities to only one entails an increase in the number of basic principles, that move means a loss, not a gain, in the type of unity generally sought by philosophy.

Smith seems to think that his dualisms should not be any more problematic than "Whitehead's distinction between abstract and concrete entities—eternal objects and actual occasions" (72). But not all distinctions are vicious dualisms, only those in which the relationship between the two types of things is so defined as to make the posited relationship seem unintelligible. Whitehead's distinction is not problematic because it is not a dualism between two types of actual or concrete things, and because the two types of things are defined so as to require each other: eternal objects can only exist in actual entities, and actual entities require eternal objects—to be an actual entity is to actualize possibilities or eternal objects.

But the dualisms that are suggested by some of Smith's statements *are* problematic. If the absolute is understood as nirguna Brahman, we can form no idea of the way a personal God (Brahman with attributes) could arise from it. (This problem is overcome if *undifferentiated* is understood to mean simplicity, the nonseparation of the attributes, instead of a complete absence of attributes, as discussed earlier.) Likewise, if Smith holds that there are, or may be, two (or more) ontologically different kinds of actual individuals, then he has the insoluble problem of mind-body interaction bequeathed to modern philosophy by Descartes. This problem would be avoided if Smith would hold consistently to that side of his thought in which he suggests a panexperientialist (panpsychist) view. Rather than moving toward this position in his reply, however, he belittles its importance. He calls it "negotiable" (72), which evidently means optional, and says that whether matter is dead or sentient "need not affect the world's significance." For the world to be significant, he says, "all that is required is that matter be intentionally created and put to good use, in the way furniture is built and pressed into the services of a home." To be sure, if something has instrumental value, it has significance. But does the question of whether it also has intrinsic value—value for itself—make no difference to its significance? Smith would not say that whether members of another race, such as Blacks, or another biological species, such as dolphins, have feelings is irrelevant to their significance. Why should it be irrelevant to those fellow creatures we call cells, organelles, molecules, atoms, and electrons?

Smith, like most moderns, seems to be worried about committing the "pathetic fallacy," of "inputing feelings to what may be inanimate

objects" (72). But why be more worried about this than the "anthropo-
centric fallacy" of assuming that only human beings and perhaps other
beings quite similar to us have feelings? After all, if we impute feelings
to something that does not have feelings, nothing has been violated except
truth (which *does* have no feelings). But if we fail to attribute feelings to
things that really do, then great harm may be done to them through the
purely instrumental, I-it relation that results. Besides having these ethical and religious benefits, the panexperientialist position helps us understand not only the mind-body relation in general, but also psychosomatic
and parapsychological relations, and God's relation to the various levels
of the world, all of which Smith believes in. I do not consider panexperientialism an optional matter, but a *conditio sine qua non* of moving beyond
the modern worldview, with its insoluble intellectual incoherences and
its disastrous ethical consequences. I also consider it a necessary condition for achieving the type of unity that philosophical theology properly
seeks.

CONCLUSION

Although most of this counterreply has been devoted to differences, my
purpose is irenic. While showing how one side of Smith's position involves
serious problems, I have suggested the existence of another side in which
those problems can be avoided. The problematic side denies the ultimate reality of evil, time, progress, and personal qualities, affirms dualisms between mind and matter and between science and theology, and
makes a virtue out of the resulting difficulties by denying the importance of self-consistency. But the positive features of Smith's vision, which
make it an attractive alternative to the modern vision, do not seem to
require these dualisms and denials. I have sought to show how these
positive features can be retained in a postmodern vision, with which one
side of Smith's thought is in harmony. I have suggested how the perfection of God, and even of reality as a whole in a strong sense, is compatible with the ultimate reality of evil and time, and with the importance of
time for progress in the realization of ultimate values. I have suggested
that, by taking *undifferentiated* or *transpersonal* to mean *simplicity* in
the sense of the identity of attributes such as love and knowledge, the
objectionable finitude of some personalistic conceptions of deity can be
overcome without resorting to a subordinationism in which the personal
side of the divine reality is regarded as derivative from an impersonal
absolute devoid of attributes. Rather, we can think of personal qualities
and the impersonal dynamism of the universe as two "aspects of a single

deity," to use Smith's phrase, while understanding this impersonal dynamism as also embodied in finite beings understood by analogy with God. From this position, the need for self-consistency, which Smith generally recognizes, can be honored without exception. This position also allows us to interpret all levels of reality in terms of one set of general principles and thus to exemplify that unity of principle which science and philosophy have always sought. Finally, I have suggested that we need a clear criterion for primordial truths, and that the best criterion is whether the ideas are inevitably presupposed in practice and have therefore been at least implicitly affirmed by human beings at all times and places. Once this criterion is recognized, the task before us is seen to be not that of resuscitating a premodern metaphysics, but the more exciting task of creating a postmodern cosmology in which primordial truths gleaned from a wide variety of traditions, including modernity, will be reconciled with each other and with the best current knowledge from the sciences.

NOTES

1. This point is discussed in *God, Power, and Evil: A Process Theodicy* (Philadelphia: Westminster Press, 1976; Lanham, Md.: University Press of America, 1990), chs. 17-18, and in *Evil Revisited* (forthcoming). The *portrayal* is attempted particularly in forthcoming books tentatively entitled *Postmodern Theology* and *Postnuclear Theology*.

2. *God, Power, and Evil* and *Evil Revisited.*

3. *God, Power, and Evil,* 22.

4. In responding to my contention that his position was based on "a peculiar idea," Smith says that it is "natural to regard dreams as less real than waking life, reflections of trees in water as less real than the trees themselves, and television dramas as of less import than those of 'real life'" and to regard the more real things as having greater worth (69). But I do not contest this point. Nor do I contest Smith's more general viewpoint, which sees "being itself as comparably graded." I endorse a hierarchical or multileveled ontology, according to which atoms have more being (which I call creative experience) than electrons (although I would not say that they are more real), macromolecules have more than atoms, living cells more yet, and multicelled animals still more. Also, in contrast with some deep ecologists, I accept the view that higher-level individuals have more intrinsic worth (because they have the capacity for richer forms of creative experience). What I called "a pecular idea" is the idea "that being finite is *ipso facto* to be in some sense evil" (29). To say that a dolphin has more intrinsic worth than a ladybug does not mean that the ladybug is in any sense evil. Nor would most people say that a DNA molecule is somehow evil because it is not a ladybug or a human being. The idea that things that are lower on the ontological scale of being are therefore evil *is* peculiar, both in the neutral sense of being

distinctive to a particular metaphysical viewpoint, and in the pejorative sense of being strange, odd, counterintuitive.

5. *God, Power, and Evil,* 301-08.

6. Emerson's famous statement occurs in his essay "Self-Reliance" (which can be found in *Ralph Waldo Emerson: Essays and Lectures,* Joel Porte, ed. [New York: The Library of America, 1983], 259-302). Emerson's concern in this essay is to encourage people to trust their own deepest thoughts, and to express them publicly, without concern for appearances, or other people's opinion of them (259, 266). The "foolish consistency" of which he speaks is the refusal to say what you think *now* because it contradicts something that you had said earlier. He says that one of the terrors "that scares us from self-trust is our consistency; a reverence for our past act or word, because the eyes of others have no other data for computing our orbit than our past acts, and we are loath to disappoint them" (265). Just before the "hobgoblin" statement, he asks: "Why drag about this corpse of your memory, lest you contradict something you have stated in this or that public place?" And just after it, he says: "Speak what you think now in hard words, and to-morrow speak what to-morrow thinks in hard words again, though it contradicts everything you said to-day" (*idem.*). Thus understood in context, Emerson's statement is unrelated to the issue of whether one should strive for self-consistency in one's philosophical theology—something Emerson himself did.

7. Alfred North Whitehead, *Process and Reality,* corr. ed., David Ray Griffin and Donald W. Sherburne, eds. (New York: The Free Press, 1978), 341.

8. A central element in Richard Rorty's case for a completely relativistic outlook, in which no justification can be given for one's own preferences beyond loyalty to one's own society and its traditions, is the rejection of all "transdisciplinary, transcultural, ahistorical criteria." See Rorty's *Consequences of Pragmatism: Essays 1972-1980* (Minneapolis: University of Minnesota Press, 1982), xxxviii, and "Postmodernist Bourgeois Liberalism," *Journal of Philosophy* 80 (1983), 583-89, esp. 585.

9. See my *A Process Christology* (Philadelphia: Westminster Press, 1973; Lanham, Md.: University Press of America, 1990), ch. 6, "Vision of Reality and Philosophical Conceptualization," and *God, Power, and Evil,* 25-27.

10. *Process and Reality,* 36.

11. Hans Küng, *Does God Exist? An Answer for Today,* Edward Quinn, trans. (Garden City, N.Y.: Doubleday, 1980), 629-30.

12. Whitehead, *Religion in the Making* (1926; Cleveland: World Publishing Co., 1960), 65, 137.

13. Whitehead, *Modes of Thought* (1938; New York: The Free Press, 1968), 174.

14. *Process and Reality,* 7.

15. *Religion in the Making,* 144.

16. *Ibid.,* 127.

17. *Ibid.,* 144.

18. The quotation is from Whitehead's *Science and the Modern World* (1925; New York: The Free Press, 1967), 187, 185.

19. *Process and Reality,* xiii; italics added.

20. *Process and Reality,* 57, 113, 117, 138, 210.

21. *Ibid.,* 123, 138-39.

22. *Ibid.,* 13.

23. *Idem.*

24. *Ibid.,* 51, 137-38, 145, 158.

25. *Ibid.,* 145, 158, 178.

26. *Ibid.,* 171.

27. *Ibid.,* 151.

28. *Idem.*

29. *Ibid.,* 153.

30. *Ibid.,* 156.

31. *Ibid.,* 6.

32. *Idem.*

33. *Ibid.,* 144.

34. *Ibid.,* 146.

35. Charles Hartshorne, *Man's Vision of God and the Logic of Theism* (1941; Hamden, Conn.: 1964), 163; see also 321.

36. *Religion in the Making,* 144; see also 66.

37. See my "The Holy, Necessary Goodness, and Morality," *Journal of Religious Ethics* 8/2 (Fall 1980), 330-49.

38. Hartshorne, *Man's Vision of God,* 116, 229; *Beyond Humanism: Essays in the Philosophy of Nature* (1937; Lincoln: University of Nebraska Press, 1968), 208-09, 316.

39. Hans Jonas, *The Phenomenon of Life: Toward a Philosophical Biology* (New York: Harper & Row, 1966), 247 n. 11.

40. See my discussion in *A Process Christology*, ch. 2, "Being Itself and Symbolic Language." One of Tillich's books was entitled *My Search for Absolutes*.

41. *Religion in the Making,* 146.

42. *Process and Reality,* 222.

43. Stephen Hawking gives support for this view in *A Brief History of Time: From the Big Bang to Black Holes* (New York: Bantam Books, 1988), 50, 116, 133, 136, 141.

44. *Process and Reality,* 225.

45. *Ibid.,* 21.

46. Nicholas Rescher, *The Riddle of Existence: An Essay in Idealistic Metaphysics* (Lanham, Md.: University Press of America, 1984).

47. *Ibid.,* 6, 67-68.

48. *Ibid.,* 22, 27, 29, 65-67.

49. *Ibid.,* 54, 62, 67, 69.

50. *Ibid.,* 58, 59, 61, 67, 69.

51. *Ibid.,* 26, 29, 30.

52. The allusion is to Joseph Needham, *Time: The Refreshing River* (New York: Macmillan, 1943).

53. Huston Smith, *Forgotten Truth: The Primordial Tradition* (New York: Harper & Row, 1977), 121.

54. See my *God and Religion in the Postmodern World* (Albany: State University of New York Press, 1988), ch. 4, "Evolution and Postmodern Theism," in which this idea is briefly discussed. A lengthier discussion is planned for a subsequent publication.

55. Stephen Jay Gould, *The Panda's Thumb* (New York: W. W. Norton, 1980), 226.

56. *Modes of Thought,* 120.

57. Whitehead, *The Function of Reason* (Boston: Beacon Press, 1958), 29.

58. I have discussed this idea more fully in "Bohm and Whitehead on Wholeness, Freedom, Causality, and Time," in David Ray Griffin, ed., *Physics and the Ultimate Significance of Time: Bohm, Prigogine, and Process Philosophy* (Albany: State University of New York Press, 1986), 127-53, esp. 140-48.

59. David Ray Griffin, ed., *The Reenchantment of Science: Postmodern Proposals* (Albany: State University of New York, 1988), 27.

60. "Introduction: of Shadows and Symbols," Ken Wilber, ed., *Quantum Questions: Mystical Writings of the World's Great Physicists* (Boston: Shambhala, 1984), 3-29, esp. 14.

61. *Ibid.,* 12.

62. *Ibid.,* 20.

63. Huston Smith, "Two Evolutions" in Leroy S. Rouner, ed., *On Nature* (Notre Dame, Ind.: University of Notre Dame Press, 1984), 50-51.

64. *Ibid.,* 51.

65. Smith believes that this view of the nature of science as oriented around the controlled experiment and upward causation is supported by an operational definition that obtains in the English-speaking West—"roughly the one that guides the National Science Foundation in its appropriation of funds" (65). I would not know how to check the accuracy of this claim. In any case, I would think a better way to discern the working definition of what counts as science in our culture would be to examine the membership of the American Association for the Advancement of Science. Among the affilliates are several in which controlled experimentation is surely not central, such as the American Anthropological Association, the American Ethnological Society, the American Geographical Society, the American Mathematical Society, the American Society for Aesthetics, and the Linguistic Society of America. There are also several in which an exclusive commitment to upward causation is not only not obvious but even seems to be rejected, at least implicitly, such as the Academy of Psychosomatic Medicine, the American Academy of Psychoanalysis, the American Society of Clinical Hypnosis, the Biofeedback Society of America, and the Parapsychological Association. (My source is the *AAAS Handbook 1988-89,* pages 81-87.) A postmodern definition of science would, therefore, to some extent involve merely an explicit recognition of the wide diversity of activities and assumptions that are already pragmatically accepted as "scientific" by working scientists themselves.

66. Smith, *Beyond the Post-Modern Mind* (New York: Crossroad Publishing Co., 1982), 71.

67. See my discussion in the introduction to *The Reenchantment of Science.*

68. For some names, see the contributors and my introduction to *The Reenchantment of Science.*

69. Smith (in n. 13) portrays me as making a stronger separation between physics and metaphysics in Whitehead's thought than I had intended (in my n. 115). What I denied was that Whitehead's metaphysical doctrine that the actual world is comprised of momentary "actual occasions" was based on Einstein's relativity theory (which Smith had claimed) or even "heavily on any particular scientific theory." I do believe (against some interpreters) that the quantum physics of the day was a significant influence on his doctrine that apparently

enduring things (such as electrons) are in reality series of discrete events. But this is a very general, metaphysical point, not tied to any one version of quantum theory. (Since writing the above, I have read an impressive paper by Christoph Wassermann [see 58 n. 115] which suggests that Whitehead's move to a cosmology of events, out of which evolved his doctrine of actual occasions, was more influenced by special relativity theory than I had thought. But the point stands that Whitehead did not accept Einstein's formulation, especially his theory of general relativity.)

70. Hartshorne, *Creative Synthesis and Philosophic Method* (Lasalle, Ill.: Open Court, 1970; Lanham, Md.: University Press of America, 1983), 9, 27. Hartshorne's point is that materialists, being experiencing beings, cannot help but implicitly affirm the existence of experiencing beings. By explicity affirming the existence of nonexperiencing beings, they have thereby implicitly affirmed dualism. Only panexperientialism, which says that all concrete things are either experiencing beings or are comprised of such, truly avoids ontological dualism. (Hartshorne, incidentally, formerly referred to his doctrine as "panpsychism," but has more recently spoken of "psychicalism"; the term "panexperientialism" is my own. One reason I prefer this term is that it more readily suggests the idea that the most fundamental actualities of the universe are momentary experiences rather than enduring individuals. Also, the term "psyche" connotes a rather high-level enduring individual.)

71. *Ibid.,* 107, 92.

72. *Beyond Humanism,* 192.

5

BEFORE SILENCE DESCENDS: A CONCLUDING APOLOGIA

Huston Smith

In responding to Griffin in our first round, I tried to speak for the perennial philosophy. In the interests of directness I now speak for myself, although I intend to reflect the primordial outlook as faithfully as possible. I address the seven topics to which Griffin has reduced his original thirteen, but not before indicating where (upon reading Griffin's counterreply) it now appears that our fundamental difference lies—at least one of them.

Griffin seems to think that there is an objective, universally applicable court of appeal that can adjudicate between worldviews, determining their truth or falsity. It consists of reason, working with the "hard-core commonsense ideas [and] rather obvious facts of immediate experience" (99). *Postmodernism,* as that word is generally used in philosophy today, refers to the collapse of faith in reason's power thus to hold court.[1] Griffin rightly points out that I should not call his reason autonomous and therefore modern, for he insists that it is not autonomous: reason in his view must be supplemented by vision. His point is well taken, but his augmented reason continues to look modern to me in claiming the power to winnow the visions that supplement it, accepting or rejecting them by the standards it imposes.

Be this as it may, my epistemology is more holistic. I see worldviews gestalting their respective data to the point where it is difficult to find neutral ground. Worlds were not made for one another. And because the furniture of each respective world (read worldview) is controlled by the style the designer has chosen (e.g., Colonial or Victorian), the chairs in my metaphysical home are not going to match well with Griffin's tables.

Stephen Pepper used to make this point with a simple diagram. Philosopher A lays out the world in this way:

but B carves it up differently:

Imposed on one another, the two sets of categories do not accord:

The overlapping octagon at the center may appear to be common ground because both A and B take it into account. But when they are pressed regarding its precise contours, we learn that A understands it to be really

whereas B sees it as

Something like this, I suspect, accounts for why, despite large areas of substantial agreement, Griffin and I are left with the frustrating feeling that the other cannot quite get things right—this despite the most attentive tutoring he is being given. Griffin tells us that "any worldview presupposes a nonrational (that is, prerational) vision of reality" (101). My vision differs from his. And because the parts of visions are no more interchangeable than the parts of a symphony or painting, the world's parts do not appear identical to us. This holds for Griffin's "hard-core commonsense ideas" as much as it does for the rest of the world. Naturally, I accept them in a rough, commonsensical way, but when Griffin defines their implications, he forces his metaphysics onto them. This point will dog my contribution to this second round of our discussion, and because it relates most directly to the second section in Griffin's counterreply, I transpose his order, treating first the subject of his second section.

I. TRUTH AND COHERENCE

Judging from Griffin's response to my initial rejoinder, I seem to have created the impression that I dislike coherence, whereas actually I like it a lot. I could even say that the reason that I believe that my view of reality is closer to the mark than his is that it *gestalts* the full range of my intuitions coherently, whereas his scheme leaves some of them dangling. Griffin either discounts them because they do not fit his grid, or fails to feel their force in the first place. The dispute is not over *coherence*. It concerns *data*.

If I spoke disparagingly of coherence initially, it was of the kind that Griffin proposes. Griffin thinks that coherence, prior to and apart from the materials it is brought to bear on, can be specified with sufficient precision and neutrality to empower it to adjudicate truth claims. Or to approach the same point from the side of data, he believes that the "commonsense truths . . . and rather obvious facts of immediate experience" (99) provide an archemedian point solid enough to serve as a fulcrum for logic in general. I am not persuaded that either of these appeals to objective criteria holds up. Asked by Griffin whether I believe "that the formal criteria of adequacy and self-consistency (or noncontradiction) are . . . neutral, universally applicable criteria" (98-99), my answer is: "I do so believe, provided the terms are kept 'vague' " — in using that word against me (99), Griffin has me exactly right.

I favor vagueness in appeals to criteria in order to protect their neutrality. Griffin quotes Whitehead's point that controlling assumptions are often based on the fact that the words and phrases of an "old established metaphysical system" have gained "a false air of adequate precision" (105) and I see this as exactly what has happened with Griffin's "commonsense ideas" and "rather obvious facts of immediate experience." The shoe is now on the other foot. Those facts and ideas are not as precise as Griffin thinks.

A look at his notion of "genuine evil" bears this out. Griffin defines it as evil that no court of appeal can completely rescind; in even the most ultimate context, it must be the case that things would have been better had the evil in question not occurred. But for me "genuine evil" is evil that evokes in normal human beings all-out feelings of abhorrence and the determination to resist it. (Moral evil is the sort that is at issue here.) Griffin, of course, thinks that my definition entails his, but quite apart from who is right, the fact that we disagree shows that we have put "obviousness" and "common sense" behind us. An all-out metaphysical storm is brewing.

I hope this shows that I do not resist logic; I resist being tied to what feels to me like Euclidian geometry after Riemann has taught us that alternatives exist. All of Whitehead's abstract, formal dicta about coherence that Griffin quotes (104) I accept wholeheartedly—proof again that they cannot referee metaphysical discernments. Contradictions *do* call for "the necessity of some readjustments." Progress in truth *is indeed* made by "evolving notions which strike more deeply into the root of reality." The goal *is* to reformulate all inherited formulations of funda-mental intuitions "so as to absorb into one system all sources of experi-ence." But Griffin seems to think that if I concur with all this and continue to think straight I will be led back to Whiteheadianism, beginning (in the order in which he introduces this section's issues) with Whitehead's view of the best possible world.

Griffin notes that we both agree that what makes a view of reality religious is its sense that things are as they ought to be—that this is the best (or at least one of the best, Griffin wants to add) of all possible worlds (96). But to believe that a world is possible we must be able to conceive it, Griffin argues, and this calls up his touchstone of coher-ence, for to conceive is to "coherently conceive" (96).

Would the quantum world ever have opened to physicists had they adopted Griffin's dictum here, I wonder in passing—but I must not let myself be distracted. When Griffin tells us that "we must limit our asser-tions about the best possible world to the best conceivable world, until someone comes up with a better world that seems, to our best understand-ing, to be genuinely conceivable" (97), my impulse is to paraphrase St. Paul on Mars Hill and exclaim, "That 'better world' is what I am showing you." But Griffin's qualifying phrase, "to our best understanding," reminds me that the showing will not avail, for Griffin's understanding is not mine. My world looks better to me because, seen in its entirety—but only then, when everything is (in principle) in view—it harbors no regret. But remove regret, says Griffin (91), and you talk gibberish, for then evil ceases to be genuine. We are back with his partisan definition of "genuine evil."

Objections do not suffice. If I say I favor consistency and coherence but not Griffin's version thereof, it is incumbent on me to enter my alternative.

Without forgetting that in the end mountains become again mountains and rivers rivers, religion begins with the fact that they are not such. This is Zen idiom for the fact that "the eyes of faith" look upon the world in a distinctive way, seeing thereby a different world. This different world must accommodate (in the sense of take into account) the unregenerated, pre-enlightenment world while at the same time subrating it. Right here, at the very start, we strike tension. (Griffin derides my position for the "strong tensions" [110] it exhibits, but religions that do not resist the world lack tonus.) To those for whom the ordinary, unregenerate world is the only world, *tension* is too weak a word; the very idea that there *is* another world contradicts their understanding of this one. How can you take seriously the history that Hegel characterized as a butcher's block, they ask rhetorically, and seriously believe with Griffin (and me) that "the world *is* the way it *ought* to be" (96)? One thinks of the determination of Camus to forge a philosophy that could be lived without lying.

To argue that the true and the seeming worlds can be reconciled—that it is possible (without either lying or becoming schizophrenic) to face the day with Bible in one hand and the morning paper in the other, as Karl Barth put the matter—I find myself appealing repeatedly to the *lingua franca* of our day, which is science. (In his *Patterns, Thinking and Cognition,* Howard Margolis says he had to look to science in order to understand politics, and I sometimes feel similarly about understanding religion.) Einstein can accommodate Newton. Larger views can honor smaller ones without being reduced to them. Coherence and conceivability remain solidly in place in such moves—moves that every alert religious consciousness traffics in constantly, I would suppose.

What makes the appeal to Einstein and Newton relevant is the notion of multiple frames of reference. Each frame legitimately possesses its own distinctive logic—different things must be said about matter at its micro-, macro-, and mega-levels. But the differences cohere because with sufficient aptitude and schooling one comes to see why each is required.

This legitimation of paradox when it is indicated is a far cry from giving it the free rein Griffin sees me permitting it (96-97). Paradoxes should not be entered into lightly, but only soberly and advisedly, which is to say: not until ineluctable evidence forces us into them. Whereupon, if one comes to sense the reasons that require them, the frustration they initially provoked gives way to delight—the "ahas" of the eureka response: so *that* was why their two sides seemed at odds; they were being viewed from different angles or planes. I see the religious paradoxes that cause Griffin to give religious geniuses poor marks as thinkers—those age-old claims for freedom *and* predestination, time *and* eternity, perfection *and* evil—as *forced* on the mystics by sensibilities that, living as they did in a less secular age than ours, were on balance more finely honed than are ours. Those sensibilities disclose data that are as remorseless as those of frontier physics in requiring paradoxical expression, with the difference that, because scientific knowledge is cumulative, its paradox-requiring profundities come later.

Where does this leave the issue of truth and coherence in our discussion? The extent to which I responded to Griffin's initial critique by coming back with the same "mistakes" must make him suspect, I fear, that I am impervious to argument. I am at odds with myself; I keep wanting to have things both ways (92, 106, 109, 121, 122). I grasp both horns of dilemmas (93). I want evil to be "genuine . . . yet not . . . genuine" (97), and so on. In a way, I think he is right about this imperviousness: our different frames of reference arm us heavily against the other's assaults. (This is the "invulnerability" with which Griffin charges me [98], and which I sense as characterizing his position as well.) I keep returning to my conviction that different visions, not arguments, regulate our conclusions; *this* is why we talk past each other so much, and why the issues between us are left, so often, unjoined. If our object is to understand each other's viewpoint, we may have gotten further if I had devoted my entire space to phenomenology: to describing as commandingly as possible the sensibilities of the mystics that *force* them to their paradoxes. Quotations from sacred texts, glossed with the esoteric angles from which the mystics approach those texts, would have figured prominently in such an enterprise, as would poetic insights. The lines from Keats's "Ode to Melancholy," for example,

> Ay, in the very temple of Delight
> Veil'd Melancholy has her sovran shrine,

to suggest how God's rapture need not be disturbed by God's perfect empathy with creaturely pain.

Still, there are places where reasoning can relieve misunderstandings, and Griffin does well to push for these. One such place concerns verbal definitions—certain words carry different connotations for the two of us. The word *reason* provides a good example; it enjoys less status in my lexicon than it does in Griffin's. For Griffin, reason has a power by which it "checks our worldview for adequacy and self-consistency" (101). I do not credit it with that power because (as previously indicated) I do not think that common sense and obvious facts provide it with a solid foundation upon which to build. My way of dealing with this problem is to supplement reason with another noetic faculty—I call it *intellect*—that works intuitively. When Griffin says that he does "not . . . believe that reason alone, apart from a substantive religious vision, can create a satisfactory worldview" (101), I would like to think that his *vision* resembles my *intellect.* There is the difference that vision, for him, *adds* furniture to the world without refashioning the pieces common sense slaps together—vision "must bow" to common sense, Griffin quotes Whitehead as saying in effect (105). But if I add a phrase to my assertion that Griffin quotes (98), saying now that "to make religion rationally intelligible [in the absence of intellect/vision] is to sound its death knell," perhaps it will seem less outrageous.

Less outrageous, perhaps, but the emendation does not reconcile our alternate estimates of reason. Griffin adheres to Whitehead's faith that reason can moniter "the coherence of such presumptions [as we] employ for the regulation of our lives" (105). Whitehead even proposes that we take as "the metaphysical rule of evidence: that we must bow to those presumptions" just mentioned (105). But I have already asserted my willingness to genuflect only as long as the presumptions remain vague. In that condition, I agree that they deserve their due. But when Griffin impresses them with his cookie cutter to give them sharp outlines, they forfeit their generic rights.

They forfeit their rights against the theologian in particular because they give more weight to the "commonsense," "rather obvious" features of human experience than "religious vision" (I like Griffin's phrase here) should allow. For Griffin and Whitehead, religious visions may *propose,* but it is common sense and the obvious that *dispose,* for reason's job is to make sure that philosophical assumptions square with the latter.[2] I can understand why philosophers might now argue this way, philosophy having ceased to take orders from theology since Descartes. But for theologians to take orders from philosophers strikes me as the same mistake—the mistake in reverse, if the medieval stance was a mistake in the first place. My religious vision not only proposes, it disposes. It disposes of process philosophy's "hard-core commonsense ideas" and "rather obvious facts of immediate experience," not by dismissing them or denying that our lives instantiate them, but by presenting them differently—in a light which, being clearer as I believe, reveals their contours more precisely.

Herein lies my focal dis-ease with theology that is process based: it accommodates theology to philosophy, religion to the world, the deepest wisdom of the ages to styles of thought that secularization has influenced profoundly. "Spiritual wisdom, from a worldly point of view, is a kind of madness," I chance to read in the course of revising this page. Process theology proposes to critique that madness from the world's perspective.

This is worth pursuing, and the longest passage that Griffin quotes from Whitehead (100) provides documentation. "In our cosmological construction," Whitehead writes,

> we are . . . left with the final opposites, joy and sorrow, good and evil, disjunction and conjunction . . . flux and permanence, greatness and triviality, freedom and necessity, God and the World. In this list, the pairs of opposites are in experience with a certain ultimate directness of intuition, except in the case of the last pair. God and the World introduce the note of interpretation.

Note that the first six sets of opposites, not the God/World contrast, are determinative. This contention is enough in itself, it seems to me, to show that Whitehead is not a theologian; he establishes other than religious data as his starting point and control. And with that fateful move, the dye is cast respecting religion: it will not receive its due. My conviction on this point sparked this entire exchange, for as Griffin reports in his section of our joint Introduction (7-8), it was on encountering my rhetorical question, "Why . . . is this loss—Process Theology—being inflicted on Christians?," that he was provoked to plans for this book. Griffin says explicitly that Whitehead's "interpretive theory of God and the World had to be adequate to the other pairs of opposites. He would *not* say that his description of, say, good and evil had to be adequate to his account of God . . . as if [God] were given with more or even equal 'directness of intuition' " (100). So much for Moses on Mount Sinai, Buddha under the Bo Tree, Saul knocked off his horse, and Muhammad driven to the edge of madness on the Night of Power. As I read Griffin and try to respond to him, I keep wondering if a point will be reached where we might say, "Here it is. *This* is where (and why) we finally differ." This may not be that point but, to quote the concluding line of *The Sting,* "It sure comes close." On pain of incoherence, process theology requires that distinctively religious deliverances— may I say revelation?—"bow" to the more "direct intuitions" of everyday life. Religion, when vital I would say, does the opposite.

I have allowed disproportionate space to this first section (Griffin's second), because I cannot deal constructively with Griffin's innumerable specific points unless the different angle from which I approach them is first indicated. Having tried to establish that alternate reference point, I now respond, stacatto, to some specific points that Griffin raises in this section.

He points out that he, too, credits God with "unsurpassable perfection" and says that "we diverge only on how to explicate the meaning of such" (99). This is true. For me, that perfection is concrete; for Griffin, it is abstract.

Griffin rightly notes that the issue is not whether his criterion for adjudicating truth-claims can be wielded objectively (101). The question is whether there exists an objective criterion to be wielded.

At one point, Griffin writes that he "do[es] not see ... how the validity of the formal criterion of adequacy to the facts of experience is contingent upon any substantive interpretation of the nature of reality" (100), but later he says that "our respective substantive positions are intertwined with our respective formal positions" (134). I do not see how these two statements mesh, but, quite apart from that, I have devoted a good part of this section to arguing that Griffin's own "formal criterion of adequacy" is tied all too tightly to a "substantive interpretation of the nature of reality"—the interpretation he thinks our commonsense ideas, rather obvious facts, and primordial truths force upon us.

I agree with Griffin that matter is not both wave and particle (101): the accurate wording is that it manifests itself as both. Being, with Griffin, a metaphysical realist, I join him in believing that there is a way that matter in itself *is*. This puts me on his side as against Hans Küng, who accepts Bohr's complementarity as a stopping place. Where I side with Bohr, against Griffin, is in not hanging onto Griffin's minority faith (shared by Einstein and Bohm) that matter's univocal essence will be found to be lodged within the perimeters in which science traffics.

Griffin's likening of my levels of reality to Hume's two levels of theory and practice (106) overlooks the fact that my higher levels include the lower in something of the way the process God includes the world. This is why I do not see the "dualistic difficulty" Griffin senses (107), but this issue belongs more directly to section seven.

The same oversight seems to prompt Griffin's assumption that I think that "the world's existence is not necessary for God" (107). I do hold (in Griffin's paraphrase of me) that "the divine reality is ... absolutely perfect and complete in every respect in itself," but it is perfect as including the world. Were the world omitted, God's infinity would be compromised. If I have written that the world does not add to God's existence, it is because it is included *in* his existence—perennialism differs from most exoteric theologies here. Rather than seeing this as "an extreme example of incoherence" (107), I feel myself to be close to the process position on this point.

II. DIVINE PERFECTION AND WORLDLY EVIL

Reading a section that gathers force as it zones in on the "pernicious" consequences of my mistaken views (95), I am all but undone by Griffin's closing concession that "a true intuition" (95) underlies my manifold errors. The intuition is this:

> that the evils of the world, while truly and ultimately evil, are part of a process that is very good on the whole; that the good in the process is not possible without the possibility and virtual inevitability of the evil; that the distinctively human evils are occurring in a long process that will eventually lead to such great and universal good that all the participants in the process will agree that the sufferings endured *en route* were worth while; and that one with a truly adequate perspective on the process—namely God—can experience the evil as evil (even feeling the sufferings of the creatures in a way analogous to our feeling of the pain in our bodily members) with serenity. (95)

Asked if I will agree with this formulation and thereby close ranks with Griffin in "presenting a unified front against the late modern denial that reality is perfect in any sense," my answer is: gladly with respect to its general intent. But scrutinized closely, the formulation—which turns out to be Griffin's philosophy compressed into a paragraph—rides roughshod over things I hold dear. (1) I do not agree that "the evils of the world [are] truly and ultimately evil." (2) Whereas Griffin sees the world as being "very good on the whole," I take it to be perfect. (3) I would tighten Griffin's claim that "the good in the process is not possible without the possibility and virtual inevitability of . . . evil," to read, "without the certainty of evil." And (4) throughout I would replace Griffin's "process" with my eternal and infinite Absolute, which subsumes time in a timeless way.

In this section, the question is how these four differences converge on the issue of the divine perfection, and Griffin points out correctly that "we differ . . . on the proper understanding of perfect power" (89). I would not have reverted from the process God to the God of classical theism had I not concluded that the traditional God is both more perfect and more powerful. More powerful, because he is the first cause of everything there is, whereas Griffin's God must work with givens that are not of his making: creativity, eternal objects, and the structure of actual occasions; more perfect, because everything—the everything for which God is solely responsible—is exactly as it should be. This, its unqualified, concrete perfection, is again something Griffin does not affirm.

On the issue of the divine perfection and worldly evil, therefore, I give God's perfection a stronger reading and the world's evil a weaker reading than does Griffin, with the result that my world emerges (in my eyes) as the superior of the two. In my world, God's perfection, tied tightly to his omnipotence, precludes the possibility of any second-rate happenings—nothing that occurs would have been better had it been otherwise. I prefer such a world to one that is dogged at every turn by irrecovable mistakes, and I revere its author more than I could a God who was unable to effect such a world.

Griffin says the reason his God cannot effect such a world is that the world in question is a logical impossibility, and for proof throws on me his hammerlock of consistency and coherence: if the possibility of indelible mistakes is removed, human freedom is removed in the same swipe. But the burden of my preceding section was that Griffin's consistency and coherence are not the neutral arbiters he assumes they are. Logics are multiple.

In saner moments, I find it quite possible to reconcile evil that is genuine in my sense of the word—to repeat, evil that evokes all the revulsion, and elicits all the resistance, that human beings are capable of—with God's ability to transmute such evil into unalloyed good. How? In some instances, we can neither say nor see how—if Griffin wants to remove God's mystery, that removes his holiness as well and I lose interest. But we can establish a logical trajectory that is firm enough to enable us to posit where the rainbow touches down on the farther shore, even though the spot itself is not in view.

That logical trajectory is established through analogies wherein things that appear blurred when held too close achieve focus when set in perspective. Viewed as a character trait, Iago's evilness is despicable, but, in the context of *Othello,* Shakespeare puts it to good use. Given Griffin's rejection of my previous appeal to the theater (93-94), it may be unwise to introduce it again, but Griffin approaches my analogy from the wrong end. If there is "no actual suffering" on stage, there is no actual resolution on stage either, so by that reading the play, being "merely 'play' " as Griffin insists, should have no impact. The point of such analogies is to demonstrate that emotions can be complex, a point that (now that the era of depth psychology is upon us) should not be obscure. Ambivalence is an obvious example, but is only the beginning. A football fumble brings groans from the stands, but it can add excitement and, if the ball is recovered, turn a routine play into a spectacular one. A couple recently recounted to me their experience with their child in a cancer ward. Their pain, through his pain in chemotherapy, was overridden by their gratitude, even exultancy, that such treatments now exist. I do not read the medieval doctrine of God's impassibility as unresponsiveness. It refers, rather, to God's capacity to "experience the evil as evil" (95) without losing his serenity and bliss (*ananda*). The differences in our two views remain, for one can be serene about a misfortune while wishing it had not occurred. And, because the God-of-process does so wish, his bliss will be less than that of the traditional God. But the point here is that Griffin knows well this most travelled of all the routes of theodicy, the route that situates evil in larger and ever larger contexts until the final one moves off canvas. He just pitches camp sooner than I do, not realizing that around the final bend ahead lies the complete vindication of the good as accomplished by the complete redemption of evil:

> . . . at the last,
> Do as the heavens have done, forget your evil;
> With them forgive yourself.
>
> (Shakespeare, *The Winter's Tale*)

Forget, not by putting the evil out of mind, but by seeing "at the last" that it never was such, so forgiveness is not even needed. Griffin would have as hard a time convincing an atheist that God's serenity and bliss are appropriate responses to "seeing people die of AIDS, watching a bloody battle, or observing the remains of thousands of people who were killed in death camps"—horrors that he uses against my position (94)—as I am having difficulty convincing him of the congruence for which I argue. But the line of argument he invokes—introducing larger contexts that place evil in perspective—is no different from the one I employ.

I do acknowledge, however, that Griffin's position is more conceptually accessible than mine; it is easier to imagine someone remaining serene in the face of calamities than to imagine him withholding the wish that they had not occurred. I even grant Griffin's point that my position holds moral dangers. Ancient Christians and Muslim texts have an apostle or companion saying something such as, "If I were to divulge all that I know, you would stone me." One of the disquieting signs that religion is becoming banal is the disappearance of the esoteric/exoteric distinction, with its contention that some truths are dangerous and should be reserved for initiates. I would not myself have initiated this debate which Griffin brought into being.

As with the section that preceded it, this section is in danger of exceeding acceptable bounds, but the key issues in Griffin's counterreply surface early. So I want to return to worldly evil as the chief phenomenological issue that separates me from Griffin, just as the chief epistemological and religious issues (treated in the preceding section) turned on the alleged neutrality of Whitehead's logical criteria of consistency and coherence.

Griffin, as he emphasizes, defines genuine evil as "anything, all things considered, without which the universe would have been better" and argues that "no one can consistently deny" its reality, for although it can be verbally denied, it will nevertheless be "presupposed in practice" (90-91). I have already registered my objection to this. What is ineluctably presupposed in practice, I contend, is an X in the world, called evil, that should be abhorred, condemned, and resisted with every ounce of energy we can muster—the full register of negative sentiments that mention of Auschwitz evokes. But that those sentiments (and yes, the victims' sufferings that prompt the sentiments) serve no constructive role in the divine economy—this metaphysical pronouncement is *not* presupposed in practice. What prescient power—the power to fathom the innermost recesses of other people's psyches—gives Griffin the right to say that no one can affirm (not just conceptually affirm, but affirm with his or her entire being, contrary, to be sure, to certain sentiments of the moment) the total rightness of things and at the same time *live* (*practice* is Griffin's word) a normally responsible life? A review of Tor Andre's *In the Garden of Murtles* points out that "trust in predestination moved the early Sufis, not to passivity as we might assume, but to action."[3] I do not know if Griffin would wish to pit the conduct of process theologians against that of the mystics, many of whom lived prodigiously active lives, or against that of the Buddha. What I can personally report is that I have not been aware of any increase in moral lassitude in my own life since deserting the process camp, although this too, I suppose, could be charged to the strength of early imprinting, or to self-deception.

How I reconcile such moral initiatives as I am capable of with God's omnipotence and untarnished beatitude I suggested in my first round, but let me reiterate. I do so in ways analogous to those of a Little Leaguer whose efforts would not be diminished by the realization (were he privy to it) that his parents' enjoyment of the afternoon—their pride in him and the way he is maturing—is not much affected by the issue that is uppermost in his mind: namely, will his team win or lose? The job of the Leager at that moment is to play ball, to give it his very best effort. And if he does not?—but let me drop the analogy. What if *I* do not live up to my moral best? All the *proximate* retributions Griffin faces await me as well: social reprisals, self-condemnation—the entire machinery of evil's disciplinary role stands ready to move in and make itself felt. But Griffin wants to say that these self-focused considerations are not enough; morality is undercut if my actions do not affect God. I am too much of a metaphysician myself to ask if history confirms him here—do atheists on balance behave worse than theists?—for I too believe that basic outlooks affect conduct. I realize, too, that his escape hatch ("they may *say* they disbelieve in God, but their actions belie the assertion") is matched by one of my own ("those who see perennialism as counselling sloth, misread it").

Consequently, because we both believe that ultimate as well as proximate considerations affect conduct, where does this leave us? As does Griffin, I believe that my life makes a difference to God; without me, God would not be infinite. But I do not believe that there is anything I can do that God is not able to transmute into perfect good; this is the esoteric reading of the Psalmist's exclamation: "Even the wrath of man shall praise him."

Beyond this, I have only two more things to say about evil. Coming back to the issue of motivation, it is important to see that evil, freedom, and selfhood must be taken together as belonging to the same package. Insofar as I take myself for a separate self—and practically speaking, who ever does otherwise?—I must accept freedom and evil as real in equal degree; to do otherwise is what Zen poet Gary Snyder called cheating. Whether within these mortal coils one ever *fully* exchanges soul (finite selfhood) for Spirit is not the question. The point is to keep the self/evil/freedom triad intact. Whether the three advance or recede in our self-estimate, they must do so together, in lockstep.[4]

The remaining point relates to a question Griffin appropriately raises (93). Even if one were to go along with "the principle of plenitude's" contention that being's infinitude requires a world in which all gradations of worth are instantiated—from seemingly inanimate matter right up to God—how are we to explain "imperfect examples of each kind (fallen angels, quirky quarks [and cancerous cells])? A good question; good enough to make me wonder whether it is permissible in discussions of this sort to confess that there are things about which one is unsure? Logically, I can repeat my appeal to the principle of plenitude and say that it requires not only that every possible gradient in kind be included, but equally, that all gradations within each kind must appear. Perennialism asserts this in its doctrine of God as All-Possibility, but I admit that my imagination is not equal to this concept. I have only the dimmest presentiment of its outworkings and retreat to the Koranic refrain, "It is easy with Allah."

III. Personal God, Transpersonal Absolute, and the Religions

God is most surely aware, and his awareness is most surely unified, which makes him personal in Griffin's definition of the word (108). But I continue (as in my first round) to find the word *personal* to be freighted with other connotations that fit God less well. I do not find it natural to speak even of electrons as persons, yet we resemble them much more than we resemble God. There are attributes of God, such as his love and responsiveness, which find ready analogues in our own experience; in carving these out of the divine infinity, I obtain my personal God—not a second God, but a limited aspect of the Godhead—which I would like to think I relate to as personally as Griffin relates to his God. And yet there remains the divine infinity which provides the backstop for this carve-out. When focusing on this infinity the emphasis is on God's difference from ourselves, and here I differ with Griffin. For although he, too, insists on differences, he is hobbled by the Whiteheadian shibboleth that God must not be an exception to metaphysical first principles. This requires that the differences he champions be differences in degree only; or, if the differences are of kind, they are formal and abstract, not concrete.[5] I, by contrast, believe that the differences separating the Godhead from human beings are concrete differences in kind. Moreover, I find that it is only differences of this sort that evoke in me full-fledged awe.[6] Differences of degree, as when time and space bottom out into their sidereal expanses, arouse intimations of awe—I find visits to a planetarium moderately awesome. But they do not leave me stupified and aghast as would a ghost if one were suddenly to materialize in my study and start dealing with me in ways I could not understand at all. My intent here is not to invoke the occult; it is to make a point. Whitehead set out to forge a set of categories that would account for everything. The metaphysician in me commends that project; we need to see things whole. But by insisting that that whole be rationally intelligible to the human mind—or where it is not, by leaving the remainder with a confession of ignorance rather than grappling with it religiously—Whitehead left too little room for regions of God that are *ganz anders,* radically other. Griffin will dispute this, to which I can only say (in anticipation) that *radical* has weaker and stronger meanings. I want its strongest meaning, in which God is emphatically an exception to metaphysical first principles insofar as these are derived from our normal experience and its extensions into science. Griffin opts for rationality; I for mysticism. Agreeing with W. T. Stace that "any writer who is honest about mysticism, as well as familiar with it, will know that it is utterly irreconcilable with all the ordinary rules of human thinking, that it blatantly breaches the laws of logic at every turn,"[7] I vehemently oppose the Whitehead/Griffin project of "rationalizing mysticism," while being prepared for Griffin's countercharge that I, for my part, mystify rationalism.

Having claimed that, instead of tabling the transrational as being simply unknown, I try to deal with it religiously, I should indicate how I do so. Here comes the "shred of analogy" for which Griffin reasonably asks (109).

I begin with standard theology: God is personal in possessing a unified experience that is responsive to all that is. But if I diagram the direction in which these considerations point my thoughts in this way, ↗, I find that I must oppose that arrow with another that points in the opposite direction: ↖ . This second arrow symbolizes the ways— concrete ways, and ways that differ in kind—in which God is *not* like us. He is timeless. He has no environment. His "unified experience" is unified to the point of being radically simple (I shall return to this), and so on. The point at which these two arrows eventually intersect is beyond our powers to imagine or even concretely conceive; this is God's ineffability. But because the point of convergence gathers into itself the contrapersonal considerations indicated by the leftward pointing arrow, there is reason to speak of the Godhead in its ineffable fullness as trans-personal. Whether this qualifies as a kind of panentheism, I leave to Griffin to decide.

That is the logic of the matter, but because it holds in tension considerations that conflict with one another, it is not easy to apply it to concrete issues without giving too much emphasis to one side or the other. Thus, I understand how my assertion that "in the last analysis God is not the kind of God who loves [humans]" would give Griffin trouble (109). It troubles me as well if I let slip the qualifier "in the last analysis," so let me explain again what that analysis unfolds. God's love is never in question; the issue relates not to God but to ourselves as *objects* of that love. Etymologically, an object is something that stands in front of something else (as in "pro*ject*"), or against something that is other than itself (as in "I ob*ject*"). Now, what if—as the very opposite of being irrelevant to God, as Griffin takes impassibility to mean—we are so *constitutive* of God (because the infinite without the finite would not be such) that the distinction becomes formal rather than experiential?—a courtesy distinction, we might say. What if, in the phrase Griffin happily introduces (115), we are "distinguishable but not separable" from God? Do I love my heart? If I think of it as something other than myself, I can be grateful to it as a distinct organ and for what it does for me, but I find such language strange. The infinite cannot be unaware of the finite, and (being unalloyed love) its love must permeate the finite. When our attention is on ourselves, we reach out for these features of the divine, rejoicing in them and drawing strength from them. But the more our attention shifts from ourselves to God, the more his attributes that differ radically and qualitatively from our own preempt the scene. "Know[ing] and lov-[ing] his creatures" (109) is not then what we experience him as doing because we, his creatures, have retired from the scene. Not God in her relation to us, but God as she is in herself, in her self-contained, effulgent glory, preempts our entire attention.

For Griffin, if the object falls from view, love does too, but I do not find this to be the case. We have come to see that, unlike fear, anxiety has no specific object, but the noetic counterpart of this has not been equally noticed. "What positive ingredient of 'knowledge' is left if we say there is nothing other . . . to know?", Griffin asks (109). Self-knowledge, I answer. And to his sequel question, "What positive ingredient of 'love' is left if there are no others to love?", the answer is: love as a character trait—as when we speak of "a loving person," without the beneficiaries of this love being in mind at all.

I continue to be dissatisfied with Griffin's dual ultimates, but what he now says (113)—especially his reemphasis of the point that creativity is abstract and therefore "not an agent which can create"—helps me to see more clearly how different are the ways in which we approach the metaphysical project. Riding the inbuilt human outreach for the one, I seek in metaphysics the single concrete reality that causes and thereby accounts for all that is. Griffin proceeds otherwise. Following Whitehead, he scrolls before himself as much of human experience as he can bring to view, and then proceeds to accommodate it to the smallest possible number of conceptual principles which, once they are isolated and interrelated, thereafter explain the full panoply.[8] He gets those explanatory principles down to four—the metaphysical ultimate (creativity), the axiological ultimate (God), eternal objects or pure possibilities, and finite actual beings (114)—and I do not question the magnitude of that achievement, given the object it sets for itself; it may indeed instance abstractive powers that, on that continuum, rival Einstein's, as Griffin, following Hartshorne, claims for Whitehead (143). But these multiple ultimates lead to curious sayings, such as "God does not create creative experience . . . because . . . How can creativity be created" (113)? Why not say, simply, that God *is* creative experience?

I can see the whole of process metaphysics poised to pounce on that statement, but we cannot go on deploying our entire systems at every turn, so let me try something different. Stepping back for a page from the presiding give-and-take of this book, let me insert a paragraph from Lord Northbourne that shows (with greater force than I could muster in equal space) how differently the metaphysical problem takes shape *for me*. It will be seen, I believe, that my approach turns more on intuitive credentials than on the rational arguments to which Griffin appeals.

Nothing is without a cause, so that behind every apparent cause lies another cause, until in the end one arrives at an ultimate cause. There cannot be a plurality of ultimate causes[9] in a single universe, though that universe be limitless in extent and in variety; for if there were more than one, either they would not be ultimate, being related one to another through the universe in question as all secondary causes are, or there would be a plurality of universes each having no relation to or communication with any other. The first alternative brings us back to where we started, and the second has no intelligible significance; therefore the ultimate cause is single. There can be any number of secondary causes, some of which may be, in relation to particular beings or situations, "relatively ultimate"; but these secondary causes and all things derived from them are permanently present either in act or in potentiality, in the single ultimate cause which is therefore absolute and indivisible plenitude, without distinction or relativity, subjectivity or objectivity; it is therefore wholly beyond any comparison and is not picturable or nameable. Yet, since by definition it comprehends all possibilities, the possibilities of distinction, separation or imperfection are not excluded from it, despite the fact that they apparently contradict its singleness; such contradiction cannot however be otherwise than illusory. Existence, etymologically a "standing apart" from the cause as well as from other things that exist, is the manifestation of those apparently contradictory possibilities; existence derives all its reality, not from itself, but from the cause that it appears to contradict. In other words the distinctiveness of all observable and specifiable things arises, not from something that belongs to them, but from the degree and kind of their deprivation. The chain of causality that leads from the cause by way of a succession of deprivations is continuous, so that nothing loses its connection with the cause; if it did so, it would cease to be; but every fresh link in the chain implies a new specification, equivalent to a new kind of obscuration or forgetfulness of the cause, a new veil of illusion between it and man who, as tradition teaches, was created last and in the image of God. In this sense, then, man himself as a distinctive being, and all that he knows as well, are but deprivation, forgetfulness and illusion; yet man alone can aspire to dispel the illusion, to see things as they are, to perfect himself.[10]

The language is uncompromising, but the statement is useful, I think, to underscore how differently Griffin and I approach the metaphysical question, and how modest, therefore, should be our expectations of the extent to which rational arguments can unite us. Even so, they can do something, so I revert to that genre by noting that Griffin's statement that his four irreducibles—God, creativity, possibilities, and finite entities—"are distinguishable but not separable" (115), seems promising. I too say that the Godhead (as infinite) entails what is other than itself (the finite), thereby creating (in the sense of giving rise to) what is other than its infinitude. Possibilities—all possibilities, as the statement just quoted points out—are actualized within it. And finitude is required, inasmuch as without it the infinite would not be such. But for me, the three derivatives are *aspects* of the one concrete universal, the God-head. Although Griffin tells me that he has said why (113), I continue not to see why he does not likewise regard his other three as God's attributes. I suppose the reason is that "ultimate" for him has only temporal-spatial meaning—*"furthest"* (115)[11]—and he sees no way to argue that God causes or accounts for the other three: "it would be nonsensical to speak of one of [Whitehead's four "ultimates"] as producing the others, as if it could have existed prior to them" (114). But causes need not be temporally prior to their effects. A table that causes a vase to stand above the floor need not be older than the vase, nor even (in principle) precede the supporting role we find it serving when we enter the room. "Of course, we dare not talk of generation in time, dealing as we are with eternal Beings," Plotinus tells us. "Were we to speak of origin in such reference, it is in the sense, merely, of cause and subordination."[12]

"What is power that is not power *in relation* to something else?", Griffin asks rhetorically (115). Agreed, but the "something else" need not be a separate entity that is equally actual. (I see Whitehead committing his own famed "fallacy of misplaced concreteness" by crediting finite entities with as much concreteness—actuality—as the infinite possesses.) We speak of having the power to move our limbs, but I do not think Griffin would want to deny that those limbs are in an important respect ourselves. I assume that he would fall back here on his "distinguishable but not separable" phrase.

Respecting the final issue Griffin introduces in this section, I do not see any great difference in our attitude toward the world's religions. I see little resemblance between Shankara's concrete nirguna Brahman and Griffin's abstract creative experience (and for comparable reasons categorically reject Griffin's characterization of my position as holding that "God is identical with the metaphysical absolute" [119] if that absolute is Griffin's), but neither of us claims that the religions are exact copies of one another. We both give some weight to the different human collectivities through which the sole God works, and neither of us wishes to privilege one religion over the others. The differences that most interest Griffin are *between* religions ("they do not *really* worship the 'same God' " [118-19]), whereas I spot the differences *within* each religion (depending on whether folk polytheism, the personal God, or the transpersonal Godhead is stage center). Griffin sees the worship of alternative "Gods" as generating different kinds of wholeness and fulfillment (salvations), which seems right provided we do not overlook commonalities that lead us to recognize them all as salvific. The commonalities strike me as more important than the differences,[13] but in this context we can waive that as a fielder's choice.

Having addressed the main topics of this section, I now address several dangling points.

Simplicity. Griffin follows Hartshorne's "true" reading of this concept, which is that "God does have personal attributes, but they are not distinct from one another," and sets this against my formulation wherein (as he quotes me) "the divine . . . dispenses with differences . . . without forfeiting any of the positive virtues, which at lower levels of being are parceled into separate faculties or components" (110). So far I do not see the difference, although I am sure that if Griffin were to press me it would become clear that I have a stronger reading of simplicity than he does. Agreeing with Plotinus, for example, that "in perfect knowing, subject and object are identical,"[14] I stand by my claim that the Godhead is "without qualities"—in the plural, *nota bene*—because within it "attributes [again in the plural, are] transcended." Because Griffin considers such wording ill-advised diction which I "should not use" (112), only provisionally is it appropriate to speak of "the Smith-Hartshorne conception of the divine simplicity."

In one passage, our positions draw very close: "The universe," Griffin writes, "is not simply a derivative, external product, but is more of an emanation [a word perennialists like], in which the infinite realm of possibilities [I would say actualities] within God are being unfolded [I would say, are eternally unfolded]. We should look at the world about us not as an external creation of a separate divine being but as a manifestation of its divine ground and center which is dialectically identical with it. That is, God both is and is not identical with the world" (111).

If I may be allowed the transpositions that I insert in brackets, I likewise agree that "the idea of a solitary One, a God [the Infinite Godhead] existing all alone without a world [the finite], . . . makes no sense" (117). And, given my ultimate denial of time, Griffin should not expect me to disagree when he says that, "The idea that God [I again substitute Godhead] has always existed but that a world of finite actualities came into existence once upon a time makes no [ultimate] sense" either (117).

IV. TIME, SOCIAL PROGRESS, GNOSTIC DUALISM, AND IMMORTALITY

Can "the temporal process . . . contribute anything of ultimate value to the divine reality?" Yes, for without it, the Infinite would not be such. Whether the slippage is in my writing or Griffin's reading, it is not the case that I do "not allow . . . the . . . experiences and achievements of human beings, and . . . the other species . . . to contribute anything to God's perfection" (123). Nor should I say what Griffin attributes to me: that because time has no ultimate reality, it therefore "has . . . no importance" (121). Together with everything else that is finite, it contributes to the divine economy which would be poorer, because not infinite, without it. Griffin is right, however, in assuming that, in my view, "what occurs in the temporal process [cannot detract] from the divine perfection" (121).[15]

My restiveness with the way my words come back at me through Griffin's reading of them helps me to see that I should be more cautious in echoing the mystics' conclusions about the unreality of time. I invariably insert the qualifier *"ultimately* unreal," and because this announces a two-tiered universe, I take it for granted that time is incontrovertibly real on the tier we directly inhabit. But for those who do not accept that distinction, I can see how misunderstandings could arise, so let me introduce a point I have not stated explicitly thus far, allowing J. N. Findlay to make it for me. "If finite distinctions [temporal distinctions are the ones in focus at the moment] can be thought to 'vanish' in certain ultimate attenuations," he writes,

> this is a vanishing in which what vanishes must be retained *qua* vanished, and must be intrinsically capable of a full reappearance. Certainly there must be a profound identification yonder [in the Absolute], to which it is however essential that it should be the point of convergence of distinct routes . . . . Dear St Teresa in her accounts of her relations to her Divine Friend here obviously strikes the correct, the experienced note: their encounters were like a light temporarily losing itself in a larger light, and yet afterwards resuming its separateness, or like water in some vessel temporarily losing itself in a larger body of water from which it could again be taken. It would be a rash and superficial interpreter who would see anything really different in the *Tat tvam asi* of the Upanishats [*sic*].[16]

Such explications may show finitude to have more status in the scheme of things than abbreviated phrases such as "ultimately unreal" suggest, but they do not affect the basic issue of whether time is in the world, or the world is in time. For me, time is in the world. It issues (causally, not temporally) from the infinite, and though in regions of that infinite it is encountered sequentially, the infinite Godhead prehends it at a glance. In that Godhead, the present, which to us is a pinched focus, achieves an all-embracing momentariness, the *punctum stans* of the Schoolmen. All happening is present in a single drop of realization; a single pulse of experience covers the entire expanse. We can no more imagine what this is like than a dog can imagine how human beings can comprehend fifteen billion light years in a thought, but we do have analogies. Traversing the edge of a table, a beetle must take in its points successively, whereas we can subsume them instantaneously. Or again, having read a story, its story line is with us atemporally, although the action sequences that we initially encountered successively are all together *there*. Because these analogies do little more than *suggest* timeless time—only faintly and infrequently do they open us to the experience of it—Griffin will not let them get off the ground. From the fact that "*our* experience is . . . temporal," he concludes that "experience as such [is] temporal" and asks what basis we have for assuming the contrary (123-24). My answer is twofold. First, because we assume that subhuman animals have less purchase on eternity than we do—they cannot grasp eternal truths—what reason have we to assume that the sequence stops with us? Second, we have the testimony of the mystics—an incredible library comprehending all climes and history.

I have said that time is derivative, but to return to an earlier point, this is a different issue from whether it had a beginning. Scientists currently tend to think that it did,[17] but Griffin points out that they only work with our cosmic epoch, which (in keeping with the Hindu "bubble gum" cosmology) could be but one in an endless sequence. I agree with Griffin on that point, but we differ as to whether, if time always was, that settles the matter, leaving it without need of further explanation. As we saw in the last section, for Griffin explanation does stop there, because if reality was never without a given feature, that feature needs, and indeed can receive, no further account. I confess to bafflement as to why, or even how, a philosopher can say that. In the preceding section, Griffin gives us his reasons, but they connect so little with my metaphysical instincts that I do not know how to respond to them.[18] It is a low blow to say that even Alan Watts had things better positioned when he began a lecture by defining a philosopher as someone who is puzzled by why there is something rather than nothing. Why do not physicists simply assume that there have always been four fundamental forces in nature and stop trying to reduce them to one? How does Griffin explain the lively little homunculi in their heads that keep shouting, "There's *got* to be one. That the four have always been around is no explanation."

If I cannot see that ubiquity settles anything—how could it, when for me *everything* has "always been" in the Godhead—Griffin is for his part baffled as to why I think the Godhead is timeless. Not on grounds of proofs, I need hardly say, insofar as these stem from the deliverances of everyday experience. My "reasons" derive from the reports of my "intellect," which (in my technical sense of that word) I have ventured to compare with Griffin's "vision"; Whitehead sounds their note well when, in beginning the final part of *Process and Reality,* he writes: "There is nothing here in the nature of proof . . . . Any cogency of argument entirely depends upon elucidation of somewhat exceptional elements in our conscious experience—those elements which may roughly be classed together as religious and moral intuitions."[19] Some things about time make it as impervious to understanding as it is threatening to our lived lives. Whitehead counters the most obvious of its threats—the perpetual perishing of experience, Kronos devouring his own children—by positing God's unfading memory. I turn the same intuitive faculties that produced Whitehead's axiological ultimate onto the unsettling features of time in its future tense to conclude that a robust God should not have to put up with those either. "Here is rest unbroken: for how can that seek change, in which all is well; what need that reach to, which holds all within itself; what increase can that desire which stands utterly achieved," Plotinus reports.[20] There is not space here to work out the whys-and-wherefores of his conclusion—which is (after all) the burden of the entire Platonic tradition in the West and virtually all of India, to cite only the obvious instances—so let me appeal to another quotation that sounds the general note. Speaking of Whitehead's cosmology specifically, but in the context of the entire nineteenth- and twentieth-century inflation of time beyond its due proportions, Windham Lewis writes:

> In this eternal manufacturing of a God . . . you co-operate, but in such a negligible way that you would be a great fool indeed to take much notice of that privilege. Looked at from the simplest human level, as a semi-religious faith, the Time-cult seems far less effective, when properly understood, than those cults which posit a Perfection already existing, eternally there, of which we are humble shadows. It would be a very irrational conceit which, if it were given the choice, would decide for the 'emergent' Time-god, it seems to me, in place, for instance, of the God of [traditional theism]. With the latter you have an achieved coexistent supremacy of perfection, impending over all your life.[21]

In the eyes of God, all is eternally well, eternally complete. *Consumatum est.* "*They* shall be changed," the Psalmist tells us, "but thou art the same" (101:27-28); and the Gospel of John repeats the thought: "Before Abraham was, I [God] *am*" (8:58). Not that the Godhead remains fixed and static like a stone, for fixity and stasis are temporal concepts, implying, as they do, a sameness that persists through time.[22] Meister Eckhart hits the right note, I believe, when he writes that "if God is God, He has it from His immutability,"[23] for aspiration is by nature uneasy. Accomplishment, being completed, is at perfect peace.

Whereas time is in God, history is in time, and I welcome Griffin's invitation to say less ambiguously whether I think history qualitatively improves or progresses. Complex forms of life on this planet arrived late in its history, so there is at least that line, or succession of dots, that angles upward. Even here there is enough ambiguity to cause Stephen Gould to insist that it is a mistake to think that natural selection works generally for the best; but be that as it may, human history exhibits no counterpart to the successive appearance of increasingly complex bodies. Or rather, because civilizations are more complex than tribes, their complexities do not host unambiguous qualitative advances. In history, currents of progress struggle against currents of decline amidst many holding patterns. Rousseau's "noble savage" was a fiction, but I have had glimpses of tribal life which, when I match them against some of the horrors of modernity, exempt me from the superstitious regard for civilization and progress that has dominated the modern West and now dominates most of the world. This has nothing to do with the fact that there are always things affecting the future that need to be done, and woe be to those who fail to put their shoulders to the wheel. The question is whether the essential needs, responsibilities, and potentialities of the human person, or for that matter, the general tenor of the quality of life, now differ fundamentally from what they have always been.

Griffin might agree that overall or "net" historical progress, as I called it in the first round, is indemonstrable, and still argue for it as an article of faith. There is something to this; stout-hearted souls "who never turn their backs but march breast forward, not doubting that the clouds will break" (Browning, slightly garbled), spark courage in us all. But when we scrutinize their creed, we see that, although *hope* is a requisite for life, only an uncompromising naturalism need situate hope on the horizontal, historical plane. Moreover, although historical hope can energize, it also has its shadow side. Some people use it as an escape from their present troubles, drawing imaginary lines across the path of time beyond which their current troubles will cease. More serious is the way abstract, utopian hopes for the future can exact concrete sacrifices from the present. "Who is this Moloch," the Russian Alexander Herzen asked as he reflected as early as 1848 on the new form of human sacrifice that the modern hope-for-progress gave rise to, the sacrifice of living human beings on the altar of abstract ideologies. "Who is this Moloch who, as the toilers approach him, instead of rewarding them, only recedes, and as a consolation to the exhausted, doomed multitudes crying '*morituri te salutant,*' can give back only the mocking answer that after their death all will be beautiful on earth?" All good ideas can be perverted, of course, and Griffin is not proposing an explicit ideology. But if the essence of ideology is the black-and-white contrast between its promises and the current state of affairs, I am fearful of the ways in which, and extent to which, preoccupation with progress can conduce to ideological thinking in this generic sense. D. H. Lawrence is only one who has warned of the way the ideal can poison the real.

Modernity can all but be defined by its transference of faith from God to historical progress. Postmodernity can all but be defined by the collapse of that faith, as our century has witnessed millions slaughtered in wars and revolutions—gas chambers, gulags, genocide, all the monstrosities for which our century will be remembered. Griffin wants to retain modernity's faith in progress in his version of postmodernism. If I do not jump to his support in this, it is because:

1. Empirically, I do not see either natural or human history proclaiming that progress is built into their matrices. Progress is a claim of faith, not a factual deliverance.
2. I do not see that human hope is contingent on that faith.
3. Neither do I think the faith is requisite for responsible action.
4. For some persons it may be requisite, but for every such person there is another who will pervert the idea for purposes of ideology or escapism. It is best, therefore, that historical progress be omitted from our collective creed. This differs from asserting that it will not occur. It simply holds back from banking on its occurring, on grounds that the perversions such banking can produce are as great as the energies it can inspire.

Griffin asks for clarification of my assertion that "Utopia is a dream, evolution a myth" (126). Its first half I stand by unequivocally. The second appeared in a context where the word *evolution* was vectored by its Darwinian meaning, only a fraction of which I consider true.[24]

I concede that my reference to Coue was inappropriate, as Griffin says (126), but as I turn now from time to what Griffin considers "the deeper issue between us [in this section], . . . the contrast between Smith's individualism and the social or ecological viewpoint" that informs his Whiteheadian vision (126), I find it difficult to see how my position, which holds that in actuality—full actuality—there *is* no individual self, can be labelled individualistic. How can a psychology in which the *jiva* or individual soul is ultimately *maya* (as in Vedanta) or *anatta* (as in Buddhism) be said to "presuppose the Cartesian doctrine of the soul" (127)?

Drawing symbolic support as it does from the nonlocality of quantum mechanics, Whitehead's socially textured self is incomparably richer than the sterile model of Descartes. It may be, however, that science is now moving toward a cosmology that would suggest that the present sharpness in which we experience our personal identities is more provisional than even Whitehead suspected. Now that super-computers are enabling us to handle the mathematics of electromagnetic forces that are thirty-nine orders of magnitude stronger than the gravitational ones that give meaning to mass and matter, the model of the three-dimensional universe that is emerging is one in which a cosmic microwave background pervades all space. Because individual entities do not "show" in this plasma background, the view suggests that the present sharpness in which we experience our personal identities may be more provisional than even Whitehead supposed. We may be less integumented and discrete than he suspected.

Gnostic dualism. Griffin sees me as succumbing to this heresy because "from Smith's perspective . . . the evolutionary process does not seem necessary . . . for the production of . . . the human soul" (128). On the contrary, I believe that it was necessary as a secondary cause. The question of whether "souls *could* be directly created (or emanated) apart from such bodies" diverts us from the question at hand to the subtle issue of the divine necessity (see my note 15), so instead of going into that I simply say that so far as we are privy to what went on, God apparently "chose" not to dispense with secondary causes.

I bow axiomatically to Griffin's reading of Whitehead, so stand corrected by his indication that, far from siding with Darwinian gradualism, Whitehead anticipated the punctuational equilibriumism of Eldridge and Gould. The sentence that Griffin quotes in support of that point—the one in which Whitehead describes God's superjective aim as "that power in history which implants into the form of process, belonging to each historical epoch, the character of a drive toward some ideal, to be realized within that period" (129)—interests me in an additional way in making me wonder if it can be used as a link to the preceding issue of gnosticism. Are we entitled to see the power Whitehead refers to here as the counterpart of the "Platonic forms" that I posit as entering history to account for the succession of species we find appearing in the fossil record?[25]

On the final topic of this section, immortality, Griffin notes that here, at least, I acknowledge "progress in the temporal process," and suggests that I "emphasize this side of [the primordial] vision" (129-30). I am prepared to do this as long as it is clearly understood: first, that the progress is one that each soul must effect for himself or herself; and second, that it occurs within the temporal process, not the Godhead. But within the temporal process, it can, and does occur. "Even the weariest river/Winds somewhere safe to sea" (Swinburne).

V. PRIMORDIAL, PREMODERN, AND POSTMODERN

Griffin makes two points in this section: that I am confused and mistaken. To begin with the "confusion": while metaphysicians describe *realities* they think are unchanging, I succumb to the *non sequitur* that *their descriptions* of those realities are unchanging (132).

It is true, of course, that their descriptions change all the time. Moreover, there can be vast derailings, of which Western metaphysics since the Middle Ages is a glaring instance. But two distinctions must be introduced: between truth and error; and between fundamental assessments and secondary accommodations. Modern metaphysics, being (on the whole) a lapse, is accounted for by the first of these distinctions; while metaphysical differences prior to Descartes are explained by the second.

Utilizing these two distinctions, perennialism claims that there is a fundamental assessment of things which, being true, is timeless and spaceless—it is primordial or all-pervading. It is not just that the *things depicted* in this assessment are timeless and spaceless; the *assessment,* too, is such. That claim cannot be read in a strictly universal way; to repeat: because not everyone sees the truth, there will always and everywhere be deviant, competing worldviews. And if massive forces (such as modern science or a police state) obtrude, they can strike history with sufficient force to throw entire epochs off course, driving the perennial philosophy underground where it flows for a time as a hidden, if vital, subterranean stream. Even so, it *survives*—additional testament to its ubiquity.

To say it as clearly as I can: There is a Way that things fundamentally and unchangingly (metaphysically) are. Human collectivities have never been without a grasp of that Way. The perennial philosophy is the articulation of that grasp. As such, it is everywhere to be found (keeping in mind the qualifications that I have entered).

So much for confusion: there is no confusion whatsoever. I believe in timeless truth, not because I overlook Griffin's distinction "between (1) the kinds of truths metaphysicians seek and (2) the attempts of metaphysicians to formulate these truths" (132). I believe in such truth because I think that the attempts of certain metaphysicians to discern them succeeded.

Griffin rejects this possibility and, doing so, rejects concomitantly perennialism's self-designation. (Confusion is now behind us and we are into the charge of mistake.) For replacement, Griffin proposes "premodern," which repudiates the claim in the original designation. Denying that the content of perennialism is universal, Griffin pegs that content to a historical period, the one that preceded modernity, while conceding that certain parts of it are sufficiently true to be retained in his postmodern platform. His rechristening carries a surface plausibility because, being timeless, the perennial was indeed present before modernity appeared. But because (as it sees things) it will also be present after modernity disappears, its early surfacing is not the point. One can reject perennialism, but to change its name as Griffin does is to turn it into a different animal. We are no longer talking about the same thing.

This should make it plain that, far from thinking "that the difference between [our outlooks] is at most a difference in degree," I am as adamant as Griffin in asserting "that there is a real difference between the two visions" (131). So what mistake do I see Griffin making in this section?

For the primordial, he looks first not to metaphysical content, but to *criteria* for determining such content. These he finds in his "hardcore commonsense ideas," which cannot be denied in practice (133). I say "his" such ideas, because it was the burden of my opening section in this chapter that the ideas he puts forward under this rubric are not in fact universal; he puts partisan, parochial spins on them. Or, more precisely, they are ambiguous in a way that makes them useless. Defined loosely enough to qualify as common sense, Griffin's "hard-core commonsense ideas" are too amorphous to adjudicate between competing metaphysical claims. (I respect the claims of time, freedom, and evil in the commonsense ways they come at us as fully as Griffin does.) But when Griffin sharpens those claims to the point where they have metaphysical bite, they cease to be primordial. In that form, it is not surprising that Griffin does "not find . . . that all the ideas considered primordial truths by Smith pass [his] test" (133). The test is weighted against perennialism from the start.

Turning the tables on me, Griffin legitimately asks what my criterion for discerning primordial truths is (133). This, too, I addressed at the start of this round, so need only repeat here that I do not believe that there *are* criteria that can be precisely formulated in independence of the data on which they are brought to bear. We must move directly to Griffin's "vision" and my "intellect," comparing their deliverances as we have been doing in this book in the faith that the common organ we designate by these alternative words will guide us incrementally to where truth lies.

VI. SCIENCE AND THEOLOGY

Griffin equates science with knowing, whereas I think of it as a certain *kind* of knowing. This difference naturally leads us to position theology differently in relation to it.

Because Griffin's definition of science sounds odd to me, I want to quote his exact words, which are: "the term *science* does mean simply knowing, or knowledge" (139). This sounds odd because we normally think of knowledge as including kinds that we do not call (or think of as being) scientific. Quite apart from whether revelation imparts knowledge, our culture's noetic standard-bearer, "The College of Arts and Sciences," points by its very name to noetic domains that science does not embrace. In the medieval university, mathematics and astronomy and geometry were classed among the seven "liberal arts," thereby making art the inclusive category. Griffin wants to reverse this by moving science to that position.

Although in the statement that I quoted, Griffin claims that his usage is descriptive, he for the most part recognizes the programmatic drive in his definition, because he grants that "we have . . . long accepted the term *science* for one method of knowing, applicable only to a limited range of objects." In fact, he proceeds to point out, we have accepted that restricted meaning of the word "for so long . . . that it is difficult at first to imagine using [science] in an inclusive way to cover all our forms of knowing and their results" (139). So why does Griffin want us to come to use it in that inclusive way?

I suspect two reasons. The first of these rides a suppressed qualifier in his initial claim that *science* means "simply knowing, or knowledge." As just noted, his shift from this purportedly descriptive definition to a normative one—what science should mean—shows his recognition that currently, at least, science does not mean knowledge *per se*. It does, however, mean somthing fairly close to that, namely effective knowledge. That science has changed the traditional world into the modern one is proof positive that it is effective. And because we all want to be effective—and want human actions generally to be effective so we can cope with the considerable problems than confront us—we want knowledge to become effective across the board. Which is to say, we want all knowledge to become scientific.

Alongside this psychological, cultural drift, I think I see a philosophical consideration that points Griffin in his chosen direction. Having, in company with modernity generally, shifted his gaze from our world's source—a creator God or emanating Godhead—to that world itself, Griffin approaches that world epistemologically. Sensitive to our need to see life whole, he searches for a single categoreal scheme that will accommodate everything; in his own words, he tries "to understand reality in terms of one set of categories" (138). Insofar as we fail in this quest, we live in the incoherence of which dualism (the topic of the next section) is a glaring, confessed instance.

This, as I say, seems to be what Griffin is reaching for. If all knowledge were scientific, it would be effective and enable us to *manage* the world—more at least than we now can. And secondly, our world would *cohere*.

The rub (as I see it) is that the "progress" he hopes for here (to throw a bridge back to section four) is not going to happen. In the charge we both hurl at each other, Griffin's program is unrealistic. He thinks that mine is unrealistic in its attempt to post "no trespassing signs" beyond which science may not go, but no one is doing that. I am not drawing a line beyond which science *may not* go. I am calling attention to a line beyond which it *cannot* go—not and remain publically effective. That line is the one that is laid down by the controlled experiment. Effective knowledge is knowledge that enables us to control. And because we can control only what is inferior to us—in Griffin's language: nonindividuated entities or individuated ones whose freedom is negligible—effective knowledge (and with it the word *science* in its now-regulative meaning) stops with the hard, exact sciences. I oversimplify: the line wavers here and there, as in the social sciences. But the logic is clear.

So Griffin's program will not succeed. Knowledge is not going to become (objectively, externally as in technology) efficacious across the board, and because efficaciousness is now pivotal in what we have come to mean by science, our language is going to continue to do what Griffin does not want it to do—to "accept . . . the term *science* for one method of knowing." Additionally, there are dangers in trying to make the term work otherwise. As I pointed out in my first round, if we try to think of extrascientific realities in scientific ways, consciously or unconsciously we will be inclined *to approach them* in scientific ways, which is to say, ways that render our knowing efficacious. Because God cannot be accommodated to this move, theology that proceeds in this vein will not come very close to God.

Turning to Griffin's critique of my views on this subject: he points out that science includes more than the controlled experiment. It certainly does. Generic science—the thread that runs through all science, premodern as well as modern—centers in careful observation of natural phenomena to discern their regularities. What modern science adds to this, as the consummate way to spot deep, underlying regularities that are not evident to the naked eye, is the controlled experiment. It is the effectiveness of this new mode of discernment that has moved the pivotal meaning of the word *science* from knowledge to effective knowledge.

Griffin thinks my assignment of "the whole" to theology and "a part" to science gives the former the lion's share. But only abstractly; science has its day in the efficacious way that it can move in on its restricted province. As Oliver Wendell Holmes once said, "science offers major help on minor problems, while religion offers minor help on major problems." Mutual respect, stemming from a fair exchange.

Griffin's remaining points relate to details. That "no one has touched or seen an electron, let alone a quark or a neutrino" (135) does not alter the fact that science deals almost exclusively with what is visible or tangible (under whatever requisite orders of magnification). Those microscopic entities enter science through being entailed by the visible or tangible.

"Smith accepts Darwinian evolutionary theory as scientific" (136). Not so. I accept the fossil record, but not Darwin's explanation for increasing complexity.[26]

"Smith's . . . part/whole relationship is not intelligible if the categories used by science and theology are different in kind" (137). Griffin's statement here is based on this interpretation: "Theology for Smith speaks in terms of downward causation . . . while science for him speaks exclusively in terms of upward causes." But I do not think that science speaks exclusively of upward causes; biologists deal routinely with teleonomies. All that science requires is that teleonomic organisms themselves originate through upward causation. My general reply to Griffin on this point is that, if science's upward causation can account for things that then work downward, there is no reason why God could not intentionally and purposively work downward to create regions of reality (the material world) wherein secondary causes work upward.

Regarding Griffin's response to my quotation of Don Cupitt (137): What Cupitt concluded to be shallow was the view that we were created by both God and evolution *as Darwin propounded it*; Cupitt explicitly refers to Darwinism twice in that short quotation. When I, for my part, ventured compatibility, it was between God's creative activity and certain limited aspects of evolutionary theory. Its claim that the more complex organisms came later is the obvious example.

"Smith believes that . . . science will . . . indefinitely remain . . . reductionistic" (138). In practice, yes, in the sense that it will (and should) continue to try to explain the complex in terms of the simple, that being the route that brings control. Strictly speaking, though, reductionism is a philosophic concept and therefore stands outside science. Scientists need not claim that their attempt succeeds, or that it tells the whole story.

Having argued uncompromisingly that science can disclose nothing that is superior to us, let me conclude this section by admitting that there may be one exception to this rule. If the so-called Anthropic Principle is more than a tautology—or perhaps a Kantian regulative principle that governs the way we think—we may be in for the noetic surprise of our age. Stephen Hawking says that the probability of there being a universe that supports life is in the order of absolute zero. It is going to be very interesting if the discipline that wrote the denial of final causes into its very charter emerges at the other end of its tunnel vision with the verdict that its findings *require* such a cause to round out its account. The conclusion would be formal; it would assert no more than that a Final Cause exists. But backed (as it would be) by the kind of knowledge that has come to persuade us most, the finding would be momentous.

VII. DUALISM, SUPERNATURALISM, AND PHILOSOPHICAL UNITY

With my transposition of Griffin's first two topics in this second round, we return in this last section to the issue that I jumped to first place: the issue of unity.

Griffin begins this section with an irony: the (to him) "surprising" fact that I charge his position with lacking unity—for having two (if not four) ultimates—when, in his words, "almost all my criticisms of Smith's position are due to what I see as a lack of unity in it" (142).

This *is* ironical, but it is also useful. For it uncovers yet another controlling reason for why Griffin and I see things differently, one that I had not seen while I was writing even the first sections of this very chapter wherein the issue of unity was stage center. Griffin points me toward this deep reason for our difference when he writes, "We have two quite different intuitions about the type of unity that philosophic throught seeks" (143). For whereas I look for unity in "a single, self-sufficient origin" from which all else derives, Griffin looks (with Hartshorne) for "a single, all-encompassing principle" in terms of which to understand the world. He considers his to be the "better exemplification of the type of unity sought by science and philosophy," and I agree if he is speaking of *modern* philosophy. But I consider that epistemological type of unity superficial compared with the premodern, ontological type. For though an "encompassing principle" brings the world to focus, providing (as it does) coherence for the way we see it, it does not explain, or try to explain, why the world is the way it is. It stops with description rather than pressing on to explanation. As for the "host of dualisms, formal and substantive" (143), that Griffin sees issuing from my position, they can be brushed aside, for internally, seen from inside that position, their referents are as mutually entailing as are Griffin's categories. It is as Griffin says: "Only ... dualisms ... in which the relationship between the two types of things is so defined as to make the posited relationship seem unintelligible ... are vicious" (144). And Griffin and I have different intelligibles.

Gratifyingly, this discussion ends with a breakthrough for me. Actually, several have occurred along the way, but let me repeat this concluding one. *Unity* for Griffin is epistemological; it resides in a single set of interrelated categories that can make intelligible, and in this sense account for, the entirety of human experience. For me the presiding unity is ontological. Its referent is an actuality—the One, Absolute, Ultimate, Infinite, Reality—from which all else proceeds. Griffin and I both have our one and our many. In fact, heightening the irony with which he begins this section, both of our unities are fourfold. His four are the categories of God, creativity, eternal objects, and the structure of actual occasions, which are united by mutual entailment, while mine are four levels of reality, which are united because the greater include the lesser and attenuate the divisions between them.

NOTES

1. See my "The Crisis in Philosophy," *Behavior* 16/1 (Spring 1988), 51-56.

2. This is the issue (raised in chapter 3) of whether God should be an exception to metaphysical principles secularly derived.

3. Philosophers Spinoza and Hobbes, and theologians Calvin and Edwards, are but four redoubtable thinkers who argued (and demonstrated) that beliefs in determinism and predestination need not counter exertion. And current philosophers of mind, such as Daniel Dennett, contend that determinism makes no difference to human freedom.

4. Because I speak elsewhere about evil and selfhood but say little about freedom, let me state unequivocally here the freedom side of our paradoxical human situation by registering the obvious. By our very nature, we are incorrigibly deliberative. Instant by instant we are doomed to decide. To be drawn off into the swamps of indecisiveness, letting events decide for us, is to throw our lives away. That will not let my God down as it would Griffin's, but each must decide for himself whether it is the way he wishes to glorify the divine.

5. For example, God "embodies [creativity] eternally" (113), whereas we do not. The eternal here is formal and abstract, not concrete.

6. "The root meaning of ... 'the holy' ... is separation: it implies the apartness of and remoteness of something. The holy is that which is out of bounds, untouchable, and altogether beyond grasp; it cannot be understood or even defined, being so totally unlike anything else. To be holy is, in essence, to be distinctly other" (Adin Steinsaltz, *The Thirteen Petalled Rose* [New York: Basic Books, 1980], 69).

7. W. T. Stace, *Mysticism and Philosophy* (Los Angeles: Jeremy P. Tarcher, 1960), 65.

8. Whitehead enunciates this procedure as follows: "The explanatory purpose of philosophy is often misunderstood. Its business is to explain the emergence of the more abstract things from the more concrete things. It is a complete mistake to ask how concrete particular fact can be built out of universals. The answer is, 'In no way.' The true philosophical question is, How can concrete fact exhibit entities abstract from itself and yet participated in by its own nature?" (*Process and Reality,* corr. ed. [New York: Free Press, 1978], 20). Whitehead misperceives the mistake here. It is not that philosophers have tried to derive the concrete from the abstract—whoever did that? The issue is whether the universals Whitehead refers to are more abstract or concrete than his particular facts.

9. I insert this endorsement by Plotinus: "Number, Quantity, is not primal: obviously before even duality there must stand the unity" (*Enneads,* V.1.5, italics added).

10. Lord Northbourne, *Looking Back on Progress* (London: Perennial Books, 1970), 40-41. Griffin says I do not "ask why the absolute, or the Godhead, is as it is" (116); but I do ask that question, and this passage that I have appropriated to speak for me contains my answer.

11. For my part, although I agree that "primordiality and ubiquity belong to the essense of ultimacy" (115), I deny that they exhaust its meaning. The notion of creative, enabling power is even more essential.

12. *Enneads,* V.1.6.

13. "The things common to all men are more important than the things peculiar to any men. Ordinary things are more valuable than extraordinary things; nay they are more extraordinary. Man is something more awful than men; something more strange. The sense of the miracle of humanity itself should be always more vivid to us than [any distinctive human] marvel" (G. K. Chesterton, *Orthodoxy* [New York: Image Books, 1959], 46-47).

14. *Enneads,* V.1.4.

15. Griffin finds two conflicting syllogisms suppressed in my discussions of this topic, but the disparity is of his own making because the premise on which

he erects his second syllogism involves a clean mistake. He assumes that I hold that if "the temporal process [were] necessary for the realization of value from the divine viewpoint]that] would imply an initial defect in God" (122), but I do not hold that. The infinite requires the finite not through lack but through definition. To argue the contrary would be equivalent to my arguing that Griffin's God is not free because it cannot will contrary to the inclusive best, whereas we both recognize that that inability is not an incapacity but a feature of God's nature.

16. J. N. Findlay, *The Transcendence of the Cave* (London: George Allen and Unwin, 1967), 135.

17. Thus, Stephen Hawking: "Many people do not like the idea that time had a beginning, probably because it smacks of divine intervention .... However, one cannot argue with a mathematical theorem and nowadays nearly everyone assumes that the universe started with a big bang singularity" (*A Short History of Time* [New York: Bantam Books, 1988], 46, 50).

18. To speak frankly, they appear to me as evidence of that "loss or weakening of the metaphysical spirit" in our time which Jacques Maritain saw as "an incalculable damage for the general order of intelligence and human affairs" (*The Degrees of Knowledge* [New York: Charles Scribner's Sons, 1959], 59). I put this statement in a note rather than the running text because it amounts to a slur on Griffin and his associates for which I apologize even as I enter it. But I say it in order (1) to echo the "passion" Griffin too registers (95), which I respect; (2) to emphasize that beneath the preponderant gentlemanliness of our printed words run currents of conviction that betray our belief that we are debating matters of major moment [Martin Buber said that no discussion group he had belonged to was worth anything unless it was totally ruthless]; and (3) to invite Griffin to come back at me with equal candor in the Afterword.

19. *Process and Reality,* 343.

20. *Enneads*, V.1.4.

21. Windham Lewis, *Time and Western Man* (Boston: Beacon Press, 1957), 438.

22. Griffin succumbs to this mistake when, again picking up one of my analogies by the wrong end, he takes me to be likening eternity to watching movie reruns and the *eternal ennui* that would result (124). An instant cannot be boring.

23. James Clark and John Skinner, eds. and trans., *Treatises and Sermons of Meister Eckhart* (New York: Octagon Books, 1983), 163-64.

24. See my "Two Evolutions," in Leroy Rouner, ed., *On Nature* (Notre Dame, Ind.: University of Notre Dame Press, 1984).

25. See my *Forgotten Truth,* 139.

26. See again my "Two Evolutions."

6

AFTERWORD

David Ray Griffin and Huston Smith

If we had expected to convert each other through the discussions in this book, or even to move the other appreciably toward our own respective positions, we would have been disappointed, but such expectations would have been naive. When people with positions they have arrived at through years of reflection engage in public exchanges, they do not expect to influence each other as much as people in their audience. Yet we have not been engaged in simply an intellectual knock-about. We have been out to sharpen our understanding of each others' positions, along with our own, to the end of seeing more clearly where our differences reside, where some unrecognized agreements may lie, and what we might appropriate.

For now, the problem is how to round off this particular dialogue—*this* dialogue, we repeat, because the ideas here generated are certain to continue to occupy us. Our decision is to let Griffin take the lead. Smith's rejoinders, pared to the bone so as not to open new sleuce-gates of argument, take the form of a running commentary, set in italics and encased in brackets, which appear within the body of Griffin's text.

GRIFFIN'S AFTERWORD, WITH SMITH'S RUNNING COMMENTARY

What I attempt in this Afterword, in which I respond to Smith's "Concluding Apologia," is both to correct some misinterpretations of my position and to state what I now see to be our basic disagreements, and yet to do this without raising any new criticisms of Smith's position which would require lengthy replies from him.

The first section I devote to the most important issue on which I cannot accept Smith's characterization of my position: the matter of hard-core commonsense beliefs (which I equate with primordial truths). In the second section, I deal *ad seriatim* with a number of misinterpretations that can be handled much more briefly. In the third section, I move from partisan defense to an attempt to state, in a neutral and accurate enough way for Smith to accept it, the fundamental differences in our positions that lie behind the rest of them.

I. HARD-CORE COMMONSENSE BELIEFS

Smith evidently means to score a point against me by saying that I am still modern in believing in reason's capacity to adjudicate between worldviews. Postmodernism is, he says, the collapse of this faith (153). But if I have thereby been caught agreeing with modernity, I do not count this a failing. I have never considered modernity unambiguously wrong; by *postmodernism,* I mean a creative synthesis of modern and premodern truths and values. What has been problematic in modern epistemology, I hold, is not the belief in some capacity to judge rationally between competing worldviews, but the acceptance of assumptions that undermine this belief. I mean especially the sensationist theory of perception. If sense-data provide the primary element in our perception, then there is no preinterpretive, given element in experience to which interpretations should attempt to be adequate. There is not even any perceptual knowledge of an actual world beyond our own experience. Truth as correspondence between ideas and their referents, as an ideal to which we should aspire, becomes meaningless. Hume brought out the solipsistic, utterly skeptical implications of this starting point, and Nietzsche and Santayana carried them through more consistently. The relativistic, nihilistic postmodernism to which Smith refers is, to a great extent, simply an attempt to carry out these implications even more completely. My constructive postmodernism, by contrast, involves the rejection, pioneered by Whitehead (with Bergson, James, and other precedents), of just those modern assumptions that led to these skeptical conclusions.

[*I agree with the main thrust here. My "intellect" is not identical with Griffin's "prehensions," but the two are alike in providing (in Griffin's words) "preinterpretive, given element(s) in experience to which interpretations should attempt to be adequate." The question is whether Griffin's interpretation of what is preinterpretively given is impartial and binding on everyone.*]

Central to this constructive postmodernism is the attention to those beliefs that we presuppose in practice, regardless of what we announce verbally in our theories. If all people do indeed presuppose them in practice, then they provide a universal, nonculturally-conditioned, nonrelativistic criterion for comparing worldviews. While different worldviews may contain many incommensurable elements, they are not wholly incommensurate if their adherents share these presuppositions in common.

[*I continue to see this as heavy-handed—similar to asserting that because all human beings do, in fact, resort to Euclidian geometry in building sundecks and so forth, alternative geometries are irrational.*]

The rejection of sensationism is crucial for this position. If presupposed in sensory perception is a more fundamental mode of perception (which Whitehead calls *prehension*), we have a reason to believe that these hard-core commonsense ideas are based upon genuine perceptions of features lying in the nature of things. Whereas relativistic, deconstructive postmodernists believe that there is nothing deep in us except what we (in a particular tradition) have put there ourselves, constructive postmodernism is open to considering some ideas as being deep in us because we have deep perceptions.

Because Smith accepts nonsensory perception, he has no *a priori* reason to reject the idea of universal primordial beliefs. Indeed, his position is based on this idea as much as mine is. (In place of *prehension*, he speaks of *intellect* as the faculty through which they are apprehended.) But we differ on the content of these beliefs and, correlatively, upon the criterion for identifying them as universal. His list does not meet my criterion, and he believes that my list of beliefs is not universal, at least as I characterize them. I will examine his arguments.

Smith accepts my examples (causality, freedom, time, ontological realism, axiological realism, evil, and ultimate meaning) as universal, but only if they are left very vague (155, 159). And at that level of vagueness, he holds, they are too amorphous to be useful in adjudicating between worldviews. I can make them precise enough to be helpful, he says, only by putting "partisan, parochial spins" on them (155, 156, 180).

As evidence that my hard-core commonsense notions are not, under my definitions, universal, Smith points to the fact that he does not accept them. He says that "the fact that we disagree shows that we have put 'obviousness'¹ and 'common sense' behind us" (156). But the fact that we disagree verbally is irrelevant. I stressed that people can and often do deny them verbally (91). The test is whether everyone inevitably presupposes them in practice, even while denying them verbally. And Smith does not deny that all people do presuppose these ideas in practice. He does deny that this fact should be taken as evidence for the ultimate truth of at least some of these features of our experience, such as freedom, evil, and time. But he does not deny that we must live as if they were real; he in fact says that they *are* real at our level, and that he does not want his denial of their ultimate reality to lessen our devotion to using our freedom to try to overcome evil with good in the temporal process. So, given *my* criterion for identifying hard-core commonsense ideas, in distinction from the criterion of verbal agreement, Smith accepts the reality of universal presuppositions, and even accepts at least some of my candidates.

[*Agreed. I do accept Griffin's criterion, and agree that it unearths universal presuppositions—as long as it is life's commonsense framework that we are talking about. But the criterion remains useless for determining whether there are other frames of reference that relativize the criterion.*]

His implicit agreement is even greater. As an example of the "partisan, parochial spins" I put on the ideas, Smith refers to my contention that "genuine evil" is "anything, all things considered, without which the universe would have been better." He thinks the more neutral, universal definition would simply define evil as anything "that should be abhorred, condemned, and resisted with every ounce of energy we can muster," with no reference to the idea that the evil makes the universe as a whole less good than it might have been. He says of this latter idea that "this metaphysical pronouncement is *not* presupposed in practice." He then asks, rhetorically:

> What prescient power . . . gives Griffin the right to say that no one can affirm (not just conceptually affirm, but affirm with his or her entire being, contrary, to be sure, to certain sentiments of the moment) the total rightness of things and at the same time live . . . a normally responsible life? (165)

Smith's implicit agreement with my point is contained in the parenthetical comment. If "certain sentiments of the moment" are affirming the opposite, then one is *not* affirming the total rightness of things with one's "entire being." And, if Smith were to retract his self-contradiction, would any of us believe him? Could any of us believe, for example, that an Amnesty International worker could be fighting against torture and genocide while affirming "the total rightness of things" with "his or her entire being?" Smith points out that I think that his definition of genuine evil entails mine. That is correct. If we really believe that something should be "abhorred, condemned, and resisted with every ounce of energy we can muster," I hold we at least implicitly believe, with at least part of our being, that that thing, to the extent that it is not prevented, will detract from the overall goodness of reality.

[*As "sentiments of the moment" are a part of one's "entire being," I cannot deny that Griffin has spotted a contradiction in my wording. But it is my experience that, if one follows the lineaments of the human spirit faithfully, sooner or later one falls into such paradoxes and contradictions, the reason being that the object one is trying to describe—the human self—is itself paradoxical: half angelic, half all too human. I continue to believe that it is possible to throw one's entire will into resisting what (in our frame of reference) appears to be unrelievedly evil, while believing that the inexhaustible resources of the Divine can make it appear otherwise from its perspective.*]

What about Smith's claim that, to the extent that my hard-core commonsense notions are formulated loosely enough to be universal, they are too vague to be useful as criteria? I have no brief against his statement that my verbal formulations of the notions are parochial, not neutral, and therefore partially inadequate. We will never, after all, have a perfectly adequate formulation of any idea until we have a perfect metaphysics, which means, probably, never. But adequacy is surely not an all-or-nothing matter. We can formulate some ideas loosely enough to be understandable to people with very different worldviews, and yet precisely enough to serve, in principle, as criteria for adjudication. To provide examples, I repeat my earlier statement of some ideas I consider primordial truths because they are presupposed in practice by everyone (even if they are denied verbally):

> causal influence (every event is influenced by other events, and influences other events), freedom (while influenced by things beyond ourselves we are not totally determined by them), time (that there is a difference between the past, which is settled, the present, which is being settled, and the future, which is still to be settled), ontological realism (other real things beyond my present experience exist), axiological realism (some things are better than other things), evil (some things happen that are worse than other

things that could have happened), and ultimate meaning (some-how what happens is ultimately meaningful). (133)

[*Griffin's concluding parenthetical statement is what I was trying to say in my preceding point. In my phraseology: somehow what happens, including the evil that happens, is ultimately meaningful.*]

I wonder how these definitions could be any looser or vaguer. (My parochial, Whiteheadian spin on them would involve a description of "actual occasions," with their "conformal feelings," "subjective forms," "subjective aims," "anticipations," "propositional feelings," and so on.) And yet they are precise enough to adjudicate between competing worldviews. For example, assuming that it is agreed that these ideas are indeed universally presupposed, and that no metaphysics contradicting them should be accepted, then Spinozism, and all solipsisms, axiological relativisms, and nihilisms are ruled out.

[*Without taking on Spinoza or endorsing the other positions Griffin mentions, the definitions in his extracted paragraph are not precise enough to adjudicate between our worldviews—his and mine—because implicit in them is the unstated assumption that they cannot be subrated by more inclusive frames of reference.*]

Smith's real claim against my appeal to hard-core commonsense ideas is not, I believe, that they are either too vague to be useful or too parochial to be universally presupposed. Rather, it is, as I will suggest in section III, that they should not be accepted as pointing to dimensions of reality that hold true at its ultimate level. Smith wonders how my recognition that "our respective substantive positions are intertwined with our respective formal positions" is consistent with my denial that "the validity of the formal criterion of adequacy to the facts of experience is contingent upon any substantive interpretation of the nature of reality" (161). A first answer is that one can maintain the latter point while recognizing that those whose substantive position is in clear violation of certain facts will be interested in belittling the importance of the criterion. [*Similarly, those who are interested in preserving the criterion will be interested in belittling criticisms directed against it.*] That is, the criterion does not become invalid just because some people belittle it. A second answer is that the difference between two positions on this issue usually does not involve the criterion of adequacy to the facts itself, but differences as to *which* alleged "facts" are most crucial. [*Same difference?*] I think they are the hard-core commonsense ideas which we inevitably presuppose in practice; Smith thinks they are the "remorseless data" received by the "intellect" of the mystics. More on this in section III.

II. Some Other Misinterpretations

The other misinterpretations of my position in Smith's concluding remarks can be corrected more briefly. I here deal *ad seriatim* with seven of the most important ones. [*Other misinterpretations? While I am sure that Griffin and I have misunderstood each other liberally in these pages, I am no further along than I was in seeing how I have misunderstood him.*]

1. Smith suggests that my position is characterized by the same kind of invulnerability to criticism with which I charged his position (158). But there is a big difference between being invulnerable in fact, in the sense of not being moved to change one's position by any of the criticisms an opponent levels against it, and being invulnerable *in principle,* in the sense that no possible criticisms could be telling. Smith's invulnerability, I charged, is of the second kind, because of his treatment of the usual criteria for judging a position, namely self-consistency and adequacy to all the facts. He says that a position cannot be finally adequate unless it is inconsistent, unless its doctrines are not coherently conceivable. He thus turns what would ordinarily be taken as arguments against his position into evidence for it. For example, after admitting that "we can neither say nor see how" God can transmute all evil into "unalloyed good," he indicates that this element of "mystery" is essential to the very "holiness" of God (163). I have not made my position invulnerable in principle in this way; indeed, that is what our whole dispute about formal criteria is about.

    [*Is it incoherent to hold that things in their ultimate nature are so marvellously mysterious as not to fit the limited structures, hence strictures, of human logic and rationality? (I do not say human "under-standing," for understanding can hold paradoxes in tension.) If it is incoherent, then our high priests of logic and consistency, the mathematicians, are themselves incoherent, for "Gödel produced an arith-metic statement that was true on one level but that denied its own truth on another level. Additionally, he showed that there was no con-ceivable way to patch the language of arithmetic . . . in order to avoid a liar's paradox" (The Sciences, December 1988:88). I do not hold invulnerable the rhetorical question with which I open this paragraph. I think it should be debated using every resource of logic and experi-ence Griffin and I can muster, some of which I have here introduced.*]

2. Just as Smith believes that certain paradoxes are forced upon us by "ineluctable" experiences (157), Smith portrays me as believing that the interpretation of reality that I propose here is "force[d] upon us" by the facts of hard-core common sense (161). But I believe that all

interpretations are, to use the current jargon, "underdetermined." That is, interpretations are never strictly dictated by observations, but always involve a creative surplus. Alternative interpretations that also "save the appearances" are always possible. I present my interpretation, my philosophical theology, not as the one and only plausible way of showing the coherence among the inevitable presuppositions of practice, but as the most plausible way known to me among past and present options. [*I understand this, and (if I did so) should not have implied the contrary.*]

3. Smith suggests that his "intellect" might be identical with my "vision" (159, 175, 180). But what he calls intellect, by which he means an intuitive way of knowing, evidently produces (or receives) rather clear propositions [*No*]—ones we can be clear enough about and confident enough of to hold in defiance of the laws of logic (as discussed in section III). What I mean by "vision," by contrast, is a preconceptual, prepropositional way of seeing reality which is largely inherited from one's culture—even in the case of visionaries who modify it significantly. It is not in itself a way of knowing; it is—even though most people do not have the self-transcendence to think of it this way— more on the order of a hypothesis about reality. A particular *vision* of reality, such as the biblical vision of the world as creation, or the Buddhist vision of all things as empty, proves itself to be true, to the extent that it does, by giving birth to a *conceptualization* of reality that is more coherent, more adequate, and more illuminating than rival visions. It is thus very different from Smith's coherence-defying [*I object*] "intellect." Smith's category would be more similar to my Whiteheadian category of "prehension," which *is* an intuitive way of knowing—although the primordial truths I think we know through prehension (such as the reality of the past, the actual world, causality, freedom, time, value, and the holy) only partly overlap with the primordial truths Smith thinks we know through the intuitive intellect. [*As I indicated, intellective knowing is not propositional, but the burden of this paragraph seems correct. My "intellection" is closer to Griffin's "prehension" than to his "vision."*]

4. Smith nowhere misunderstands my position more thoroughly than with regard to science. He thinks I want all knowledge to be scientific so that "it would be effective and enable us to *manage* the world" (182). In my proposal for an expanded science, however, I spoke of including as part of "scientific knowledge" the wisdom that most things *cannot* be completely controlled, and that some things can be controlled even less than others. To help make the point stand out, I even proposed a "prayer for postmodern scientists," modeled upon the prayer by Reinhold Niebuhr appropriated by Alcoholics Anonymous (140). And I concluded:

Once knowledge based on control and sought for the sake of control is no longer the inclusive ideal within science itself, the insatiable desire to control which has possessed our culture can be exorcised. The attitude of 'letting be' could then come to pervade our male-female relations, our parent-child relations, our international relations, and our relations with the rest of nature. (140)

That Smith could so completely misunderstand my proposal is evidently due to the fact that he has so thoroughly equated "science" with controlling knowledge that he automatically reads any proposal for an expanded science to mean a proposal for expanded control. My proposal goes in exactly the opposite direction. Smith's response, in saying that I want to make science the inclusive category (181), fails to acknowledge that my proposal for overcoming lines of demarcation can equally be read as making philosophy or theology the inclusive subject (139).

[*We seem to be in a complete muddle on this one—it is the one point in the book where I feel the need of a third-party facilitator to help us see what is occurring. I understand that Griffin is not arguing for more control, and we both favor an overview— worldview—that throws all knowledge into perspective. Is anything more than terminology, then, at stake?*

It is science's talent for producing proofs-and-powers that has caused us to promote it to first place among our ways of knowing. Because that is what has effected its exalted status, I favor keeping the word tied tightly to domains and procedures where it can exercise this capacity. Does Griffin want to enlarge science's referent to encourage it to produce proofs-and-power on the issues that philosophy, theology and art now ponder? If not—if (with me) he does not see proofs-and-powers as available in these domains—I do not see why he is adamant in insisting that future reflection (which always has and always will take into account *what science has demonstrated) be itself called science.*

In short, if the intent of the closing sentence in Griffin's preceding paragraph is to turn science *into a synonym for* philosophy *or* theology, *I do not understand why he wishes to do that. It does not jeopardize our sense of the whole to recognize that different modes of knowing (of which science is one) are appropriate for understanding different parts of the whole.*]

5. Believing that the drive for unity manifested in science, philosophy, and theology seeks a single source from which all else arises, Smith compares my contentment with a plurality of ultimate realities (God,

finite actualities, eternal objects, creativity) to the contentment of a (second-rate) scientist with the present four forces of physics. Smith says: "Why do not physicists simply assume that there have always been four fundamental forces in nature and stop trying to reduce them to one? . . . That the four have always been around is no explanation" (174-75). But there is a crucial difference between physics and metaphysics. Physics deals with contingent features of our particular world. None of the four forces appears to be a necessary feature of reality which would necessarily exist in any possible world. There is, therefore, no good reason to believe that "the four have always been around." And none of these forces depends upon all the others for its very meaning. Metaphysics, by contrast, seeks to discern those features of our world that are necessary, that would be exemplified in any world whatsoever. To say that something, such as God or eternal possibilities, has always existed, because it exists necessarily, is to give the only kind of explanation for it that is either possible or necessary. Furthermore, the ideal of coherence is that the basic elements of existence, however many are posited, should not be definable in abstraction from each other. Actualities, for example, make no sense apart from possibilities, because they are actualizations of possibilities; and possibilities make no sense apart from actualities, because they are nothing but possibilities to be actualized. Creativity makes no sense apart from actualities in which it is embodied; and actuality, understood as the creative unification of a many, presupposes the reality of creativity. Likewise, if God is the soul of the universe, that all-inclusive creative unification which makes the many finite things into a unity, then neither God nor the world can be understood apart from the other. There is no reason, therefore, to make the kind of unity sought by science the standard for that sought by the philosophical theologian. (Smith's suggestion that it should be seems, in fact, to run counter to his general program.) Smith and I largely concur on eternal possibilities and creativity, because Smith agrees that they have always been, and I agree that they do not exist apart from God. The point of divergence is the world: I see it as comprised of events that are as actual as God (if inferior in every other way),[2] while Smith regards all worldly events as mere attributes of God (171).

[*Though I am not persuaded that Griffin's four metaphysical ultimates are required by every possible world—they are not the ultimates in mine—I see that it was inappropriate to liken those ultimates to the four forces in physics.*]

6. Smith says that I hold that, "if time always was, that settles the matter, leaving it without need of further explanation" (174). But, I do not

believe in time as an absolute, as if it could exist apart from temporal events. And these temporal events provide a kind of explanation. Time exists only because of the conformal inclusion by present events of prior events and the anticipation by these present events of subsequent events. Time in this most general sense has always existed, by hypothesis, because there have always been events including prior events and anticipating future ones.[3] Smith and I seem close on this point, because he says that time arises causally but not temporally (174). We disagree, of course, insofar as he believes that this means that time is not ultimately real (172, 173), and that all events—including those that are future for us as well as past and present—can be prehended in the Godhead in "a single pulse of experience" (174). Our difference here is due to the fact, mentioned in the previous point, that I think the actual events constituting the world are fully actual, whereas Smith considers them less real than God, as mere attributes of God.

7. Smith wonders how I could call his position individualistic, given his view that the individual soul is ultimately illusory (178). This is a good question—with a good answer. Smith's position on this topic, as on most, contains two levels. Just as he treats time, evil, freedom, and modern science's upward causation as wholly real at one level, and as wholly unreal from the ultimate perspective [*I balk at "wholly." The finite is contained in the infinite and thereby "prefigured" there.*], he accepts an individualistic view of the self at one level while rejecting the reality of individuals altogether at the ultimate level. I had referred to this two-tiered account by speaking of "the Hindu doctrine of the *atman,* which is essentially independent of all relations (except to Brahman, which might ... be a relation of identity [127])." The individualism at the phenomenal level is again reflected in Smith's statement that any progress made in the world is progress "that each soul must effect for himself or herself" (179). What I mean by a more ecological view of the self is one in which each individual is seen to be largely constituted by its relations to (prehensions of) the elements (including the other people) in its environment, even though it is also true that we always have some society-transcending freedom, so that individual effort is important. This is why I believe that social progress—creating a better social environment—is important for individual well-being. From this standpoint, Smith's view *is* too individualistic (while being ultimately too anti-individualistic).

8. Smith persists in portraying me as having something called "faith in progress," in the sense of "banking on its occurring" (177). But, as I pointed out in my counterreply, I talked only "about the possibility

and desirability of progress, not its inevitability" (126). Smith evidently thinks I need to be reminded of "all the monstrosities for which our century will be remembered," which led to the collapse of the modern faith in progress. But I am the one, not Smith, who considers such events ultimately evil. Smith doubts whether "the general tenor of the quality of life" differs fundamentally from what it has always been; in other words, he doubts that it has improved (176). But I think that this general tenor is in many crucial respects *worse* now, under the impact of modernization. This is why I call for movement toward a *postmodern* world. I believe in inevitable decline no more than in inevitable progress. Modernity with its horrors is a contingent development, resulting from human decisions; it can likewise be transcended through human decisions. This transcendence is not inevitable, but it is possible and desirable. This hope for progress is why this book series exists.

[*We nuance different aspects of the issue, but I see no real difference between us here.*]

III. OUR FUNDAMENTAL DIFFERENCES: A FINAL SUMMARY

We have both spoken of the intellectual drive for unity, to see a seemingly disparate set of data or principles as manifestations of an underlying fact or principle. And this drive has been exemplified in our discussion. After beginning with fourteen points of disagreement in the first exchange, we reduced this to seven in the second. More important, we both from the outset tried to identify one or two underlying, controlling issues, from which the others followed. I continue this attempt here, seeking to state the underlying differences as I see them more precisely than before and therefore in a way more illuminating of the various surface differences.

Our differences on the various issues we have debated seem to lie in two fundamentally different visions, each of which has a substantive and a formal dimension. The substantive dimension is the way God and the world (including the human mind) are related, while the formal dimension involves the status of our mind's rational criteria in forming and evaluating a worldview.

In my vision, which is *pan-en-theistic,* the relation of God and the world is analogous to that of the human soul or mind to its body, with the mind and body understood as distinct and equally real while being intimately related.[4] God and a world presuppose each other and are intimately interrelated but they are not simply identical. Not only does the divine soul of the universe transcend the multiplicity of finite things, having a unity of creative experience in response to the world; each finite unity also transcends God, in the sense of having a partially self-determining unity of experience that is influenced but not wholly determined by God. Because God and the world are really distinct in the sense that each has its own creativity by which it partially transcends the other, worldly freedom, evil, and time can all be taken as ultimately real without impugning God's goodness and unity.

In Smith's vision, which can be called *pantheistic* (although I do not think he uses this word), the relation of God to the world is analogous to that of the human being as a whole to its body. Our bodily parts, in Smith's view, are parts of us and, in abstraction from the whole psychophysical organism, cannot be regarded as equally actual (171). The world is thus not distinct from God, except in the sense that the finite part is distinct from the infinite whole of which it is a part. Eternal possibilities, creativity, and finite things are "God's attributes" (171). The world is a manifestation of God (or better, the Godhead) and thereby has no self-determining power with which to transcend divine determination; freedom, evil, and time must therefore be taken as ultimately unreal.

[*This is interesting. I had not thought of things in this way, but the contrasting analogies are suggestive.*]

Correlative with these contrasting substantive visions are two contrasting formal attitudes toward the human mind's rational criteria. Smith's vision implies that these criteria must finally be overridden, while my vision encourages their being pressed to the hilt and not overridden. At the center of this difference are those features of experience that I associate with "hard-core common sense." We inevitably live as if time, freedom, and evil were real. Smith agrees, stressing that he does not mean anything he says to lead people to take them less seriously in the way they live. But in Smith's vision these things are not ultimately real. For example, he defines "genuine evil" as that which "should be abhorred, condemned, and resisted with every ounce of energy we can muster" (165), but then says that from the ultimate standpoint these events are not really evil, that everything has always been "exactly as it should be" (162). The same dual perspective is needed for freedom and time: we are to live as if they were real—because at our level they are—while knowing that they are not ultimately real. Because of the need for this dual perspective, Smith cannot take those features of experience that we inevitably presuppose in practice as clues to the ultimate nature of reality. They cannot be taken as "facts" to which a theory must be "adequate" in its ultimate account of things. A view such as mine, then, that defines these features of experience so as to make them ultimately real is seen as putting "parochial" spins on them (180).

Smith's substantive vision, with its dual perspective, also entails that human rationality's law of noncontradiction must be relativized. Events must be said to be evil and yet not evil, our actions must be said to be free and yet wholly determined by God,[5] and time must be said to be real and yet unreal. Smith begins his concluding statement by affirming that he likes coherence, sounding surprised that he had created the impression that he did not (155). But he quite quickly modifies his attachment to coherence, saying that he does not like the kind of coherence I favor, according to which the formal meaning of coherence can be specified apart from the content to which it is applied (155). He later adds that certain "remorseless data" provide "ineluctable evidence" that forces us (or at least the mystics with the sensibilities to recognize this evidence) to adopt paradoxes, such as "freedom *and* predestination, time *and* eternity, perfection *and* evil" (157-58). Eventually, he tells us that "logics are multiple" (163), and that the mysticism he endorses "is utterly irreconcilable with all the ordinary rules of human thinking, that it blatantly breaches the laws of logic at every turn" (167). If this is not the same as disliking coherence, then—to use Smith's line from *The Sting* (160)—"It sure comes close." [*I like coherence, but do not require that the whole of reality conform to our capacity for it.*]

In my own view, nothing militates against using those features of our experience that we inevitably presuppose in practice as clues to the ultimate nature of reality, and as criteria with which to judge the adequacy of any worldview. There is also no reason to try to belittle or subvert the law of noncontradiction. In fact, besides providing no reason to relativize the criteria of adequacy and coherence, this postmodern vision provides strong incentive to emphasize them. The idea that all individuals, from God to electrons, embody creative experience encounters strong initial incredulity, especially because modern thought has conditioned people to think of matter as insentient and (internally) inert. Advocates of postmodern theology seek to overcome this prejudice against its basic idea by showing how the supposition of insentient matter leads to either dualism or materialism, both of which involve terminal cases of inadequacy and incoherence, and by showing that the doctrine of panexperientialism, while being initially startling to modern minds, leads to an unprecedentedly adequate and self-consistent account of reality. Postmodern theology therefore claims to beat modern thought, which gave up the appeal to revelation in favor of experience and reason, at its own game.

It might seem strange, given the appeal of most types of theology to revelation, that postmodern theology would rest its case on experience and reason alone rather than appealing to revelation. It does speak of revelation, but not to argue the truth of its case. It does not, in other words, claim that certain ideas are true because they came from divine revelation. This sets it apart from premodern forms of theology. Insofar as postmodern theology does think of some ideas as resulting from divine revelation to a greater degree than others, it seeks to establish their truth first. The reason for this epistemic approach is also rooted in the understanding of the God-world relation. Because all creatures have their own creativity *vis-à-vis* divine creativity, and because human beings have a very high degree of this power to be self-determining in relation to the divine influence upon them, no human ideas can be thought to have been directly implanted by God. All human ideas, whether about God or the world, are largely free interpretations. Although there is a prelinguistic, preinterpretive, "given" element in experience, including a direct experience of God, all conscious ideas are constructed by the creative power of human experience. The premodern idea of "revealed theology" must therefore be totally abolished. *All* theological ideas are human constructions. Accepting this idea fully, postmodern theology must rest its claim to truth wholly upon the intrinsic convincingness of its ideas, and this means upon their self-consistency, adequacy to all the facts of experience, and illuminating power.

Smith, by contrast, does seem to believe that certain ideas [*No. Not ideas.*] are revealed to the receptive mind (or what he calls the "intellect"), and that this revealed status provides the warrant for considering them true. I discussed this difference between our positions previously (25-26, 41, 100, 119-20), but it now seems to me, especially in the light of Smith's concluding comments, to be even more important than I had thought. I have already pointed out Smith's belief that mystics are forced into paradoxes by "remorseless data," which suggests that certain ideas are rather straightforwardly given to them. Perhaps even more revealing of his beliefs is his complaint that my position is too secular, that "it accommodates theology to philosophy, religion to the world," and his statement that "Whitehead is not a theologian" because "he establishes other than religious data as his starting point and control" (159, 160).

This characterization at first glance appears to be based on a misunderstanding. Whitehead states in the Preface to *Science and the Modern World,* his first book in metaphysics, that he means to give religious, aesthetic, and ethical intuitions as much importance as those of natural science in constructing his cosmology. He not only does so in this and later writings, but stresses the point repeatedly. Indeed, Smith even quotes a passage in which Whitehead says that his argument in the final part of

Process and Reality "depends upon elucidation of somewhat exceptional elements in our conscious experience—those elements which may roughly be classed together as religious and moral intuitions" (175). As for my position, I had pointed out that it depends upon a "religious vision," and upon "religious, aesthetic, and moral intuitions as well as sensory perceptions" (101). It might seem, then, that Smith has misunderstood.

But that would be to misinterpret Smith's position. He holds that for a position to be authentically religious, or theological, it is not enough to include distinctively religious data among the other types. The religious data must exert a controlling role over all the others. He is not sure, he says, that the medieval stance, in which philosophy took orders from theology, was a mistake (159). He says, "My religious vision not only proposes, it disposes" (159). And his remark that Whitehead is not a theologian was evoked by Whitehead's statement that the pair of opposites "God and the World" is not given in experience with the same directness of intuition as good and evil, freedom and necessity, and flux and permanence. Smith retorts: "So much for Moses on Mount Sinai, Buddha under the Bo Tree, Saul knocked off his horse, and Muhammad driven to the edge of madness on the Night of Power" (160). Smith's retort is meaningful here only if he believes not only that these were powerful religious experiences (which I also believe), but also that inherent in the experience, as more of a given element than an interpretation, was a rather clear idea of God (which I do not believe). Smith can hold this position because of his belief that God fully determines worldly events.

Given this position—that propositions are revealed, and that these revealed propositions should be allotted the controlling role in the formation of one's theological position—all of Smith's other claims about reason's criteria follow. When the idea of the God-world relation and the criterion of noncontradiction clash, it is the latter that must budge. The same is true for all those other ideas that we inevitably presuppose in practice.

[*Not believing that propositions are revealed, I would not say "that a rather clear idea of God" was contained in the experiences to which I allude. Griffin was closer to the mark earlier (191) when he likened my intellections to his preconceptual prehensions.*]

The relation between the substantive vision of the God-world relation and the formal position on the role of reason in religious thought is mutually supporting in each of our positions. While Smith's view of God's omnipotence allows for his doctrine of revealed propositions [*No.*], mine rules it out. While Smith's position on reason and revelation allows for his doctrine of the God-world relation, mine rules it out. While my doctrine of the God-world relation implies that a theological position should be tested in terms of its overall adequacy and self-consistency, Smith's doctrine implies that those tests cannot be ultimate. [*My wording would be: "... imples that those tests are contextual and cannot be abstractly formulated with sufficient precision to have clout."*] And while my view of the role of reason in theological construction encourages various moves designed to make the God-world relation rationally intelligible, such as the distinction between the world's creativity and God's, and the idea that God should be understood as the chief exemplification of metaphysical principles rather than an exception to them, Smith's view leads him to find this doctrine of God inadequate precisely because it *is* rationally intelligible: only a paradoxical view evokes religious awe and worship (163, 167).

[*This is a fair characterization as long as we keep in mind that, for me, reason operates in a restricted region of the mind's domain.*]

This combination of substantive and formal differences seems to lie behind our differences on the various other issues. These differences seem ultimate, not based on any other, more deepseated differences, and not negotiable. We do, as we have pointed out, agree on many things, against the dominant worldview of late modernity: the rejection of a relativistic, reductionistic, nihilistic view of reality, the acceptance of primordial truths and an enchanted nature, the rootage of our world in a perfect creator, and so on. Because our differences are also far-reaching, we present two alternatives to the currently dominant worldview. Whether readers incline more to one than to the other (if to either) will probably depend more upon whether their ultimate intuitions, substantive and formal, agree more with Smith's or mine, than upon any arguments either of us has introduced against the other's view or in favor of his own. But I hope [*As do I.*] that our arguments have nevertheless been useful in helping some readers think through their own positions, whether by attraction or by repulsion.

I wish to close by saying that this dialogue has been very helpful to me, and to thank Huston Smith for making it possible and for being such a congenial discussion partner. We did not hesitate while engaged in battle to speak sharply, sometimes even sarcastically (readers surely enjoyed, for example, Huston's remark that he was "all but undone by Griffin's closing concession that 'a true intuition' underlies my manifold errors" [162]). But we could not have had a better relationship off the field. [*I heartily agree.*]

NOTES

1. I probably should not have used the term *obvious,* which Smith cites several times. I introduced it in stating what "the principle of adequacy is gen-

erally taken to mean," namely, "adequacy to the rather obvious facts of immediate experience" (99). I then specified the "hard-core commonsense ideas" as the most important subclass of these "rather obvious facts of immediate experience." In this brief discussion, I failed to point out that the hard-core commonsense ideas, such as temporality and freedom, which point to metaphysical or necessary features of experience, are generally less obvious than more contingent features of experience, such as present sensory data. A more complete discussion would also need to point out that some of the hard-core commonsense ideas, such as the idea of the holy, are even less obvious than others, such as the reality of time. It would be better to strike the word *obvious* altogether, leaving the focus on the fact that the ideas are inevitably presupposed in practice. The real distinction I had in mind is that between the more "given" and the more "interpretive" features of experience; theories need to be adequate to the former, not necessarily to the latter.

2. In note 18, Smith apologizes for his statement that my position on this point is an example of that "loss or weakening of the metaphysical spirit" in our time which Jacques Maritain saw as "an incalculable damage for the general order of intelligence and human affairs" and invites me to come back at him with equal candor in this Afterword. But I wonder why any apology is necesssary because, from Smith's view, the "incalculable damage" only occurs at the level of appearances; from the ultimate standpoint, there are no "second-rate happenings," and my theology is part of that "everything for which God is solely responsible" which is "exactly as it should be." I am saying just what I should say, because "nothing that occurs would have been better had it been otherwise" (163), and "there is [not] anything I can do that God is not able to transmute into perfect good" (166). In fact, without me and my theology, according to Smith's principles, God's concrete perfection would not exist (166, 173). [*It is important to keep in mind that the levels in the perennial outlook must honor in full the principles by which each is organized—one cannot skip back and forth. Thus, it is true that* for God *"nothing that occurs would have been better had it been otherwise," but as we are not God, that principle does not hold for us, or for the history about which Griffin and I are both concerned.*]

If I *were* to come back at Smith in this Afterword, it would be on his attempt to provide analogies to indicate how one can reconcile this belief with the insistence that evil should still evoke revulsion and resistance in us (163). He says he knows a couple whose pain evoked by their child's chemotherapy "was overridden by their gratitude, even exultancy, that such treatments now exist." But surely they were not pleased that their child got cancer so that it could experience the wonders of chemotherapy! And yet that is what would be necessary if we were to have an analogy with Smith's God, whose bliss in the face of this misfortune is not even marred by "wishing it had not occurred" (164) [*We do not know (1) all the "karmic" factors that may have been working themselves out in the order, (2) how the child and its parents may have advanced spiritually through the way they endured it, or (3) what the eventual destinies of the persons affected will be, destinies that may present this trauma in a new light. I*

*write this, however, only under duress, for as I pointed out in introducing this
example, it borders on obscenity to raise these considerations when it is the
suffering of others, not one's own, that is being considered.*] I also would note
that, after having earlier said that, if anything in his doctrine, correctly understood, leads anyone to resist evil less, that would be proof that his doctrine is
wrong (70), he now admits that his doctrine "holds moral dangers" (164). He has
not thereby contradicted himself, because his assertion that the doctrine is not
morally harmful has always included the proviso that it be correctly understood,
and his present point is that some esoteric doctrines "should be reserved for
initiates" who, presumably, would understand them correctly. (He adds: "I would
not myself have initiated this debate which Griffin brought into being." But the
doctrine of the absolute, concrete perfection of reality as a whole was published
by Smith and many others long before I initiated this dialogue.) I would argue,
however, that this doctrine, insofar as it is really affirmed at the conscious level,
would *almost inevitably* encourage *some* slackening in *some* people's resistance
to at least *some* forms of evil. But these are things that I would argue if I were
responding again to Smith's views, which would then require a further counterresponse. Because I am only providing a concluding Afterword, in which partisan comments are limited to corrections of misinterpretations of my position, I
must simply let stand unchallenged several points in Smith's defense of his own
position with which I strongly disagree.

3. I have developed this idea in the introduction to David Ray Griffin, ed.,
*Physics and the Ultimate Significance of Time: Bohm, Prigogine, and Process
Philosophy* (Albany: State University of New York Press, 1987).

4. Smith suggests that it would be strange to say "I love my heart" (168).
But if love is most fundamentally sympathy, or compassion, meaning feeling the
feelings of another *with* the other, then we do love our hearts—as becomes
clearest perhaps during a heart attack (which my father had while I was involved
in this interchange): we feel the heart's pain as our own pain. I find this relation
of dialectical identity, or identity with difference, more accurate for understanding my relation to my body than that of strict identity, and more helpful for
thinking of God's relation to the world.

5. In his note 3, Smith seems to endorse the view that freedom and determinism are compatible.

NOTES ON AUTHORS
AND CENTERS

DAVID RAY GRIFFIN, editor of the SUNY Series in Constructive Post-modern Thought, is author of *God, Power, and Evil* and *God and Religion in the Postmodern World,* co-author of *Process Theology* and *Varieties of Postmodern Theology,* and editor of *The Reenchantment of Science: Postmodern Proposals* and *Spirituality and Society: Postmodern Visions.* He is professor of philosophy of religion at the School of Theology at Claremont and Claremont Graduate School, founding president of the Center for a Postmodern World, and executive director of the Center for Process Studies, 1325 North College, Claremont, California 91711.

HUSTON SMITH is author of *The Religions of Man, Purposes of Higher Education, Condemned to Meaning, Forgotten Truth,* and *Beyond the Post-Modern Mind.* He is Thomas J. Watson Professor of Religion and Distinguished Adjunct Professor of Philosophy, Emeritus, Syracuse University. He is currently affiliated with the Graduate Theological Union, and resides at 130 Avenida Drive, Berkeley, California 94708.

This series is published under the auspices of the Center for a Postmodern World and the Center for Process Studies.

The Center for a Postmodern World is an independent nonprofit organization in Santa Barbara, California, founded by David Ray Griffin. It promotes the awareness and exploration of the postmodern worldview and encourages reflection about a postmodern world, from postmodern art, spirituality, and education to a postmodern world order, with all this implies for economics, ecology, and security. One of its major projects is to produce a collaborative study that marshals the numerous facts supportive of a postmodern worldview and provides a portrayal of a postmodern world order toward which we can realistically move. It is located at 2060 Alameda Padre Serra, Suite 101, Santa Barbara, California 93103.

The Center for Process Studies is a research organization affiliated with the School of Theology at Claremont and Claremont University Center and Graduate School. It was founded by John B. Cobb, Jr., Director, and David Ray Griffin, Executive Director. It encourages research and reflection upon the process philosophy of Alfred North Whitehead, Charles Hartshorne, and related thinkers, and upon the application and testing of this viewpoint in all areas of thought and practice. This center sponsors conferences, welcomes visiting scholars to use its library, and publishes a scholarly journal, *Process Studies,* and a quarterly *Newsletter.* It is located at 1325 North College, Claremont, California 91711.

Both centers gratefully accept (tax-deductible) contributions to support their work.

Index